casseroles
and one-pots

HOMESTYLE

casseroles
and one-pots

MURDOCH BOOKS

contents

Good, wholesome food

This is one of the most useful cookbooks you will ever own; the recipes in it cut across seasons, cuisines and the courses of a menu. For many cooks (and diners), soups, casseroles, curries, stews and other 'one-pot' meals are among the most beloved fare ever. Generally made by slowly simmering ingredients in stock or other liquid, such dishes open the door to a world of delicious possibilities. Whether you're wishing to concoct a warming winter soup to serve for lunch, a light broth to kick off a dinner party, or a wholesome casserole for a family meal, there's a recipe here to suit any occasion, whim or craving. All the comforting classics, such as hot beef borscht, chicken paprika with dumplings, and sausage and chickpea stew are in this collection, as are more exotic offerings. The zingy flavour of duck and pineapple curry, prawn laksa or vindaloo, for example, bring the adventure of Asia to your table while Middle Eastern accents (in dishes such as lamb with quince and lemon, lamb kefta, and Moroccan chicken), will entice with their exotic spiciness.

With the exception of most of the seafood recipes, these are dishes that can be made in advance—indeed, many stews, casseroles and curries actually improve in flavour if left in the fridge overnight. These are also the types of recipes that lend themselves to being doubled in quantity so there are plenty of leftovers to freeze; there is nothing more convenient than having a few meals on hand for when time to cook runs short. Fish and seafood is best cooked just before needed (as it can become chewy and dry) and recipes containing these are less suitable for freezing. Other meats—particularly stewing cuts of beef and lamb—are nearly impossible to over-cook, making meaty braises and stews good choices for novice cooks. Don't be daunted by lengthy cooking times—curries, stews, soups and the like need little supervision after their initial preparation. Apart from an occasional quick stir or skim, they can be left to gently bubble away, undisturbed. The only thing to really worry about with the recipes in this collection is the quality of your stock; whether fish, vegetable, beef or chicken stock, always use a good one (home-made is best) for the most delectable results.

Soups

Minestrone

PREPARATION TIME: 25 MINUTES + OVERNIGHT SOAKING | TOTAL COOKING TIME: 2 HOURS | SERVES 6

125 g (4½ oz) dried borlotti (cranberry) beans
1 large onion, roughly chopped
2 garlic cloves
2 tablespoons roughly chopped flat-leaf (Italian) parsley
60 g (2¼ oz) pancetta, chopped
60 ml (2 fl oz/¼ cup) olive oil
1 celery stalk, halved lengthways, cut into 1 cm (½ inch) slices
1 carrot, halved lengthways, cut into 1 cm (½ inch) slices
1 potato, diced
2 teaspoons tomato paste (concentrated purée)
400 g (14 oz) tin chopped tomatoes
6 basil leaves, roughly torn
2 litres (70 fl oz/8 cups) chicken stock
2 thin zucchini (courgettes), cut into 1.5 cm (⅝ inch) slices
115 g (4 oz/¾ cup) shelled peas
60 g (2¼ oz) green beans, trimmed, cut into 4 cm (1½ inch) lengths
80 g (2¾ oz) silverbeet leaves, shredded
75 g (2½ oz) ditalini or small pasta

PESTO
2 large handfuls basil
20 g (¾ oz) lightly toasted pine nuts
2 garlic cloves
100 ml (3½ fl oz) olive oil
25 g (¾ oz/¼ cup) grated parmesan cheese

1 Put the borlotti beans in a large bowl, cover with water and soak overnight. Drain and rinse under cold water.

2 Place the onion, garlic, parsley and pancetta in a food processor and process until finely chopped. Heat the oil in a saucepan, add the pancetta mixture and cook over low heat, stirring occasionally, for 8–10 minutes.

3 Add the celery, carrot and potato, and cook for 5 minutes, then stir in the tomato paste, tomato, basil and borlotti beans. Season with black pepper. Add the stock and bring slowly to the boil. Cover and simmer, stirring occasionally, for 1½ hours.

4 Season, and add the zucchini, peas, green beans, silverbeet and pasta. Simmer for 8–10 minutes, or until the vegetables and pasta are *al dente*.

5 To make the pesto, combine the basil, pine nuts and garlic with a pinch of salt in a food processor. Process until finely chopped. With the motor running, slowly add the olive oil. Transfer to a bowl and stir in the parmesan and ground black pepper to taste. Serve the soup, along with crusty bread. Add the pesto on top as desired.

NUTRITION PER SERVE
Protein 9 g; Fat 30 g; Carbohydrate 20 g; Dietary Fibre 5.3 g; Cholesterol 9 mg; 1593 kJ (380 Cal)

Cook the processed onion, garlic, parsley and pancetta mixture.

Simmer the soup until the pasta and vegetables are *al dente*.

Stir the grated parmesan into the finely chopped basil mixture.

Mulligatawny

PREPARATION TIME: 20 MINUTES | TOTAL COOKING TIME: 1 HOUR 15 MINUTES | SERVES 4

30 g (1 oz) butter

375 g (13 oz) chicken thigh cutlets, skin and fat removed

1 large onion, finely chopped

1 apple, peeled, cored and diced

1 tablespoon curry paste

2 tablespoons plain (all-purpose) flour

750 ml (26 fl oz/3 cups) chicken stock

50 g (1¾ oz/¼ cup) basmati rice

1 tablespoon chutney

1 tablespoon lemon juice

60 ml (2 fl oz/¼ cup) cream

1 Gently heat the butter in a large heavy-based saucepan. Cook the chicken on medium–high heat for 5 minutes, or until browned, then remove and set aside. Add the onion, apple and curry paste to the pan. Cook for 5 minutes, or until the onion is soft. Stir in the flour and cook for 2 minutes, then add half the stock. Continue stirring until the mixture boils and thickens.

2 Return the chicken to the pan with the remaining stock. Stir until boiling, then reduce the heat, cover and simmer for 1 hour. Add the rice for the last 15 minutes of cooking.

3 Remove the chicken from the pan. Remove the meat from the bones, shred and return to the pan. Add the chutney, lemon juice and cream, and season to taste.

Once the mixture has thickened, return the browned chicken thighs to the pan.

Add the chutney, lemon juice and cream at the end of cooking.

NUTRITION PER SERVE
Protein 25 g; Fat 16 g; Carbohydrate 25 g; Dietary Fibre 2 g; Cholesterol 28 mg; 1396 kJ (333 Cal)

Hot beef borscht

PREPARATION TIME: 30 MINUTES | TOTAL COOKING TIME: 2 HOURS 50 MINUTES | SERVES 4–6

500 g (1 lb 2 oz) stewing beef, cut into cubes
500 g (1 lb 2 oz) beetroot
1 onion, finely chopped
1 carrot, cut into short strips
1 parsnip, cut into short strips
75 g (2½ oz/1 cup) finely shredded cabbage
sour cream, to serve
snipped chives, to serve

1 Put the beef and 1 litre (35 fl oz/4 cups) water in a large heavy-based saucepan, and bring slowly to the boil. Reduce the heat, cover and simmer for 1 hour. Skim the surface of the stock to remove the fat as required.

2 Cut the stems from the beetroot, wash well and place in a large, heavy-based saucepan with 1 litre (35 fl oz/4 cups) water. Bring to the boil, then reduce the heat and simmer for 40 minutes, or until tender. Drain, reserving 250 ml (9 fl oz/ 1 cup) of the liquid. Allow to cool, then peel and grate the beetroot.

3 Remove the meat from the stock and cool. Skim any remaining fat from the surface of the stock. Return the meat to the stock and add the onion, carrot, parsnip, beetroot and reserved beetroot liquid. Bring to the boil, reduce the heat, cover and simmer for 45 minutes.

4 Stir in the cabbage and simmer for a further 15 minutes. Season to taste. Serve with the sour cream and chives.

To avoid stains, wear rubber gloves to grate the cooled beetroot.

Pour the reserved beetroot liquid into the soup and bring to the boil.

NUTRITION PER SERVE (6)
Protein 20 g; Fat 10 g; Carbohydrate 10 g; Dietary Fibre 5 g; Cholesterol 80 mg; 940 kJ (225 Cal)

Bouillabaisse

PREPARATION TIME: 30 MINUTES + 5 MINUTES SOAKING | TOTAL COOKING TIME: 1 HOUR 15 MINUTES | SERVES 6

60 ml (2 fl oz/¼ cup) olive oil
1 large onion, chopped
2 leeks, sliced
4 garlic cloves, crushed
500 g (1 lb 2 oz) ripe tomatoes, peeled and
   roughly chopped
1–2 tablespoons tomato paste (concentrated
   purée)
6 flat-leaf (Italian) parsley sprigs
2 bay leaves
2 thyme sprigs
1 fennel sprig
¼ teaspoon saffron threads
2 kg (4 lb 8 oz) seafood trimmings (fish
   heads, bones, shellfish remains)
1 tablespoon Pernod or Ricard liqueur
4 potatoes, cut into 1.5 cm (⅝ inch) slices
1.5 kg (3 lb 5 oz) fish fillets, such as blue-eyed
   cod, bream, red fish and snapper, cut into
   large chunks (see NOTE)

TOASTS
½ baguette, cut into twelve 1.5 cm (⅝ inch)
   slices
2 large garlic cloves, halved

ROUILLE
3 slices day-old Italian white bread, crusts
   removed
1 red capsicum (pepper), seeded and
   quartered
1 small red chilli, seeded and chopped
3 garlic cloves, crushed
1 tablespoon chopped basil leaves
80 ml (2½ fl oz/⅓ cup) olive oil

1   Heat the oil in a large saucepan over low
heat. Cook the onion and leek for 5 minutes
without browning. Add the garlic, tomato and
1 tablespoon of the tomato paste. Simmer for
5 minutes. Stir in 2 litres (70 fl oz/8 cups) cold
water, then add the parsley sprigs, bay leaves,
thyme, fennel, saffron and seafood trimmings.
Bring to the boil, then reduce the heat and
simmer for 30–40 minutes.

2   Strain the stock into a large saucepan,
pressing out the juices and discarding the solids.
Set aside 60 ml (2 fl oz/¼ cup) stock. Add the
Pernod to pan and stir in extra tomato paste if
needed to enrich the colour. Season with salt
and pepper. Bring to the boil and add potato,
then reduce the heat and simmer for 5 minutes.

3   Add the blue-eyed cod and bream, cook for
2–3 minutes, then add the red fish and snapper,
and cook for 5–6 minutes, or until cooked.

4   To make the toasts, toast the bread until
golden on both sides. While still warm, rub with
the garlic.

5   To make the rouille, soak the bread in
enough cold water to cover, for 5 minutes.
Cook the capsicum, skin side up, under a
hot grill (broiler) until the skin blackens and
blisters. Place in a sealable plastic bag and leave
to cool, then peel away the skin. Roughly chop
the flesh. Squeeze bread dry and place in a food
processor with capsicum, chilli, garlic and basil.
Process to a smooth paste. While processing,
gradually add the oil until the consistency
resembles mayonnaise. Thin the sauce with
1–2 tablespoons of reserved fish stock. Season.

6   To serve, place two pieces of toast in the
base of six soup bowls. Spoon in the soup and
fish pieces and serve with the rouille.

NOTE: *Try to use at least four different varieties
of fish, choosing a range of textures and flavours.
Rascasse, where available, is traditional, but cod,
bass, john dory, halibut, monkfish, turbot, hake
and red mullet can also be used. Shellfish such as
lobster, scallops and mussels can be used.*

HINT: *Make sure the plastic bag is firmly sealed
when you place the capsicum inside. This ensures
it sweats and makes it easier to peel off the skin.*

NUTRITION PER SERVE
Protein 60 g; Fat 30 g; Carbohydrate 40 g; Dietary
Fibre 5.5 g; Cholesterol 175 mg; 2838 kJ (678 Cal)

Simmer the onion, leek, garlic, tomato and tomato paste for 5 minutes.

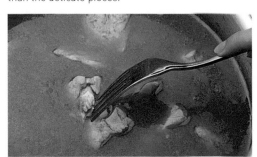
Cook the firmer-fleshed fish pieces slightly longer than the delicate pieces.

Rub the halved garlic cloves over the toasted bread slices while they are still warm.

Vietnamese fish and noodle soup

PREPARATION TIME: 30 MINUTES + 5 MINUTES SOAKING | TOTAL COOKING TIME: 20 MINUTES | SERVES 4

1 teaspoon shrimp paste
150 g (5½ oz) mung bean vermicelli
2 tablespoons peanut oil
6 garlic cloves, finely chopped
1 small onion, thinly sliced
2 long red chillies, chopped
2 lemongrass stems (white part only), thinly
    sliced
1.25 litres (44 fl oz/5 cups) chicken stock
60 ml (2 fl oz/¼ cup) fish sauce
1 tablespoon rice vinegar
4 ripe tomatoes, peeled, seeded and chopped
500 g (1 lb 2 oz) firm white fish fillets (snapper
    or blue-eyed cod), cut into 3 cm (1¼ inch)
    pieces
1 large handful mint, torn
1 very large handful coriander (cilantro) leaves
90 g (3¼ oz/1 cup) bean sprouts, trimmed
1 tablespoon mint, extra
1 tablespoon coriander (cilantro) leaves, extra
2 long red chillies, extra, sliced
lemon wedges, to serve

1   Wrap the shrimp paste in foil and place
under a hot grill (broiler) for 1 minute. Set aside.

2   Soak the vermicelli in boiling water for
3–4 minutes. Rinse under cold water, drain and
then cut into 15 cm (6 inch) lengths.

3   Heat the oil in a heavy-based saucepan
over medium heat. Add the garlic and cook for
1 minute, or until golden. Add the onion, chilli,
lemongrass and paste, and cook, stirring, for a
further minute. Add the stock, fish sauce, vinegar
and tomato. Bring to the boil, then reduce the
heat to medium and simmer for 10 minutes. Add
the fish and simmer gently for 3 minutes, or until
cooked. Stir in the mint and coriander.

4   Divide noodles and sprouts among bowls
and ladle the soup on top. Top with extra mint,
coriander and chilli. Serve with lemon wedges.

Remove the seeds from the peeled tomato with a teaspoon.

Gently simmer the fish pieces in the soup until they are cooked.

NUTRITION PER SERVE
Protein 33 g; Fat 13 g; Carbohydrate 21 g; Dietary
Fibre 5.5 g; Cholesterol 74 mg; 1405 kJ (335 Cal)

Chicken and coconut milk soup

PREPARATION TIME: 30 MINUTES + 5 MINUTES SOAKING | TOTAL COOKING TIME: 15 MINUTES | SERVES 8

150 g (5½ oz) dried rice vermicelli
1 lime
4 small red chillies, seeded and chopped
1 onion, chopped
2 garlic cloves, crushed
4 thin slices fresh ginger, finely chopped
2 lemongrass stems (white part only), chopped
1 tablespoon chopped coriander (cilantro)
    leaves
1 tablespoon peanut oil
750 ml (26 fl oz/3 cups) chicken stock
685 ml (23½ fl oz/2¾ cups) coconut milk
500 g (1 lb 2 oz) chicken tenderloins, cut into
    thin strips
4 spring onions (scallions), chopped
150 g (5½ oz) fried tofu puffs, sliced
90 g (3¼ oz/1 cup) bean sprouts
3 teaspoons soft brown sugar

1   Soak the vermicelli in boiling water for 5 minutes. Drain, cut into short lengths.

2   Remove the lime zest with a vegetable peeler and cut it into long, thin strips.

3   Place the chilli, onion, garlic, ginger, lemongrass and coriander into a food processor and process in short bursts for 20 seconds, or until smooth.

4   Heat the oil in a large heavy-based saucepan over medium heat. Add the chilli mixture and cook, stirring frequently, for 3 minutes, or until fragrant. Add the stock, coconut milk and lime zest strips, and bring to the boil. Add the chicken and cook, stirring, for 4 minutes, or until tender.

5   Add the spring onion, tofu, bean sprouts and brown sugar, and season with salt. Stir over medium heat for 3 minutes, or until the spring onion is tender. Divide the noodles among eight bowls and pour the soup over the top. Garnish with chilli and coriander.

NUTRITION PER SERVE
Protein 20 g; Fat 25 g; Carbohydrate 19 g; Dietary Fibre 3.5 g; Cholesterol 44 mg; 1555 kJ (370 Cal)

Remove the lime zest with a vegetable peeler, and cut it into long, thin strips.

Process the chilli, onion, garlic, ginger, lemongrass and coriander until smooth.

Chinese pork and noodle soup

PREPARATION TIME: 25 MINUTES + OVERNIGHT REFRIGERATION + 1 HOUR REFRIGERATION | TOTAL COOKING TIME: 4 HOURS | SERVES 4–6

STOCK

1.5 kg (3 lb 5oz) chicken bones (chicken necks, backs, wings), washed

3 garlic cloves, sliced

2 slices fresh ginger, 1 cm (½ inch) thick

4 spring onions (scallions), (white part only)

150 g (5½ oz) Chinese cabbage, shredded

1 tablespoon peanut oil

2 teaspoons sesame oil

4 garlic cloves, crushed

1 tablespoon grated fresh ginger

300 g (10½ oz) minced (ground) pork

1 egg white

¼ teaspoon ground white pepper

2 tablespoons light soy sauce

1 tablespoon Chinese rice wine

1½ tablespoons cornflour (cornstarch)

1 very large handful coriander (cilantro) leaves, finely chopped

6 spring onions (scallions), extra, thinly sliced

200 g (7 oz) fresh thin egg noodles

1 To make the stock, place the bones and 3.5 litres (122 fl oz/14 cups) water in a large saucepan and bring to a simmer—do not boil. Cook for 30 minutes, removing any scum that rises to the surface. Add the garlic, ginger and spring onion, and cook, partially covered, at a low simmer for 3 hours. Strain through a fine sieve, then cool. Cover and refrigerate overnight. Remove the layer of fat from the surface once it has solidified.

2 Bring a large saucepan of water to the boil and cook the cabbage for 2 minutes, or until soft. Drain the cabbage, cool and squeeze out the excess water.

3 Heat the peanut oil and 1 teaspoon of the sesame oil in a small frying pan, and cook the garlic and ginger for 1 minute, or until the garlic just starts to brown. Allow to cool.

4 Combine the pork, cabbage, garlic mixture, egg white, white pepper, soy sauce, rice wine, cornflour, half the coriander and half the spring onion. Cover and refrigerate for 1 hour. Shape tablespoons of the mixture into balls.

5 Bring 1.5 litres (52 fl oz/6 cups) of the stock (freeze the leftover stock) to the boil in a wok over high heat. Reduce the heat to medium and simmer for 1–2 minutes. Add the pork balls and cook, covered, for 8–10 minutes, or until they rise to the surface and are cooked through.

6 Bring a large saucepan of water to the boil. Cook the noodles for 1 minute, then drain and rinse. Divide among serving bowls and ladle the soup and pork balls on top. Garnish with the remaining spring onion, coriander leaves and sprinkle over remaining sesame oil.

NUTRITION PER SERVE (6)
Protein 17 g; Fat 9.5 g; Carbohydrate 23 g; Dietary Fibre 2 g; Cholesterol 35 mg; 1030 kJ (245 Cal)

Place all the meatball ingredients in a bowl and combine with your hands.

Once the pork balls have been shaped, add them to the wok one by one.

The pork balls are cooked when they rise to the surface of the stock.

Roast duck and noodle broth

PREPARATION TIME: 25 MINUTES + 25 MINUTES SOAKING | TOTAL COOKING TIME: 10 MINUTES | SERVES 4–6

3 dried shiitake mushrooms
1 Chinese roast duck (1.5 kg/3 lb 5 oz)
500 ml (17 fl oz/2 cups) chicken stock
2 tablespoons light soy sauce
1 tablespoon Chinese rice wine
2 teaspoons sugar
400 g (14 oz) fresh flat rice noodles
2 tablespoons oil
3 spring onions (scallions), thinly sliced
1 teaspoon finely chopped fresh ginger
400 g (14 oz) bok choy (pak choy), leaves
    separated
¼ teaspoon sesame oil

1   Soak the mushrooms in 250 ml (9 fl oz/1 cup) boiling water for 20 minutes. Drain, reserving the liquid and squeezing the excess liquid from the mushrooms. Discard the stems and thinly slice the caps.

2   Remove the skin and flesh from the duck. Discard the fat and carcass. Finely slice the duck meat and the skin (you need about 400 g/14 oz of duck meat).

3   Place the stock, soy sauce, rice wine, sugar and the reserved mushroom liquid in a saucepan over medium heat. Bring to a simmer and cook for 5 minutes.

4   Meanwhile, place the rice noodles in a heatproof bowl, cover with boiling water and soak briefly. Gently separate the noodles with your hands and drain well. Divide evenly among large soup bowls.

5   Heat the oil in a wok over high heat. Add the spring onion, ginger and mushroom, and cook for several seconds. Transfer to the broth with the bok choy and duck meat, and simmer for 1 minute, or until the duck has warmed through and the bok choy has wilted. Ladle the soup on the noodles and drizzle sesame oil on each serving. Serve immediately.

Once the shiitake mushrooms have been soaked, thinly slice the caps.

NUTRITION PER SERVE (6)
Protein 17 g; Fat 24 g; Carbohydrate 31 g; Dietary Fibre 2 g; Cholesterol 77 mg; 1695 kJ (405 Cal)

Vietnamese beef noodle soup

PREPARATION TIME: 15 MINUTES + 40 MINUTES FREEZING + 5 MINUTES SOAKING | TOTAL COOKING TIME: 30 MINUTES | SERVES 4

400 g (14 oz) rump steak, trimmed
1 litre (35 fl oz/4 cups) beef stock
½ onion
1 star anise
1 cinnamon stick
1 tablespoon fish sauce
pinch ground white pepper
200 g (7 oz) fresh thin round rice noodles
2 spring onions (scallions), thinly sliced
30 mint leaves
90 g (3¼ oz/1 cup) bean sprouts, trimmed
1 small white onion, thinly sliced
1 small red chilli, thinly sliced

1 Wrap the meat in plastic wrap and freeze for 30–40 minutes, or until partially frozen. Thinly slice the meat across the grain.

2 Place the stock in a large heavy-based saucepan with the onion half, star anise, cinnamon stick, fish sauce, white pepper and 500 ml (17 fl oz/2 cups) water, and bring to the boil over high heat. Reduce the heat to low–medium and simmer, covered, for 20 minutes. Discard the onion, star anise and cinnamon stick.

3 Meanwhile, cover the noodles with boiling water and gently separate. Drain and refresh with cold water. Divide the noodles and spring onion among the serving bowls. Top with equal amounts of beef, mint leaves, bean sprouts, onion slices and chilli. Ladle the simmering broth into the bowls, and serve.

NOTE: *It is important that the broth is kept hot as the heat will cook the slices of beef.*

Thinly slice the partially frozen steak across the grain.

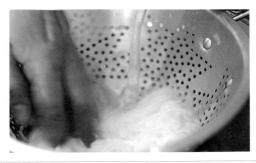

Rinse the noodles well in a colander, under cold running water.

NUTRITION PER SERVE
Protein 28 g; Fat 5.5 g; Carbohydrate 24 g; Dietary Fibre 2 g; Cholesterol 64 mg; 1100 kJ (265 Cal)

Chicken laksa

PREPARATION TIME: 30 MINUTES + 10 MINUTES SOAKING | TOTAL COOKING TIME: 35 MINUTES | SERVES 4–6

1½ tablespoons coriander seeds

1 tablespoon cumin seeds

1 teaspoon ground turmeric

1 onion, roughly chopped

1 tablespoon roughly chopped fresh ginger

3 garlic cloves

3 lemongrass stems (white part only), sliced

6 candlenuts or macadamias (see NOTES)

4–6 small red chillies, sliced

2–3 teaspoons shrimp paste, roasted (see
    NOTES)

1 litre (35 fl oz/4 cups) chicken stock

60 ml (2 fl oz/¼ cup) oil

400 g (14 oz) chicken thigh fillets, cut into
    2 cm (¾ inch) pieces

750 ml (26 fl oz/3 cups) coconut milk

4 makrut (kaffir lime) leaves

2½ tablespoons lime juice

2 tablespoons fish sauce

2 tablespoons grated palm sugar (jaggery) or
    soft brown sugar

250 g (9 oz) dried rice vermicelli

90 g (3¼ oz/1 cup) bean sprouts, trimmed

4 fried tofu puffs, cut into matchsticks

1 very large handful mint leaves

2 large handfuls coriander (cilantro) leaves

lime wedges, to serve

NUTRITION PER SERVE (6)
Protein 22 g; Fat 43 g; Carbohydrate 40 g; Dietary
Fibre 5 g; Cholesterol 58 mg; 2620 kJ (625 Cal)

1 Dry-fry (no oil) the coriander and cumin seeds in a frying pan over medium heat for 1–2 minutes, or until fragrant, tossing to prevent burning. Grind finely in a mortar with a pestle.

2 Place all the spices, onion, ginger, garlic, lemongrass, nuts, chillies and shrimp paste in a food processor or blender. Add 125 ml (4 fl oz/½ cup) of the stock and blend to a fine paste.

3 Heat the oil in a large saucepan over low heat and cook the paste for 3–5 minutes, stirring to prevent it burning. Add remaining stock and bring to the boil over high heat. Reduce heat to medium and simmer for 15 minutes, or until reduced slightly. Add the chicken and simmer for 4–5 minutes, or until cooked through.

4 Add the coconut milk, makrut leaves, lime juice, fish sauce and palm sugar, and simmer for 5 minutes over low–medium heat. Do not bring to the boil, as the coconut milk will split.

5 Meanwhile, place the vermicelli in a heatproof bowl, cover with boiling water and soak for 6–7 minutes, or until softened. Drain and divide among large serving bowls with the bean sprouts. Ladle the hot soup over the top and garnish with some tofu strips, mint and coriander leaves. Serve with a wedge of lime.

NOTES: *Raw candlenuts are slightly toxic so must be cooked before use.*

To roast the shrimp paste, wrap the paste in foil and place under a hot grill (broiler) for 1 minute.

Dry-fry the coriander and cumin seeds over medium heat, tossing constantly.

Place the spices, onion, ginger, garlic, chillies, nuts lemongrass, and shrimp paste in a food processor.

Simmer the laksa for 5 minutes over low–medium heat, taking care not to let it boil.

Smoked haddock chowder

PREPARATION TIME: 20 MINUTES I TOTAL COOKING TIME: 35 MINUTES I SERVES 4–6

500 g (1 lb 2 oz) smoked haddock
1 potato, diced
1 celery stalk, diced
1 onion, finely chopped
50 g (1¾ oz) butter
1 bacon slice, rind removed, finely chopped
2 tablespoons plain (all-purpose) flour
½ teaspoon mustard powder
½ teaspoon worcestershire sauce
250 ml (9 fl oz/1 cup) full-cream (whole) milk
2 very large handfuls chopped flat-leaf (Italian) parsley
60 ml (2 fl oz/¼ cup) cream

1 To make the fish stock, put the fish in a frying pan, cover with water and bring to the boil. Reduce the heat and simmer for 8 minutes, or until the fish flakes easily. Drain, reserving the fish stock, then peel, bone and flake the fish.

2 Put the potato, celery and onion in a medium saucepan, and pour over enough of the reserved fish stock to cover the vegetables. Bring to the boil, then reduce the heat and simmer for 8 minutes, or until the vegetables are tender.

3 Melt the butter in a large saucepan over low heat. Increase heat to medium–high, add the bacon and cook, stirring, for 3 minutes. Add the flour, mustard and worcestershire sauce, and stir until combined. Cook for 1 minute. Remove from the heat and gradually pour in the milk, stirring continuously until smooth. Return to the heat and stir for 5 minutes, until the mixture comes to the boil and has thickened. Stir in the vegetables and remaining stock, then add the parsley and fish. Simmer over low heat for 5 minutes, or until heated through. Season to taste, and serve with cream, if desired.

NOTE: *Chowder is a thick, hearty soup, made with seafood, fish, vegetables or chicken.*

Lay the fish on paper towels to drain well, then peel, bone and flake into small pieces.

Gradually add the milk, stirring continuously with a wooden spoon.

NUTRITION PER SERVE (6)
Protein 20 g; Fat 10 g; Carbohydrate 8 g; Dietary Fibre 1 g; Cholesterol 90 mg; 970 kJ (230 Cal)

Portuguese chicken broth with rice

PREPARATION TIME: 15 MINUTES I TOTAL COOKING TIME: 1 HOUR I SERVES 6

2.5 litres (87 fl oz/10 cups) chicken stock
1 onion, cut into thin wedges
1 teaspoon grated lemon zest
1 mint sprig
500 g (1 lb 2 oz) potatoes, chopped
1 tablespoon olive oil
2 boneless, skinless chicken breasts
200 g (7 oz/1 cup) long-grain rice
2 tablespoons lemon juice
mint leaves, to garnish

1   Combine the chicken stock, onion, lemon zest, mint sprig, potato and olive oil in a large saucepan. Slowly bring to the boil, then reduce the heat, add the chicken breasts and simmer gently for 20–25 minutes, or until the chicken is cooked through.

2   Remove the chicken breasts and discard the mint sprig. Cool the chicken, then cut it into thin slices.

3   Meanwhile, add the rice to the saucepan and simmer for 25–30 minutes, or until the rice is tender. Return the sliced chicken to the saucepan, add the lemon juice and stir for 1–2 minutes, or until the chicken is warmed through. Season, and serve garnished with mint leaves.

NOTE: *Rice and potato absorb liquid on standing, so serve immediately.*

NUTRITION PER SERVE
Protein 20 g; Fat 5 g; Carbohydrate 38 g; Dietary
Fibre 2 g; Cholesterol 37 mg; 1197 kJ (286 Cal)

Simmer the chicken for 20–25 minutes, or until cooked through.

Once it has cooled, slice the cooked chicken into thin strips.

Add the rice to the pan and simmer until the rice is tender.

Barley soup with golden parsnips

PREPARATION TIME: 30 MINUTES + OVERNIGHT SOAKING | TOTAL COOKING TIME: 2 HOURS 20 MINUTES | SERVES 6

200 g (7 oz) pearl barley
1 tablespoon oil
2 onions, chopped
2 garlic cloves, finely chopped
2 carrots, chopped
2 potatoes, chopped
2 celery stalks, chopped
2 bay leaves, torn in half
2 litres (70 fl oz/8 cups) chicken stock
125 ml (4 fl oz/½ cup) full-cream (whole) milk
40 g (1½ oz) butter
3 parsnips, cubed
1 teaspoon soft brown sugar
chopped flat-leaf (Italian) parsley, to serve

NUTRITION PER SERVE
Protein 7 g; Fat 10 g; Carbohydrate 40 g; Dietary Fibre 8 g; Cholesterol 20 mg; 1190 kJ (285 Cal)

1 Soak the barley in water overnight. Drain. Place in a saucepan with 2 litres (70 fl oz/ 8 cups) water. Bring to the boil, then reduce the heat and simmer, partially covered, for 1¼ hours, or until tender. Drain the barley.

2 Heat the oil in a large saucepan, add the onion, garlic, carrot, potato and celery, and cook for 3 minutes. Stir well and cook, covered, for 15 minutes over low heat, stirring occasionally.

3 Add the barley, bay leaves, stock, milk, 2 teaspoons of salt and 1 teaspoon of pepper. Bring to the boil, then reduce the heat and simmer the soup, partially covered, for around 35 minutes. If the soup is too thick, add about 250 ml (9 fl oz/1 cup) cold water, a little at a time, until it reaches your preferred consistency.

4 While the soup is simmering, melt the butter in a frying pan, add the parsnip and toss in the butter. Sprinkle with the sugar and cook until golden brown and tender. Serve the parsnip on top of the soup and sprinkle with the parsley and, if desired, season with cracked black pepper.

Using a sharp knife, chop the carrots, potatoes and the celery.

Add the drained barley to the cooked vegetables and stir through.

Sprinkle the soft brown sugar over the parsnip in the frying pan.

Spiced lentil soup

PREPARATION TIME: 10 MINUTES + 20 MINUTES STANDING | TOTAL COOKING TIME: 50 MINUTES | SERVES 4

1 eggplant (aubergine)
60 ml (2 fl oz/¼ cup) olive oil
1 onion, finely chopped
2 teaspoons brown mustard seeds
2 teaspoons ground cumin
1 teaspoon garam masala
¼ teaspoon cayenne pepper (optional)
2 large carrots, cut into cubes
1 celery stalk, diced
400 g (14 oz) tin chopped tomatoes
100 g (3½ oz/1 cup) puy or small blue-green
    lentils
1 litre (35 fl oz/4 cups) chicken stock
2 large handfuls coriander (cilantro) leaves,
    roughly chopped
125 g (4½ oz/½ cup) plain yoghurt

1 Cut the eggplant into cubes, place in a colander, sprinkle with salt and leave for 20 minutes. Rinse well and pat the eggplant dry with paper towels.

2 Heat the oil in a large saucepan over medium heat. Add the onion and cook for 5 minutes, or until softened. Add the eggplant, stir to coat in oil and cook for 3 minutes, or until softened.

3 Add the spices and the cayenne pepper (if using) and cook, stirring, for 1 minute, or until fragrant and the mustard seeds begin to pop. Add the carrot and celery and cook for 1 minute. Stir in the tomato, lentils and stock and bring to the boil. Reduce the heat and simmer for 40 minutes, or until the lentils are tender and the liquid is reduced to a thick stew-like soup. Season to taste with salt and freshly ground black pepper.

4 Stir the coriander into the soup just before serving. Ladle the soup into four warmed bowls and serve with a dollop of the yoghurt on top.

Add the spices to the onion and eggplant mixture, and stir until fragrant.

Simmer the mixture until it is thick and the lentils are tender.

NUTRITION PER SERVE
Protein 11 g; Fat 16 g; Carbohydrate 20 g; Dietary
Fibre 8.5 g; Cholesterol 5 mg; 1148 kJ (274 Cal)

Pasta and bean soup

PREPARATION TIME: 15 MINUTES + OVERNIGHT SOAKING + 10 MINUTES RESTING | TOTAL COOKING TIME: 1 HOUR 45 MINUTES | SERVES 4

200 g (7 oz) dried borlotti (cranberry) beans (see NOTE)
60 ml (2 fl oz/¼ cup) olive oil
90 g (3¼ oz) piece pancetta, finely diced
1 onion, finely chopped
2 garlic cloves, crushed
1 celery stalk, thinly sliced
1 carrot, diced
1 bay leaf
1 rosemary sprig
1 flat-leaf (Italian) parsley sprig
400 g (14 oz) tin chopped tomatoes, drained
1.6 litres (56 fl oz) vegetable stock
2 tablespoons finely chopped flat-leaf (Italian) parsley
150 g (5½ oz) ditalini or other small dried pasta
extra virgin olive oil, to serve
grated parmesan cheese, to serve

1   Place the beans in a large bowl, cover with cold water and soak overnight. Drain and rinse.

2   Heat the oil in a large saucepan, add the pancetta, onion, garlic, celery and carrot, and cook over medium heat for 5 minutes, or until golden. Season. Add the bay leaf, rosemary, parsley sprig, tomato, stock and beans. Bring to the boil. Reduce heat and simmer for 1½ hours, or until tender. Add boiling water if needed.

3   Discard the bay leaf, rosemary and parsley sprigs. Scoop out 250 ml (9 fl oz/1 cup) of the mixture and purée in a food processor. Return to the pan, season, and add chopped parsley and pasta. Simmer for 6 minutes, or until *al dente*. Remove from heat and set aside for 10 minutes. Serve drizzled with olive oil, sprinkled with parmesan and pepper if desired.

NOTE: *If you prefer, you can use three 400 g (14 oz) tins drained borlotti beans. Simmer with the other vegetables for 30 minutes.*

NUTRITION PER SERVE
Protein 13 g; Fat 20 g; Carbohydrate 38 g; Dietary Fibre 7.5 g; Cholesterol 12 mg; 1643 kJ (393 Cal)

Purée 250 ml (9 fl oz/1 cup) of the bean mixture in a food processor.

Add the dried pasta to the soup and simmer until it is *al dente*.

Avgolemono with chicken

PREPARATION TIME: 30 MINUTES | TOTAL COOKING TIME: 30 MINUTES | SERVES 4

1 onion, halved

2 cloves

1 carrot, cut into chunks

1 bay leaf

500 g (1 lb 2 oz) boneless, skinless chicken
    breasts

75 g (2½ oz/⅓ cup) short-grain rice

3 eggs, separated

60 ml (2 fl oz/¼ cup) lemon juice

2 tablespoons chopped flat-leaf (Italian)
    parsley

4 thin lemon slices, to garnish

NUTRITION PER SERVE
Protein 35 g; Fat 6.5 g; Carbohydrate 18 g; Dietary
Fibre 1.5 g; Cholesterol 198 mg; 1145 kJ (274 Cal)

1 Stud the onion halves with the cloves and then place in a large saucepan with 1.5 litres (52 fl oz/6 cups) water. Add the carrot, bay leaf and chicken. Season with salt and freshly ground black pepper. Slowly bring to the boil, reduce the heat and simmer for 10 minutes, or until chicken is cooked.

2 Strain the stock into a clean saucepan, reserving the chicken and discarding the vegetables. Add the rice to the stock, bring to the boil, then reduce the heat and simmer for 15 minutes, or until tender. Tear the chicken into shreds.

3 Whisk the egg whites until stiff peaks form, then beat in the yolks. Slowly beat in the lemon juice. Gently stir in 150 ml (5 fl oz) of the hot (not boiling) soup and beat thoroughly. Add the egg mixture to the soup and stir gently over low heat until thickened slightly. It should still be quite thin. Do not let it boil or the eggs may scramble. Add the shredded chicken, and season to taste.

4 Set aside for 3–4 minutes to allow the flavours to develop, then sprinkle with the parsley. Garnish with lemon slices and serve.

Simmer the chicken breasts for 10 minutes, or until cooked.

Whisk the egg whites until stiff peaks form, then beat in the yolks, then the lemon juice.

Add the shredded chicken breasts to the soup, and season to taste.

Chunky vegetable soup

PREPARATION TIME: 20 MINUTES + OVERNIGHT SOAKING | TOTAL COOKING TIME: 1 HOUR 5 MINUTES | SERVES 6

100 g (3½ oz/½ cup) dried red kidney beans
    or borlotti (cranberry) beans (see NOTE)
1 tablespoon olive oil
1 leek, halved lengthways, chopped
1 small onion, diced
2 carrots, chopped
2 celery stalks, chopped
1 large zucchini (courgette), chopped
1 tablespoon tomato paste (concentrated
    purée)
1 litre (35 fl oz/4 cups) vegetable stock
400 g (14 oz) pumpkin (winter squash), cut
    into 2 cm (¾ inch) cubes
2 potatoes, cut into 2 cm (¾ inch) cubes
crusty wholemeal bread, to serve

1   Put the beans in a large bowl, cover with cold water and soak overnight. Rinse, then transfer to a saucepan, cover with cold water and cook on medium–high for 45 minutes, or until just tender. Drain and set aside.

2   Meanwhile, heat the oil in a large saucepan. Add the leek and onion, and cook over medium heat for 2–3 minutes without browning, or until they start to soften. Add the carrot, celery and zucchini, and cook for 3–4 minutes. Add the tomato paste and stir for a further 1 minute. Pour in the stock and 1.25 litres (44 fl oz/5 cups) water, and bring to the boil. Reduce the heat to low and simmer for 20 minutes.

3   Add the pumpkin, potato and beans, and simmer on low–medium heat for a further 20 minutes, or until the vegetables are tender and the beans are cooked. Season to taste. Serve immediately with crusty bread.

NOTE: *To save time, use a 400 g (14 oz) tin of red kidney beans instead of dried beans. Rinse well and leave out Step 1.*

Using a sharp knife, cut the peeled pumpkin into large cubes.

Add the vegetables and beans, and simmer until the vegetables are cooked.

NUTRITION PER SERVE
Protein 7.5 g; Fat 4 g; Carbohydrate 19 g; Dietary Fibre 7 g; Cholesterol 0 mg; 600 kJ (143 Cal)

Lentil and silverbeet soup

PREPARATION TIME: 20 MINUTES + OVERNIGHT REFRIGERATION | TOTAL COOKING TIME: 3 HOURS 20 MINUTES | SERVES 6

CHICKEN STOCK
1 kg (2 lb 4 oz) chicken bones (chicken necks, backs, wings), washed
1 small onion, roughly chopped
1 bay leaf
3–4 flat-leaf (Italian) parsley sprigs
1–2 oregano or thyme sprigs

280 g (10 oz/1½ cups) brown lentils, washed
850 g (1 lb 14 oz) silverbeet (Swiss chard)
60 ml (2 fl oz/¼ cup) olive oil
1 large onion, finely chopped
4 garlic cloves, crushed
2 large handfuls finely chopped coriander (cilantro) leaves
80 ml (2½ fl oz/⅓ cup) lemon juice
lemon wedges, to serve
crusty bread, to serve

1 To make the stock, place all the stock ingredients in a large saucepan, add 3 litres (105 fl oz/12 cups) water and bring to the boil. Skim any scum from the surface. Reduce the heat and simmer for 2 hours. Strain the stock, discarding the bones, onion and herbs. Chill overnight.

2 Skim any fat from the stock. Place the lentils in a large saucepan and add the stock and 1 litre (35 fl oz/4 cups) water. Bring to the boil, then reduce the heat and simmer, covered, for 1 hour.

3 Meanwhile, remove the stems from the silverbeet and shred the leaves. Heat the oil in a saucepan over medium heat and cook the onion for 2–3 minutes, or until transparent. Add the garlic and cook for 1 minute. Add the silverbeet and toss for 2–3 minutes, or until wilted. Stir the mixture into the lentils. Add the coriander and lemon juice, season, and simmer, covered, for 15–20 minutes. Serve with the lemon wedges and crusty bread.

NUTRITION PER SERVE
Protein 52 g; Fat 15 g; Carbohydrate 20 g; Dietary Fibre 11 g; Cholesterol 83 mg; 1782 kJ (425 Cal)

Skim any fat from the surface of the stock before adding the lentils.

Add the coriander and lemon juice to the silverbeet and lentil mixture.

Lamb hotpot

PREPARATION TIME: 40 MINUTES + 1 HOUR REFRIGERATION | TOTAL COOKING TIME: 2 HOURS | SERVES 4

2 tablespoons olive oil

8 lamb shanks

2 onions, sliced

4 garlic cloves, finely chopped

3 bay leaves, torn in half

1–2 teaspoons hot paprika

2 teaspoons sweet paprika

1 tablespoon plain (all-purpose) flour

60 g (2¼ oz/¼ cup) tomato paste
    (concentrated purée)

1.5 litres (52 fl oz/6 cups) vegetable stock

4 potatoes, chopped

4 carrots, sliced

3 celery stalks, thickly sliced

3 tomatoes, seeded and chopped

NUTRITION PER SERVE
Protein 70 g; Fat 15 g; Carbohydrate 30 g; Dietary
Fibre 8 g; Cholesterol 170 mg; 2200 kJ (525 Cal)

1   To make the lamb stock, heat 1 tablespoon of the oil in a large heavy-based saucepan over medium heat. Brown the shanks well in two batches, then drain on paper towels.

2   Add the remaining oil to the pan and cook the onion, garlic and bay leaves over low heat for 10 minutes, stirring regularly. Add the paprikas and flour and cook, stirring, for 2 minutes. Gradually add the combined tomato paste and vegetable stock. Bring to the boil, stirring continuously, and return the shanks to the pan. Reduce the heat to low and simmer, covered, for 1½ hours, stirring occasionally.

3   Remove and discard the bay leaves. Remove the shanks, allow to cool slightly and then cut the meat from the bone. Discard the bone. Cut the meat into pieces and refrigerate. Refrigerate for about 1 hour, or until fat forms on the surface and it can be spooned off.

4   Return the meat to the stock along with the potato, carrot and celery, turn the heat up to medium–high and bring to the boil. Reduce the heat and simmer for 15 minutes. Season, and add the chopped tomato to serve.

Halve the tomatoes and carefully scoop out the seeds with a teaspoon.

Brown the shanks in two batches, remove with tongs and drain on paper towels.

Spoon off the layer of fat that forms on the surface of the soup.

Miso with ramen

PREPARATION TIME: 15 MINUTES + 15 MINUTES SOAKING | TOTAL COOKING TIME: 15 MINUTES | SERVES 4

1 teaspoon finely chopped dried wakame

180 g (6¼ oz) fresh ramen noodles

100 g (3½ oz) silken firm tofu, cut into 1.5 cm (⅝ inch) cubes

2 spring onions (scallions), thinly sliced on the diagonal

1¾ teaspoons dashi granules

2–3 tablespoons red miso (see NOTE)

2 teaspoons mirin (sweet rice wine)

2 teaspoons Japanese soy sauce

1 Soak the wakame in a bowl of tepid water for 15 minutes. Drain and set aside.

2 Cook the noodles in a large saucepan of boiling salted water for 2 minutes, or until cooked through. Drain and rinse, then divide among warmed serving bowls. Place the tofu and spring onion on top.

3 Meanwhile, bring 1.25 litres (44 fl oz/5 cups) water to the boil in a large saucepan. Reduce the heat to low and add the dashi granules, stirring for 30 seconds, or until dissolved.

4 In a bowl, combine the miso with 250 ml (9 fl oz/1 cup) of the dashi stock, whisking until smooth. Return the miso mixture to the pan of stock and stir until combined—be careful not to boil the broth as this will diminish the flavour of the miso. Add the mirin, soy sauce and wakame, and gently heat for 1 minute, then stir to combine. Ladle the broth over the noodles, tofu and spring onion, and serve immediately.

NOTE: *Shiro (white) miso can be used instead of red miso, however the flavour will not be as strong—adjust to taste.*

With a very sharp knife, chop the dried wakame into fine pieces.

NUTRITION PER SERVE
Protein 9 g; Fat 3 g; Carbohydrate 28 g; Dietary Fibre 2.5 g; Cholesterol 6 mg; 735 kJ (175 Cal)

Soba noodle and vegetable soup

PREPARATION TIME: 15 MINUTES + 5 MINUTES SOAKING | TOTAL COOKING TIME: 10 MINUTES | SERVES 4

250 g (9 oz) soba noodles

2 dried shiitake mushrooms

2 litres (70 fl oz/8 cups) vegetable stock

120 g (4¼ oz) snow peas (mangetout), cut into
thin strips

2 small carrots, cut into thin 5 cm (2 inch)
strips

2 garlic cloves, finely chopped

6 spring onions (scallions), cut into
5 cm (2 inch) lengths and thinly sliced
lengthways

3 cm (1¼ inch) piece fresh ginger, cut into
matchsticks

80 ml (2½ fl oz/⅓ cup) soy sauce

60 ml (2 fl oz/¼ cup) mirin (sweet rice wine)
or sake

90 g (3¼ oz/1 cup) bean sprouts, trimmed

1 Cook the noodles according to the packet instructions, then drain.

2 Soak the mushrooms in 125 ml (4 fl oz/ ½ cup) boiling water until soft. Drain, reserving the liquid. Discard the stems and slice the caps.

3 Combine the vegetable stock, mushrooms, reserved liquid, snow peas, carrot, garlic, spring onion and ginger in a large saucepan. Bring slowly to the boil, then reduce the heat to low and simmer for 5 minutes, or until the vegetables are tender. Add the soy sauce, mirin and bean sprouts. Cook for a further 3 minutes.

4 Divide the noodles among serving bowls. Ladle the soup and vegetables over the noodles and garnish with coriander.

After soaking the mushrooms, drain, discard the stems and thinly slice the caps.

Simmer the vegetables for 5 minutes, or until they are tender.

NUTRITION PER SERVE
Protein 13 g; Fat 1.5 g; Carbohydrate 30 g; Dietary
Fibre 6 g; Cholesterol 11 mg; 1124 kJ (270 Cal)

Prawn laksa

PREPARATION TIME: 45 MINUTES + 5 MINUTES SOAKING | TOTAL COOKING TIME: 50 MINUTES | SERVES 4

1 kg (2 lb 4 oz) raw prawns (shrimp)
80 ml (2½ fl oz/⅓ cup) oil
2–6 small red chillies, seeded
1 onion, roughly chopped
3 garlic cloves, halved
2 cm x 2 cm (¾ inch x ¾ inch) piece fresh ginger or galangal, chopped
3 lemongrass stems (white part only), chopped
1 teaspoon ground turmeric
1 tablespoon ground coriander
2 teaspoons shrimp paste
625 ml (21½ fl oz/2½ cups) coconut cream
2 teaspoons grated palm sugar (jaggery) or soft brown sugar
4 makrut (kaffir lime) leaves, crushed
1–2 tablespoons fish sauce
200 g (7 oz) packet fish balls
190 g (6¾ oz) fried tofu puffs
250 g (9 oz) dried rice vermicelli
125 g (4½ oz) bean sprouts, trimmed
1 large handful mint leaves, to serve
coriander (cilantro) leaves, to serve

1   Peel the prawns and gently pull out the dark vein from each prawn back, starting at the head end. Reserve the heads, shells and tails. Cover and refrigerate the prawn meat.

2   Heat 2 tablespoons of the oil in a wok or large saucepan and add the prawn shells, tails and heads. Stir over medium heat for 10 minutes, or until orange, then add 1 litre (35 fl oz/4 cups)water. Bring to the boil, then reduce the heat and simmer for 15 minutes. Strain the stock through a fine sieve and reserve the liquid. Discard the shells and clean the pan.

3   Finely chop the chillies (use two for mild flavour, increase for hot), and process with the onion, garlic, ginger, lemongrass, turmeric, coriander and 60 ml (2 fl oz/¼ cup) of the prawn stock in a food processor.

4   Heat the remaining oil in the pan, add the chilli mixture and shrimp paste, and stir over medium heat for 3 minutes, or until fragrant. Pour in the remaining stock and simmer for 10 minutes. Add the coconut cream, palm sugar, makrut leaves and fish sauce, and simmer for 5 minutes. Add the prawns and simmer for 2 minutes, or until firm and light pink. Add the fish balls and fried tofu puffs, and simmer gently until just heated through.

5   Soak the rice vermicelli in a bowl of boiling water for 2 minutes, then drain and divide among serving bowls. Top with the bean sprouts and ladle the soup over the top. Garnish with the mint and coriander.

NUTRITION PER SERVE
Protein 58 g; Fat 58 g; Carbohydrate 71 g; Dietary Fibre 9 g; Cholesterol 514 mg; 4331 kJ (1031 Cal)

Stir and toss the prawn heads, shells and tails until the heads turn bright orange.

Process the chilli, onion, garlic, ginger, lemongrass, spices and stock.

Add the prawns to the pan and simmer until they turn light pink.

Pork, corn and noodle soup

PREPARATION TIME: 15 MINUTES | TOTAL COOKING TIME: 30 MINUTES | SERVES 4

2 small fresh corn cobs

200 g (7 oz) dried ramen noodles

2 teaspoons peanut oil

1 teaspoon grated fresh ginger

1.5 litres (52 fl oz/6 cups) chicken stock

2 tablespoons mirin (sweet rice wine)

200 g (7 oz) piece Chinese barbecued pork (char siu), thinly sliced

3 spring onions (scallions), sliced on the diagonal

20 g (¾ oz) unsalted butter (optional, see NOTE)

1 Remove the corn kernels from the cob using a sharp knife.

2 Cook the ramen noodles in a large saucepan of boiling water for 4 minutes, or until tender. Drain, then rinse in cold water.

3 Heat the oil in a large saucepan over high heat. Stir-fry the ginger for 1 minute. Add the chicken stock and mirin and bring to the boil. Reduce the heat and simmer for 8 minutes.

4 Add the pork slices and cook for 5 minutes, then add the corn kernels and two-thirds of the spring onion, and cook for a further 4–5 minutes, or until the corn is tender.

5 Separate the noodles by running them under hot water, then divide them among four deep bowls. Ladle on the soup, then place 1 teaspoon butter on each serving. Garnish with the remaining spring onion and serve immediately.

NOTE: *This soup is traditionally served with the butter on top. However, for a healthier option, it can be omitted.*

Cut the barbecued pork into thin slices, using a small sharp knife.

Remove the kernels from the corn cobs by cutting down the cob with a knife.

NUTRITION PER SERVE
Protein 23 g; Fat 10.5 g; Carbohydrate 42 g; Dietary Fibre 3 g; Cholesterol 77 mg; 1510 kJ (360 Cal)

Eight-treasure noodle soup

PREPARATION TIME: 20 MINUTES + 20 MINUTES SOAKING | TOTAL COOKING TIME: 20 MINUTES | SERVES 4

10 g (¼ oz) dried shiitake mushrooms

375 g (13 oz) fresh thick hokkein (egg) noodles

1.2 litres (42 fl oz/5 cups) chicken stock

60 ml (2 fl oz/¼ cup) light soy sauce

2 teaspoons Chinese rice wine

200 g (7 oz) boneless, skinless chicken breasts, cut into 1 cm (½ inch) strips on the diagonal

200 g (7 oz) Chinese barbecued pork (char siu), cut into 5 mm (¼ inch) slices

¼ onion, finely chopped

1 carrot, cut into 1 cm (½ inch) sliced on the diagonal

120 g (4¼ oz) snow peas (mangetout), cut in half on the diagonal

4 bulb spring onions (scallions), thinly sliced

1 Soak the mushrooms in boiling water for 20 minutes, or until soft. Drain and squeeze out any excess liquid. Discard the stems and thinly slice the caps.

2 Bring a large saucepan of water to the boil and cook the noodles for 1 minute, or until cooked through. Drain, then rinse with cold water. Divide evenly among four deep warmed serving bowls.

3 Meanwhile, bring the chicken stock to the boil in a large saucepan over high heat. Reduce the heat to medium and stir in the soy sauce and rice wine. Simmer for 2 minutes. Add the chicken and pork and cook for 2 minutes, or until the chicken is cooked and the pork is heated through. Add the onion, carrot, snow peas, mushrooms and half the spring onion, and cook for 1 minute, or until the carrot is tender.

4 Divide the vegetables and meat among the serving bowls and ladle on the hot broth. Garnish with the remaining spring onion.

NUTRITION PER SERVE
Protein 42 g; Fat 7 g; Carbohydrate 61 g; Dietary Fibre 4 g; Cholesterol 109 mg; 1995 kJ (475 Cal)

Drain and squeeze any liquid out of the shiitake mushrooms before slicing.

Add the meat to the stock and cook until the chicken is cooked and pork is warmed through.

Hot and sour soup

PREPARATION TIME: 40 MINUTES + OVERNIGHT REFRIGERATION + 10 MINUTES STANDING | TOTAL COOKING TIME: 4 HOURS | SERVES 6

STOCK
1.5 kg (3 lb 5 oz) chicken bones (chicken
    necks, backs, wings), washed
2 slices fresh ginger, 1 cm (½ inch) thick
4 spring onions (scallions), (white part only)

200 g (7 oz) boneless, skinless chicken
    breasts, cut into 2 cm (¾ inch) pieces
2 tablespoons garlic and red chilli paste
60 ml (2 fl oz/¼ cup) light soy sauce
¾ teaspoon ground white pepper
115 g (4 oz) baby corn, quartered lengthways
80 ml (2½ fl oz/⅓ cup) Chinese black vinegar
4 fresh shiitake mushrooms, stems removed,
    caps thinly sliced
100 g (3½ oz) enoki mushrooms, trimmed
    and separated
65 g (2¼ oz) fresh black wood fungus, cut
    into 1 cm (½ inch) strips
200 g (7 oz) fresh Shanghai noodles
200 g (7 oz) firm tofu, cut into 2.5 cm
    (1 inch) cubes
30 g (1 oz/¼ cup) cornflour (cornstarch)
3 eggs, lightly beaten
1 teaspoon sesame oil
2 spring onions (scallions), thinly sliced on
    the diagonal, to garnish

1 To make the stock, place the bones and 3.5 litres (121 fl oz/14 cups) water in a large saucepan to simmer—do not boil. Cook for 30 minutes, removing the surface scum. Add ginger and any spring onion, and cook, partially covered, at a low simmer for 3 hours. Strain and cool. Cover and refrigerate overnight. Remove fat from the surface.

2 Bring 2 litres (70 fl oz/8 cups) of stock to the boil in a saucepan over high heat (freeze any remaining stock). Reduce heat to medium, add the chicken, garlic and chilli paste, soy sauce and white pepper, and stir to combine. Simmer, covered, for 10 minutes, or until the chicken is cooked. Add the corn, vinegar, mushrooms, wood fungus, noodles and tofu. Season with salt, and gently simmer for 5 minutes—do not stir.

3 Combine the cornflour and 60 ml (2 fl oz/¼ cup) water. Slowly stir into soup until combined and just thickened. Simmer, then slowly pour the egg over the surface. Turn off the heat, allow to stand for 10 minutes, then stir in the sesame oil. Garnish with spring onion and serve.

Cut the ends off the enoki mushrooms, then separate the stems

NUTRITION PER SERVE
Protein 23 g; Fat 9.5 g; Carbohydrate 31 g; Dietary
Fibre 3.5 g; Cholesterol 128 mg; 1265 kJ (300 Cal)

Clam chowder

PREPARATION TIME: 25 MINUTES I TOTAL COOKING TIME: 45 MINUTES I SERVES 4

30 g (1 oz) butter
2 bacon slices, finely chopped
1 large onion, finely chopped
4 potatoes, cut into small cubes
500 ml (17 fl oz/2 cups) fish stock
1 bay leaf
125 ml (4 fl oz/½ cup) full-cream (whole) milk
4 x 105 g (3½ oz) tins baby clams (vongole),
    drained and chopped
2 tablespoons finely chopped parsley
250 ml (9 fl oz/1 cup) cream
parsley, extra, to garnish

1   Heat the butter in a large saucepan. Cook the bacon and onion for 2–3 minutes, or until softened. Stir in the potato. Cook for a further 2–3 minutes, then gradually pour on the stock. Add the bay leaf.

2   Bring the mixture to the boil, then reduce the heat and simmer, covered, for 20 minutes, or until the potato is cooked. Simmer for 10 minutes, or until the soup is reduced and slightly thickened. Discard the bay leaf.

3   Add the milk, clams, parsley and cream. Stir to gently reheat, but do not allow the soup to boil. Season with salt and freshly ground black pepper. Sprinkle with parsley to serve.

NUTRITION PER SERVE
Protein 20 g; Fat 40 g; Carbohydrate 20 g; Dietary Fibre 3 g; Cholesterol 250 mg; 2090 kJ (500 Cal)

Peel and cut the potatoes into strips and then into small cubes.

Remove the bay leaf from the chowder with a pair of tongs.

Add the milk, chopped clams and parsley, and pour in the cream.

Mexican bean chowder

PREPARATION TIME: 20 MINUTES + OVERNIGHT SOAKING | TOTAL COOKING TIME: 1 HOUR 20 MINUTES | SERVES 6

155 g (5½ oz/¾ cup) dried red kidney beans

165 g (5¾ oz/¾ cup) dried Mexican black beans (see NOTE)

1 tablespoon oil

1 onion, chopped

2 garlic cloves, crushed

½–1 teaspoon chilli powder

1 tablespoon ground cumin

2 teaspoons ground coriander

2 x 400 g (14 oz) tins chopped tomatoes

750 ml (26 fl oz/3 cups) vegetable stock

1 red capsicum (pepper), chopped

1 green capsicum (pepper), chopped

440 g (15½ oz) tin corn kernels

2 tablespoons tomato paste (concentrated purée)

grated cheddar cheese, to serve

sour cream, to serve

1 Soak the kidney beans and black beans in separate bowls in plenty of cold water overnight. Drain. Place in a large saucepan, cover with water and bring to the boil. Reduce the heat and simmer for 45 minutes, or until tender. Drain.

2 Heat the oil in a large saucepan, add the onion and cook over medium heat until soft. Add the garlic, chilli powder, cumin and coriander, and cook for 1 minute. Stir in the tomato, stock, capsicum, corn and tomato paste. Cook, covered, for 25–30 minutes. Add the beans during the last 10 minutes of cooking. Stir occasionally.

3 Serve topped with the grated cheddar and a spoonful of sour cream.

NOTE: *Mexican black beans are also known as black turtle beans.*

Soak the red kidney beans and black beans in separate bowls overnight.

Add the tomato, stock, capsicum, corn and the tomato paste.

Chickpea and herb dumpling soup

PREPARATION TIME: 30 MINUTES | TOTAL COOKING TIME: 35 MINUTES | SERVES 4

1 tablespoon oil
1 onion, chopped
2 garlic cloves, crushed
2 teaspoons ground cumin
1 teaspoon ground coriander
¼ teaspoon chilli powder
2 x 300 g (10½ oz) tins chickpeas, drained
875 ml (30 fl oz/3½ cups) vegetable stock
2 x 400 g (14 oz) tins chopped tomatoes
1 tablespoon chopped coriander (cilantro)
    leaves

DUMPLINGS
125 g (4½ oz/1 cup) self-raising flour
25 g (1 oz) butter, chopped
2 tablespoons grated parmesan cheese
2 tablespoons mixed chopped herbs (chives,
    flat-leaf (Italian) parsley and coriander
    (cilantro) leaves)
60 ml (2 fl oz/¼ cup) full-cream (whole) milk
crusty bread, to serve

1 Heat the oil in a large saucepan and cook the onion over medium heat for 2–3 minutes, or until soft. Add the garlic, cumin, ground coriander and chilli, and cook for 1 minute, or until fragrant. Add the chickpeas, stock and tomato. Bring to the boil, then reduce the heat and simmer, covered, for 10 minutes. Stir in the coriander leaves.

2 To make the dumplings, sift the flour into a bowl and add the chopped butter. Rub the butter into the flour with your fingertips until it resembles fine breadcrumbs. Stir in the parmesan and mixed fresh herbs. Make a well in the centre, add the milk and mix with a flat-bladed knife until just combined. Bring the dough together into a rough ball, divide into eight portions and roll into small balls.

3 Add the dumplings to the soup, cover and simmer for 20 minutes, or until a skewer comes out clean when inserted into the centre of the dumplings. Serve with cracked black pepper and crusty bread.

NUTRITION PER SERVE
Protein 17 g; Fat 16 g; Carbohydrate 50 g; Dietary Fibre 12 g; Cholesterol 23 mg; 1767 kJ (422 Cal)

Stir the chopped coriander into the simmering chickpea mixture.

Add the milk to the dumpling mixture and mix with a flat-bladed knife.

Pierce the dumplings with a skewer to test if they are cooked.

Casseroles

Chicken and mushroom casserole

PREPARATION TIME: 20 MINUTES + 5 MINUTES SOAKING | TOTAL COOKING TIME: 1 HOUR | SERVES 4

20 g (¾ oz) dried porcini mushrooms

1.5 kg (3 lb 5 oz) chicken pieces

30 g (1 oz/¼ cup) seasoned plain (all-purpose) flour

2 tablespoons oil

1 large onion, chopped

2 garlic cloves, crushed

60 ml (2 fl oz/¼ cup) chicken stock

80 ml (2½ fl oz/⅓ cup) white wine

400 g (14 oz) tin whole peeled tomatoes

1 tablespoon balsamic vinegar

3 thyme sprigs

1 bay leaf

300 g (10½ oz) field mushrooms, thickly sliced

thyme leaves, extra, to garnish

NUTRITION PER SERVE
Protein 11 g; Fat 18.5 g; Carbohydrate 56 g; Dietary Fibre 8.5 g; Cholesterol 8.5 mg; 1809 kJ (432 Cal)

1 Preheat the oven to 180°C (350°F/Gas 4). Put the porcini mushrooms in a bowl and cover with 60 ml (2 fl oz/¼ cup) boiling water. Leave for 5 minutes, or until the mushrooms are rehydrated.

2 Lightly toss the chicken in the seasoned flour to coat, and shake off any excess.

3 Heat the oil in a flameproof casserole dish, and cook the chicken over medium heat in batches until well browned all over. Set aside. Add the onion and garlic to the casserole dish, and cook for 3–5 minutes, or until the onion softens. Stir in the chicken stock.

4 Return the chicken to the dish with the porcini mushrooms (and any remaining liquid), wine, tomatoes, vinegar, thyme sprigs and bay leaf. Cover and bake for 30 minutes.

5 After 30 minutes, remove the lid and add the field mushrooms. Return to the oven and cook, uncovered, for 15–20 minutes, or until the sauce thickens slightly. Garnish with thyme leaves and serve with a salad.

Cover the porcini mushrooms with boiling water and soak until rehydrated.

Lightly toss the chicken pieces in the flour and shake off any excess.

Add the chicken to the casserole dish and cook in batches until brown.

Lamb with borlotti beans

PREPARATION TIME: 20 MINUTES + OVERNIGHT SOAKING | TOTAL COOKING TIME: 2 HOURS | SERVES 6

200 g (7 oz/1 cup) dried borlotti (cranberry)
  beans
1 tablespoon olive oil
12 lamb loin chops
1 onion, finely chopped
1 celery stalk, chopped
1 carrot, chopped
3 garlic cloves, finely chopped
½ teaspoon dried chilli flakes
1 teaspoon cumin seeds
500 ml (17 fl oz/2 cups) lamb or chicken stock
2 bay leaves
60 ml (2 fl oz/¼ cup) lemon juice
2 large handfuls parsley, chopped
1 tablespoon shredded mint

1   Soak the beans overnight in cold water. Drain, rinse well and set aside.

2   Preheat the oven to 180°C (350°F/Gas 4). Heat the oil in a large heavy-based saucepan. Brown the lamb over high heat in batches, then transfer to a casserole dish.

3   Add the onion, celery and carrot to the pan, and cook over low heat for 10 minutes, or until soft and golden. Add the garlic, chilli and cumin seeds, and cook for 1 minute, then transfer to the casserole dish.

4   Add the stock, beans and bay leaves. Cover tightly and bake for 1½–1¾ hours, or until the lamb is very tender and the beans are cooked. Season with salt and freshly ground black pepper. Stir in the lemon juice, parsley and mint just before serving.

When the oil is hot, brown the lamb over high heat in batches.

Add the onion, celery and carrot to the saucepan, and cook until soft and golden.

NUTRITION PER SERVE
Protein 30 g; Fat 8 g; Carbohydrate 20 g; Dietary Fibre 5 g; Cholesterol 65 mg; 1185 kJ (280 Cal)

Seafood casserole with feta and olives

PREPARATION TIME: 20 MINUTES | TOTAL COOKING TIME: 35 MINUTES | SERVES 4

500 g (1 lb 2 oz) fresh mussels
2 tablespoons olive oil
1 large onion, sliced
2 x 400 g (14 oz) tins chopped tomatoes
2 lemon zest strips
1 tablespoon chopped lemon thyme
80 ml (2½ fl oz/⅓ cup) dry vermouth or
    white wine
1 teaspoon sugar
12 raw king prawns (shrimp), peeled and
    deveined, leaving the tails intact
750 g (1 lb 10 oz) firm white fish fillets, cut
    into bite-sized pieces
12 black olives
125 g (4½ oz) feta cheese, cubed

1   Discard any broken mussels, or open ones that don't close when tapped on the work surface. Scrub the rest of the mussels and remove the hairy beards. Place the mussels in a saucepan of simmering water. As soon as the shells open, place the mussels in a bowl of cold water, discarding any unopened ones. Open them up and leave the mussels on their half shells, discarding the other half.

2   Preheat the oven to 180°C (350°F/Gas 4). Heat the oil in a large heavy-based saucepan and cook the onion over low heat for 5 minutes, or until soft but not brown. Add the tomato, lemon zest, lemon thyme, vermouth and sugar. Bring to the boil, and season to taste. Reduce the heat, cover and simmer for 10 minutes.

3   Place all the seafood in a shallow ovenproof dish and cover with the hot sauce. Bake, covered, for 10 minutes. Add the olives and feta, covering the seafood with the sauce. Bake for 10 minutes, or until heated through. Serve immediately.

NUTRITION PER SERVE
Protein 70 g; Fat 25 g; Carbohydrate 10 g; Dietary
Fibre 4 g; Cholesterol 313 mg; 2430 kJ (580 Cal);

Peel and devein the prawns, and cut the fish into bite-sized pieces.

Scrub the mussels, remove the hairy beards, then place in a saucepan of simmering water.

Beef and artichoke casserole

PREPARATION TIME: 30 MINUTES | TOTAL COOKING TIME: 2 HOURS 15 MINUTES | SERVES 4–6

2 tablespoons olive oil
1 kg (2 lb 4 oz) stewing beef, cut into large cubes
2 red onions, sliced
4 garlic cloves, crushed
1 teaspoon cumin seeds
2 teaspoons ground cumin
1 teaspoon ground coriander
2 teaspoons sweet paprika
1 tablespoon plain (all-purpose) flour
500 ml (17 fl oz/2 cups) beef stock
1 teaspoon grated lemon zest
1 tablespoon soft brown sugar
1 tablespoon tomato paste (concentrated purée)
60 ml (2 fl oz/¼ cup) lemon juice
4 globe artichokes
90 g (3¼ oz/½ cup) black olives

1 Preheat the oven to 180°C (350°F/Gas 4). Heat half the oil in a large heavy-based frying pan. Brown the meat in batches over medium–high heat, then transfer to a large casserole dish.

2 Add the remaining oil to the frying pan and cook the onion over medium heat for 5 minutes, or until soft. Add the garlic, cumin seeds, cumin, coriander and paprika, and cook for 1 minute.

3 Add the flour, cook for 30 seconds, then remove from the heat. Add the stock, return to the heat and stir until the mixture bubbles. Add to the meat with the lemon zest, sugar and tomato paste. Cover tightly and bake for 1½ hours.

4 Meanwhile, add the lemon juice to a bowl of water. Cut the top third from each artichoke, trim the stem to 5 cm (2 inches) and cut away the dark outer leaves. Cut the artichokes in half lengthways. Remove the prickly lavender-topped leaves in the centre and scoop out the hairy choke. Drop the artichokes into the lemon-water until ready to use.

5 Drain the artichokes and add to the casserole, covering them in the liquid. Cover and bake for 30 minutes, or until tender. For a thicker gravy, cook uncovered for 15 minutes more. Season, and stir in the olives to serve.

NUTRITION PER SERVE (6)
Protein 40 g; Fat 12 g; Carbohydrate 8 g; Dietary Fibre 2 g; Cholesterol 112 mg; 1212 kJ (290 Cal)

Add the garlic and spices to the fried onion, and cook for 1 minute.

Cut the trimmed artichokes in half lengthways and place them in the lemon-water.

Drain the artichokes and add them to the casserole, covering them with the liquid.

Veal and fennel casserole

PREPARATION TIME: 20 MINUTES I TOTAL COOKING TIME: 2 HOURS 15 MINUTES I SERVES 4–6

1 tablespoon oil
30 g (1 oz) butter
4 veal shanks, cut into 4 cm (1½ inch) pieces
  (see NOTE)
1 large onion, sliced
1 garlic clove, crushed
2 celery stalks, thickly sliced
3 carrots, thickly sliced
2 small fennel bulbs, quartered
30 g (1 oz/¼ cup) plain (all-purpose) flour
425 g (15 oz) tin chopped tomatoes
80 ml (2½ fl oz/⅓ cup) white wine
250 ml (9 fl oz/1 cup) chicken stock
1 tablespoon chopped thyme plus extra,
  to garnish
12 black olives

1   Preheat the oven to 180°C (350°F/Gas 4).
Heat the oil and butter in a large heavy-based
saucepan and brown the meat quickly in batches
on both sides over high heat. Transfer to a large,
shallow casserole dish.

2   Add the onion and garlic to the saucepan,
and cook over medium heat until soft. Add the
celery, carrot and fennel, and cook for 2 minutes.
Add the flour, stir until golden, then add the
tomato, wine, stock and thyme. Bring to the
boil, reduce the heat and simmer for 5 minutes,
or until thickened. Season with salt and freshly
ground black pepper.

3   Add the sauce to the veal; cover and bake for
1½–2 hours, or until tender. Scatter with extra
thyme and olives to serve.

NOTE: *Many butchers sell veal shanks already
cut into pieces. You will need 12 medium pieces
for this recipe.*

Trim the leaves and base from the celery stalks,
then cut into thick slices.

Heat the oil and butter, then brown the meat in
batches over high heat.

NUTRITION PER SERVE (6)
Protein 20 g; Fat 8 g; Carbohydrate 10 g; Dietary
Fibre 3 g; Cholesterol 80 mg; 840 kJ (200 Cal)

Chicken, leek and sweet potato one-pot

PREPARATION TIME: 15 MINUTES | TOTAL COOKING TIME: 1 HOUR 40 MINUTES | SERVES 4

600 g (1 lb 5 oz) orange sweet potato
2 tablespoons olive oil
1.5 kg (3 lb 5 oz) chicken pieces
1 leek, cut into 2 cm (¾ inch) slices
2 garlic cloves, crushed
2 tablespoons plain (all-purpose) flour
500 ml (17 fl oz/2 cups) chicken stock
2 tablespoons thyme leaves

1 Preheat the oven to 220°C (425°F/Gas 7). Peel the sweet potato and cut it into chunks. Heat 1 tablespoon of the oil in a large flameproof casserole dish. Cook the chicken in batches for 3–4 minutes, or until browned. Set aside. Add the remaining oil and cook the leek and garlic for 2 minutes, or until soft.

2 Add the flour to the dish and cook, stirring, for about 1 minute to brown the flour. Gradually add the stock, stirring until the sauce boils and thickens. Remove from the heat. Return the chicken to the dish.

3 Add the sweet potato and half the thyme. Bake, covered, for 1½ hours, or until the chicken is cooked through and the sweet potato is tender. Season, and scatter with the remaining thyme. Serve with steamed rice.

NUTRITION PER SERVE
Protein 80 g; Fat 25 g; Carbohydrate 25 g; Dietary Fibre 4 g; Cholesterol 260 mg; 2778 kJ (665 Cal)

Brown the chicken pieces, in batches, until they are browned all over.

Gradually add the stock to the flour mixture, then stir until the sauce boils and thickens.

Add the orange sweet potato pieces to the casserole dish containing the chicken and stock.

Whole fish casserole

PREPARATION TIME: 30 MINUTES + 2 HOURS MARINATING | TOTAL COOKING TIME: 1 HOUR 35 MINUTES | SERVES 4–6

1.25 kg (2 lb 12 oz) whole red bream or red snapper, cleaned

1 lemon

1 lemon, sliced, extra

60 ml (2 fl oz/¼ cup) olive oil

800 g (1 lb 12 oz) potatoes, thinly sliced

3 garlic cloves, thinly sliced

1 large handful finely chopped parsley

1 small red onion, thinly sliced

1 small dried chilli, seeded and finely chopped

1 red capsicum (pepper), cut into thin rings

1 yellow capsicum (pepper), cut into thin rings

2 bay leaves

3–4 thyme sprigs

60 ml (2 fl oz/¼ cup) dry sherry

NUTRITION PER SERVE (6)
Protein 39 g; Fat 12 g; Carbohydrate 20 g; Dietary Fibre 3 g; Cholesterol 104 mg; 1462 kJ (349 Cal)

1 Cut off and discard the fins from the fish and place it in a large non-metallic dish. Cut 2 thin slices from one end of the whole lemon and reserve. Squeeze the juice from the rest of the lemon inside the fish. Add 2 tablespoons of the oil. Refrigerate, covered, for 2 hours.

2 Preheat the oven to 190°C (375°F/Gas 5) and lightly oil a shallow earthenware baking dish large enough to hold the whole fish. Spread half the potato on the base and scatter the garlic, parsley, onion, chilli and capsicum on top. Season with salt and pepper. Cover with the rest of the potato. Pour in 80 ml (2½ fl oz/⅓ cup) water and sprinkle the remaining oil over the top. Cover with foil and bake for 1 hour.

3 Increase the oven temperature to 220°C (425°F/Gas 7). Season the fish inside and out with salt and pepper, and place the bay leaves and thyme inside the cavity. Make three or four diagonal slashes on each side. Cut the reserved lemon slices in half and fit these into the slashes on one side of the fish, to resemble fins. Nestle the fish into the potatoes with extra lemon slices on top. Bake, uncovered, for 30 minutes, or until the fish is cooked through and the potato is golden and crusty.

4 Pour the dry sherry over the fish and return to the oven for 3 minutes. Serve straight from the dish.

Scatter the garlic, parsley, onion, chilli and capsicum on top of the potato.

Make three or four diagonal slashes on each side of the stuffed fish.

Cassoulet

PREPARATION TIME: 20 MINUTES + OVERNIGHT SOAKING | TOTAL COOKING TIME: 4 HOURS | SERVES 6

500 g (1 lb 2 oz) dried haricot beans
1.5 litres (52 fl oz/6 cups) beef stock
2 tablespoons oil
500 g (1 lb 2 oz) pork spareribs, trimmed
250 g (9 oz) diced lamb
250 g (9 oz) garlic or spiced sausage
125 g (4½ oz) bacon, cut into cubes
2 onions, chopped
2 carrots, chopped
2 garlic cloves, crushed
1 bay leaf
1 parsley sprig
1 thyme sprig
6 black peppercorns
160 g (5½ oz/2 cups) fresh breadcrumbs
60 g (2¼ oz) butter, chilled and grated

1   Soak the beans overnight in water.

2   Drain the beans and place in a large saucepan with the stock. Bring slowly to the boil, then reduce the heat and simmer for 1 hour, or until tender. Drain the beans, reserving the liquid.

3   Heat the oil in a frying pan. Brown the pork, lamb, sausage and bacon in several batches. Remove and drain on paper towels. Add the onion, carrot and garlic to the pan, and brown well.

4   Preheat the oven to 160°C (315°F/Gas 2–3). Layer the meats, beans and vegetables in a large casserole dish. Tie the herbs and peppercorns together in a small piece of muslin (cheesecloth), and add to the dish. Pour over the liquid from the beans, cover and bake for 2 hours.

5   Remove and discard the herb bag. Combine the breadcrumbs and butter, and sprinkle over the top of the casserole. Return to the oven for 30 minutes, or until the crust is golden and crisp.

Place the soaked haricot beans in a large saucepan with the beef stock.

Add the onion, carrot and garlic to the frying pan, and brown well.

NUTRITION PER SERVE
Protein 55 g; Fat 36 g; Carbohydrate 56 g; Dietary Fibre 19 g; Cholesterol 123 mg; 3140 kJ (750 Cal)

Chicken and red wine casserole

PREPARATION TIME: 15 MINUTES | TOTAL COOKING TIME: 1 HOUR 50 MINUTES | SERVES 4–6

30 g (1 oz) butter
125 g (4½ oz) bacon, roughly chopped
1.5 kg (3 lb 5 oz) skinless chicken pieces
350 g (12 oz) baby onions
2 tablespoons plain (all-purpose) flour
750 ml (26 fl oz/3 cups) red wine
250 g (9 oz) mushrooms, sliced

1 Preheat the oven to 180°C (350°F/Gas 4). Melt the butter in a large flameproof casserole dish over medium heat. Add the bacon and cook until golden, then remove. Add the chicken pieces and cook, in batches, for 4–5 minutes, or until browned. Remove. Add the onions and cook for 2–3 minutes, or until browned, then remove from the dish.

2 Stir the flour into the juices in dish, then remove from the heat and slowly pour in the red wine, while stirring. Return to the heat, bring to the boil and return the bacon and chicken to the dish. Cover and bake for 1 hour. Return the onions to the dish and add the mushrooms. Cook for a further 30 minutes. Season to taste with salt and freshly ground black pepper. This dish is delicious served with mashed potato.

NUTRITION PER SERVE (6)
Protein 65 g; Fat 11 g; Carbohydrate 11 g; Dietary Fibre 2 g; Cholesterol 150 mg; 2040 kJ (487 Cal)

Cook the whole onions in the casserole dish until they are browned.

Return the cooked bacon and chicken pieces to the casserole dish.

Lamb shanks with puy lentils

PREPARATION TIME: 25 MINUTES | TOTAL COOKING TIME: 1 HOUR 45 MINUTES | SERVES 4

80 ml (2½ fl oz/⅓ cup) olive oil
4 French-trimmed lamb shanks
   (280 g/10 oz each)
6 garlic cloves, unpeeled
1 onion, thinly sliced
1 red capsicum (pepper), sliced
2 garlic cloves, crushed
400 g (14 oz) tin chopped tomatoes
250 ml (9 fl oz/1 cup) white wine
1 bay leaf
1 cinnamon stick
2 orange zest strips
320 g (11¼ oz) puy or tiny blue-green lentils
400 g (14 oz) tin cannellini beans, rinsed
   and drained
2 spring onions (scallions), sliced
pinch saffron threads
1 teaspoon ground coriander
1 teaspoon ground cumin
2 tablespoons chopped flat-leaf (Italian)
   parsley

1   Preheat the oven to 200°C (400°F/Gas 6). Heat half the oil in a large flameproof casserole dish, add the shanks in batches and cook over medium heat for 4 minutes, or until brown on all sides. Remove from the dish.

2   Place the unpeeled garlic cloves on a baking tray and drizzle with half the remaining oil.

3   Add the onion, capsicum and crushed garlic to the dish and cook until golden. Stir in the tomato, wine, bay leaf, cinnamon stick and orange zest, return the shanks to the dish, then cover and transfer to the oven. Cook for 1 hour, then uncover and cook for a further 30 minutes, or until tender and the meat just falls off the bone. Keep warm. Add the garlic clove tray to the oven 15 minutes before the meat is ready. Cook until soft. Cool slightly, then peel.

4   Meanwhile, place the lentils in a saucepan, cover with 1.5 litres (52 fl oz/6 cups) water and bring to the boil. Cook over high heat for 20 minutes, or until tender. Drain, reserving the liquid.

5   Place the peeled garlic cloves in a food processor with the beans and a dash of the reserved lentil cooking liquid, and process until smooth and creamy. Season to taste. Cover and keep warm. Add more liquid if it starts to thicken and dry out.

6   Heat the remaining oil in a large frying pan, add the spring onion and spices, and cook over medium heat for 3 minutes, or until fragrant. Stir in the lentils and parsley, and cook until warmed through.

7   Place a mound of lentils on each plate, stand the shanks in the lentils and drizzle with some of the cooking liquid. Serve a spoonful of the bean purée on the side.

NOTE: *French-trimmed lamb shanks are lamb shanks that have the meat scraped back to make a neat lamb 'drumstick'. You can use regular lamb shanks instead.*

NUTRITION PER SERVE
Protein 70 g; Fat 35 g; Carbohydrate 45 g; Dietary Fibre 2 g; Cholesterol 130 mg; 3437 kJ (820 Cal)

Cook the lamb shanks in batches until brown all over.

Add the onion, capsicum and garlic to the dish, and cook until golden.

Cook the lamb shanks until the meat is just falling off the bone.

Chicken paprika with dumplings

PREPARATION TIME: 20 MINUTES I TOTAL COOKING TIME: 1 HOUR 10 MINUTES I SERVES 4–6

2 tablespoons oil
1.6 kg (3 lb 8 oz) chicken, cut into 10 pieces
1 large onion, chopped
1 garlic clove, crushed
1 teaspoon sweet paprika
1 teaspoon dried thyme
2 tablespoons plain (all-purpose) flour
125 ml (4 fl oz/½ cup) chicken stock
400 g (14 oz) tin chopped tomatoes
2 carrots, cut into 2cm (¾ in) pieces

DUMPLINGS
125 g (4½ oz/1 cup) self-raising flour
20 g (¾ oz) butter, chopped
2 teaspoons finely chopped flat-leaf (Italian) parsley
2 teaspoons finely chopped chives
½ teaspoon mixed dried herbs
80 ml (2½ fl oz/⅓ cup) buttermilk

1   Heat the oil in a frying pan. Brown the chicken in batches over medium–high heat, and place in a very deep 3 litre (105 fl oz/12 cup) casserole dish.

2   Add the onion and garlic to the pan, stirring until soft. Reduce the heat to low. Add the paprika, thyme and flour, and cook, stirring, for 2 minutes. Gradually stir in the stock. Add the tomato, and season. Pour the mixture over the chicken. Add the carrot. Cover and bake for 30 minutes.

3   To make the dumplings, sift the flour into a bowl. Rub in the butter until fine and crumbly. Stir in the herbs and almost all the buttermilk. Mix to a soft dough, adding more buttermilk if necessary. Turn the dough out onto a floured surface and gather into a ball. Divide into eight portions and roll each into a ball. Arrange the dumplings on top of the casserole. Bake, uncovered, for 20 minutes. Serve immediately.

Rub the butter into the flour until the mixture is fine and crumbly.

Divide the dough into eight and roll each portion into a ball.

NUTRITION PER SERVE (6)
Protein 44 g; Fat 36 g; Carbohydrate 25 g; Dietary Fibre 3 g; Cholesterol 200 mg; 2480 kJ (595 Cal)

Fish and lemongrass casserole

PREPARATION TIME: 15 MINUTES | TOTAL COOKING TIME: 45 MINUTES | SERVES 4

4 fish cutlets (200 g/7 oz each)
seasoned plain (all-purpose) flour
2–3 tablespoons peanut oil
2 onions, sliced
2 lemongrass stems (white part only), finely
   chopped
4 makrut (kaffir lime) leaves, shredded
1 teaspoon ground cumin
1 teaspoon ground coriander
1 teaspoon finely chopped fresh red chilli
185 ml (6 fl oz/¾ cup) chicken stock
375 ml (13 fl oz/1½ cups) coconut milk
1 large handful coriander (cilantro) leaves,
   chopped, plus extra leaves to garnish
2 teaspoons fish sauce
lime wedges, to serve

1   Preheat the oven to 180°C (350°F/Gas 4). Toss the fish lightly in the flour, and gently shake off excess. Heat half the oil in a large heavy-based frying pan and cook fish over medium heat until lightly browned on both sides. Transfer to a shallow ovenproof dish.

2   Heat the remaining oil in the frying pan. Cook the onion and lemongrass, stirring, for 5 minutes, or until the onion softens. Add the makrut leaves, ground spices and chilli, and stir for 2 minutes, or until fragrant.

3   Add the stock and coconut milk to the onion mixture, and bring to the boil. Pour over the fish, then cover and bake for 30 minutes, or until the fish is tender.

4   Transfer the fish to a serving plate. Stir the chopped coriander and the fish sauce into the remaining sauce, and season to taste with salt and freshly ground black pepper. Pour the sauce over the fish to serve. Garnish with extra coriander leaves and serve with lime wedges.

NUTRITION PER SERVE
Protein 35 g; Fat 40 g; Carbohydrate 6 g; Dietary
Fibre 1 g; Cholesterol 105 mg; 2040 kJ (490 Cal)

Finely chop the white part of the lemongrass stems, and shred the makrut leaves.

Heat half the peanut oil and brown the lightly floured fish over medium heat.

Navarin of lamb

PREPARATION TIME: 25 MINUTES | TOTAL COOKING TIME: 1 HOUR 35 MINUTES | SERVES 4

8 lamb noisettes (see NOTES)

seasoned plain (all-purpose) flour

2 tablespoons oil

2 celery stalks, sliced thinly

12 baby carrots, peeled (see NOTES)

12 new potatoes, halved

6 thyme sprigs

1 large handful flat-leaf (Italian) parsley, chopped

2 onions, chopped

2 garlic cloves, crushed

40 g (1½ oz/⅓ cup) plain (all-purpose) flour

625 ml (21½ fl oz/2½ cups) chicken stock

250 ml (9 fl oz/1 cup) red wine

60 g (2¼ oz/¼ cup) tomato paste (concentrated purée)

chopped flat-leaf (Italian) parsley, extra, to garnish

1 Toss the lamb in the seasoned flour, shaking off the excess. Preheat the oven to 180°C (350°F/Gas 4).

2 Heat the oil in a heavy-based saucepan. In batches, brown the lamb well on both sides over medium–high heat. Remove from the heat, drain well on paper towels, then transfer to a greased, 3 litre (105 fl oz/12 cup) casserole dish. Top with the celery, carrots, potatoes, thyme sprigs and parsley.

3 Cook the onion and garlic in the same saucepan, stirring over medium heat for 5–10 minutes, or until the onion is soft.

4 Add the flour and stir for 1 minute, or until the onion is coated. Add the stock, wine and tomato paste and stir until the sauce boils and thickens. Pour the sauce over the lamb and vegetables. Bake, covered, for 1¼ hours, or until the lamb is tender. Carefully remove the string from the lamb, and sprinkle with extra parsley to serve.

NOTES: *A noisette is a round slice of meat, cut from a boned loin and tied with string to hold its shape. For this recipe you could also use a boned leg of lamb, cut into 3 cm (1¼ inch) cubes.*

If baby carrots are not available, use four sliced carrots instead.

NUTRITION PER SERVE
Protein 40 g; Fat 60 g; Carbohydrate 60 g; Dietary Fibre 10 g; Cholesterol 120 mg; 4050 kJ (970 Cal)

Add the lightly floured lamb to the hot oil and brown well all over.

Add the stock, wine and tomato paste to the softened onion mixture.

Beef and vegetable casserole

PREPARATION TIME: 40 MINUTES | TOTAL COOKING TIME: 1 HOUR 45 MINUTES | SERVES 6

cooking oil spray

500 g (1 lb 2 oz) lean round steak, cut into
 2 cm (¾ inch) cubes

1 onion, sliced

3 garlic cloves, crushed

2 teaspoons ground cumin

1 teaspoon dried thyme leaves

2 bay leaves

400 g (14 oz) tin chopped tomatoes

500 g (1 lb 2 oz) potatoes, chopped

2 large carrots, thickly sliced

4 zucchini (courgettes), thickly sliced

250 g (9 oz) mushrooms, halved

250 g (9 oz) yellow squash, halved

2 tablespoons tomato paste (concentrated
 purée)

125 ml (4 fl oz/½ cup) red wine

2 large handfuls parsley, chopped

1 Preheat the oven to 180°C (350°F/Gas 4). Spray a deep non-stick frying pan with cooking oil spray and fry the steak in batches until it is browned all over. Remove the meat from the pan. Spray the pan again, add the onion and cook until lightly golden. Add the garlic, cumin, thyme and bay leaves, and stir for 1 minute.

2 Return the meat and any juices to the frying pan, tossing to coat the meat with the spices. Add 375 ml (13 fl oz/1½ cups) water and the tomato, scraping the bottom of the pan. Simmer for 10 minutes, or until thickened. Transfer the mixture to a large casserole dish with the potato, carrot, zucchini, mushrooms, squash, tomato paste and wine.

3 Bake, covered, for 1 hour. Stir well, then uncover and bake for a further 20 minutes. Remove the bay leaves, season, stir in the parsley and serve.

Discard any excess fat and sinew from the steak, and cut the steak into cubes.

When the onion is golden, add the garlic, cumin, thyme and bay leaves.

NUTRITION PER SERVE
Protein 25 g; Fat 4 g; Carbohydrate 20 g; Dietary
Fibre 6.5 g; Cholesterol 50 mg; 930 kJ (220 Cal)

Boston baked beans

PREPARATION TIME: 25 MINUTES + AT LEAST 6–8 HOURS SOAKING | TOTAL COOKING TIME: 1 HOUR 35 MINUTES | SERVES 4–6

350 g (12 oz/1¾ cups) dried cannellini beans
 (see NOTES)
1 whole ham hock
2 onions, chopped
2 tablespoons tomato paste (concentrated
 purée)
1 tablespoon worcestershire sauce
1 tablespoon molasses
1 teaspoon French mustard
45 g (1½ oz/¼ cup) soft brown sugar
125 ml (4 fl oz/½ cup) tomato juice

1 Cover the beans with cold water and soak for
6–8 hours, or overnight.

2 Drain the beans, rinse them well and place in
a large saucepan. Add the ham hock and cover
with cold water. Bring to the boil, then reduce
the heat and simmer, covered, for 25 minutes, or
until the beans are tender. Preheat the oven to
160°C (315°F/Gas 2–3).

3 Remove the ham hock from the saucepan
and set aside to cool. Drain the beans, reserving
250 ml (9 fl oz/1 cup) of the cooking liquid. Trim
the ham of all skin, fat and sinew, then chop the
meat and discard the bone.

4 Transfer the meat and beans to a 2 litre
(70 fl oz/8 cup) casserole dish. Add the reserved
liquid and all the remaining ingredients. Mix
gently, then cover and bake for 1 hour. Serve
with hot buttered toast.

NOTES: *Any type of dried bean can be used in
this recipe.*

*To quick-soak beans, place them in a pan, add
hot water to cover, bring slowly to the boil, then
remove from the heat. Leave to soak for 1 hour
before draining and using.*

NUTRITION PER SERVE (6)
Protein 28 g; Fat 5 g; Carbohydrate 30 g; Dietary
Fibre 2 g; Cholesterol 60 mg; 1090 kJ (260 Cal)

Place the drained beans in a large saucepan, add
the ham hock and cover with cold water.

Trim the ham of all fat, skin and sinew, then
roughly chop the meat.

Caramel pork with Shanghai noodles

PREPARATION TIME: 15 MINUTES | TOTAL COOKING TIME: 2 HOURS 30 MINUTES | SERVES 4

500 g (1 lb 2 oz) Shanghai noodles

700 g (1 lb 9 oz) boneless pork belly

2 teaspoons peanut oil

150 g (5½ oz) caster (superfine) sugar

5 garlic cloves, crushed

5 slices fresh ginger, 5 mm (¼ inch) thick

2 lemongrass stems (white part only), bruised

1 teaspoon white pepper

500 ml (17 fl oz/2 cups) chicken stock

70 ml (2¼ fl oz) fish sauce

100 g (3½ oz) tinned bamboo shoots,
    drained well

4 spring onions (scallions), cut into 3 cm
    (1¼ inch) pieces

1 tablespoon lime juice

1 tablespoon chopped coriander (cilantro)
    leaves (optional)

1 bunch bok choy (pak choy), (optional)

1 Cook the Shanghai noodles in a large saucepan of boiling water for 4–5 minutes, or until tender. Rinse, drain and cut the noodles into 10 cm (4 inch) lengths.

2 Preheat the oven to 180°C (350°F/Gas 4). Cut the pork belly across the grain into 1 cm (½ inch) thick slices, then cut each slice into 2 cm (¾ inch) pieces. Heat the oil in a 4 litre (140 fl oz/16 cup) flameproof casserole dish over medium–high heat. Cook the pork in two batches for 5 minutes, or until it starts to brown all over. Remove the pork and drain off the fat.

3 Add the sugar and 2 tablespoons water to the casserole dish, stirring until the sugar has dissolved and scraping up any sediment that may have stuck to the bottom. Increase heat to high and cook for 2–3 minutes without stirring until dark golden, being careful not to burn—you should just be able to smell the caramel.

4 Return the pork to the casserole dish, then stir in the garlic, ginger, lemongrass, white pepper, stock, 2 tablespoons of the fish sauce and 375 ml (12 fl oz/1½ cups) water. Place the dish in the oven and bake, covered, for 1 hour, then remove the lid and cook for a further 1 hour, or until the pork is very tender. Carefully remove the ginger and the lemongrass stems.

5 Add the noodles to the casserole dish with the bamboo shoots, spring onion, lime juice and remaining fish sauce, and stir to combine. Return the dish to the oven for a further 10 minutes to heat through. Stir in the coriander, if desired, and serve with steamed bok choy and steamed Asian greens, if desired.

NUTRITION PER SERVE
Protein 49 g; Fat 7.5 g; Carbohydrate 73 g; Dietary Fibre 4 g; Cholesterol 166 mg; 2305 kJ (550 Cal)

Cut the pork belly across the grain into slices, then into pieces.

Return all the browned pork belly pieces to the casserole dish.

Carefully remove the ginger slices and lemongrass from the casserole.

Sweet and sour meatballs

PREPARATION TIME: 20 MINUTES | TOTAL COOKING TIME: 1 HOUR 20 MINUTES | SERVES 4–6

1 kg (2 lb 4 oz) lean minced (ground) beef
80 g (2¾ oz/1 cup) fresh breadcrumbs
1 egg, lightly beaten
1 tablespoon worcestershire sauce
1 tablespoon chilli sauce
1 tablespoon chopped flat-leaf (Italian) parsley
2 tablespoons oil

SAUCE
2 tablespoons soft brown sugar
80 ml (2½ fl oz/⅓ cup) white vinegar
2 tablespoons barbecue sauce
2 tablespoons tomato sauce (concentrated
    purée)
500 ml (17 fl oz/2 cups) pineapple juice
1 tablespoon cornflour (cornstarch)

1 large cucumber, halved, seeded and cut into
    matchsticks
1 large carrot, cut into matchsticks
1 red capsicum (pepper), cut into matchsticks
440 g (15½ oz) tin pineapple pieces, drained

1   Preheat the oven to 160°C (315°F/Gas 2–3).
Combine the beef, breadcrumbs, egg, sauces and
parsley in a large bowl. Using your hands, mix
well. Using 2 teaspoons of the mixture at a time,
roll into balls.

2   Heat the oil in a heavy-based frying pan.
Cook meatballs in batches over medium heat for
3 minutes, or until browned. Drain.

3   To make the sauce, place the sugar, vinegar,
sauces and juice in a medium saucepan. Cook
over medium heat until the sugar has dissolved.
Bring to the boil, then remove from the heat.
Blend the cornflour with 2 tablespoons water.
Add to the pan. Stir over medium heat for
3 minutes, or until it boils and thickens. Place
the meatballs and remaining ingredients in a
casserole dish. Pour the sauce over the top.
Bake for 1 hour. Serve with rice.

Cut the cucumbers in half lengthways, then use a
teaspoon to scoop out the seeds.

Cook the meatballs in batches, then place on to
paper towels to drain.

NUTRITION PER SERVE (6)
Protein 38 g; Fat 19 g; Carbohydrate 41 g; Dietary
Fibre 2.5 g; Cholesterol 117 mg; 2015 kJ (480 Cal)

Fish, ginger and tomato hotpot

PREPARATION TIME: 20 MINUTES + 20 MINUTES SOAKING | TOTAL COOKING TIME: 1 HOUR | SERVES 4

1 tablespoon peanut oil
1 onion, cut into thin wedges
1 small red chilli, sliced
3 garlic cloves, finely chopped
2 cm x 2 cm (¾ inch x ¾ inch) piece fresh
    ginger, cut into matchsticks
½ teaspoon ground turmeric
400 g (14 oz) tin chopped tomatoes
1 litre (35 fl oz/4 cups) chicken stock
1 tablespoon tamarind purée
80 g (2¾ oz) dried rice stick noodles
600 g (1 lb 5 oz) snapper fillets, skin removed,
    cut into 3 cm (1¼ inch) cubes
coriander (cilantro) leaves, to garnish

1 Preheat the oven to 220°C (425°F/Gas 7).
Heat the oil in a frying pan over medium–high
heat, and cook the onion for 1–2 minutes, or
until softened. Add the chilli, garlic and ginger,
and cook for a further 30 seconds. Add the
turmeric, tomato, stock and tamarind purée,
and bring to the boil over high heat. Transfer to
a 2.5 litre (87 fl oz/10 cup) heatproof hotpot or
casserole dish and bake, covered, for 40 minutes.

2 Place the rice stick noodles in a large
heatproof bowl and cover with warm water. Soak
the noodles for 15–20 minutes, or until *al dente*.
Drain, rinse and drain again.

3 Remove the hotpot from the oven and stir
in the drained noodles. Add the fish cubes,
then cover and return to the oven for a further
10 minutes, or until the fish is cooked through.
Serve garnished with coriander leaves.

Using tongs, gently add the fish cubes to the
hotpot mixture.

NUTRITION PER SERVE
Protein 36 g; Fat 8 g; Carbohydrate 24 g; Dietary
Fibre 3 g; Cholesterol 92 mg; 1310 kJ (315 Cal)

Lion's head meatballs

PREPARATION TIME: 20 MINUTES + OVERNIGHT REFRIGERATION + 20 MINUTES SOAKING | TOTAL COOKING TIME: 4 HOURS 45 MINUTES | SERVES 4

CHICKEN STOCK
1.5 kg (3 lb 5 oz) chicken bones (chicken necks, backs, wings), washed (see NOTE)
2 slices fresh ginger, cut into 1 cm (½ inch) thick slices
4 spring onions (scallions)

6 dried Chinese mushrooms
100 g (3½ oz) mung bean vermicelli
600 g (1 lb 5 oz) minced (ground) pork
1 egg white
4 garlic cloves, finely chopped
1 tablespoon finely grated fresh ginger
1 tablespoon cornflour (cornstarch)
1½ tablespoons Chinese rice wine
6 spring onions (scallions), thinly sliced
2 tablespoons peanut oil
60 ml (2 fl oz/¼ cup) light soy sauce
1 teaspoon sugar
400 g (14 oz) bok choy (pak choy), halved lengthways, leaves separated

1 To make the stock, place the bones and 3.5 litres (122 fl oz/10 cups) water in a large saucepan and bring to a simmer—do not let it boil. Remove the surface scum over the next 30 minutes. Add ginger and spring onions, and cook, partially covered, at a low simmer for 3 hours. Strain and cool. Cover and refrigerate overnight. Remove the layer of fat from the surface once it has solidified.

2 Soak the Chinese mushrooms in 250 ml (9 fl oz/1 cup) boiling water for 20 minutes. Drain. Discard the stems and thinly slice the caps. Meanwhile, place the vermicelli in a heatproof bowl, cover with boiling water and soak for 3–4 minutes, or until soft. Drain and rinse. Preheat the oven to 220°C (425°F/Gas 7).

3 Place the pork, egg white, garlic, ginger, cornflour, rice wine, two-thirds of the spring onion and salt, to taste, in a food processor. Process until smooth. Divide mixture into eight portions and roll into balls with wet hands.

4 Place 500 ml (17 fl oz/2 cups) of the stock (freeze any remaining stock) in a large saucepan and bring to the boil over high heat. Remove from the heat and keep warm.

5 Heat the oil in a wok over high heat. Fry the meatballs in batches for 2 minutes each side, or until golden, but not cooked through. Drain.

6 Place the meatballs, mushrooms, soy sauce and sugar in a 2.5 litre (87 fl oz/10 cup) casserole dish, and cover with the hot stock. Bake, covered, for 45 minutes. Add the bok choy and noodles and bake, covered, for another 10 minutes. Sprinkle with the remaining spring onion, and serve.

NOTE: *To save time, use 500 ml (17 fl oz/ 2 cups) of purchased stock instead of making your own.*

NUTRITION PER SERVE
Protein 35 g; Fat 20 g; Carbohydrate 22 g; Dietary Fibre 4 g; Cholesterol 97 mg; 1720 kJ (410 Cal)

Form the mince mixture into eight large balls using wet hands.

Add the bok choy and noodles to the dish containing the meatballs.

Tagine of lamb with quince and lemon

PREPARATION TIME: 25 MINUTES | TOTAL COOKING TIME: 2 HOURS 10 MINUTES | SERVES 4

1.5 kg (3 lb 5 oz) boned shoulder of lamb, cut into 12 even pieces
1 onion, finely chopped
2 garlic cloves, crushed
1 cinnamon stick
1 teaspoon ground ginger
½ teaspoon saffron threads
1 large quince, peeled, seeded and cut into 12 pieces
1 teaspoon ground cinnamon
90 g (3¼ oz/¼ cup) honey
½ preserved lemon (see NOTE)
1 handful chopped flat-leaf (Italian) parsley, to garnish

1 Trim the lamb of excess fat and place in a large saucepan. Add the onion, garlic, cinnamon stick, ginger and saffron, and enough cold water to cover. Slowly bring to the boil, stirring occasionally. Reduce the heat, cover and simmer for 45 minutes. Transfer the meat to a large casserole dish and set aside.

2 Add the quince, ground cinnamon and honey to the cooking liquid, and simmer for 15 minutes, or until the quince is tender. Discard the cinnamon stick; remove the quince and add to the meat, reserving the liquid.

3 Preheat the oven to 180°C (350°F/Gas 4). Boil the cooking liquid for 30 minutes, or until reduced by half, then pour over the meat and quince. Remove and discard the flesh from the lemon. Slice the zest thinly, then add to the meat. Cover and bake for 40 minutes, or until the meat is tender. Sprinkle with parsley and serve with couscous.

NOTE: *Preserved lemons are available from specialty stores.*

HINT: *As you work, place the peeled quince in water with a little lemon juice to prevent discolouring.*

Add the quince, ground cinnamon and honey to the cooking liquid.

Remove and discard the flesh from the preserved lemon and thinly slice the zest.

NUTRITION PER SERVE
Protein 80 g; Fat 15 g; Carbohydrate 20 g; Dietary Fibre 3 g; Cholesterol 250 mg; 2160 kJ (515 Cal)

Beef carbonnade

PREPARATION TIME: 15 MINUTES | TOTAL COOKING TIME: 3 HOURS 25 MINUTES | SERVES 4

1 leek, green part only
1 bay leaf
1 thyme sprig
1 celery leaf sprig
4 parsley sprigs
40 g (1½ oz) butter
1 tablespoon oil
1 kg (2 lb 4 oz) chuck or stewing steak, cubed
2 onions, sliced
2 garlic cloves, crushed
2 tablespoons plain (all-purpose) flour
375 ml (13 fl oz/1½ cups) brown ale or stout
1 long baguette
2 teaspoons French mustard
2 teaspoons butter, extra, softened

1 To make a bouquet garni, wrap the green part of the leek around the bay leaf, thyme, celery leaf and parsley sprigs, then tie together with string. Leave a long tail for easy removal.

2 Preheat the oven to 180°C (350°F/Gas 4). Heat the butter and oil in a large saucepan, and cook the steak in batches for 3–4 minutes, or until well browned. Remove from the pan. Reduce the heat and cook the onion and garlic for 4 minutes, or until soft. Sprinkle in the flour, stir well, then cook for 1 minute. Combine the ale with 375 ml (12 fl oz/1½ cups) water, and pour into the pan. Stir well, scraping the pan to incorporate any ingredients that are stuck to the base. Bring to the boil and return the meat to the pan. Add the bouquet garni and return to the boil. Transfer to a 2.5 litre (87 fl oz/10 cup) casserole dish, cover with foil and bake for 2½ hours.

3 Cut the bread into 2 cm (¾ inch) slices and spread with the combined mustard and extra butter. Remove the dish from the oven, take out the bouquet garni and skim off the fat. Top the casserole with bread slices, mustard side up, and press gently to soak up the juices. Return to the oven and cook, uncovered, for another 30–40 minutes, until the bread toasts.

NUTRITION PER SERVE
Protein 60 g; Fat 25 g; Carbohydrate 30 g; Dietary Fibre 3.5 g; Cholesterol 195 mg; 2455 kJ (585 Cal)

Leave a long tail of string on the bouquet garni for easy removal.

Cook the steak in batches in a large saucepan until well browned all over.

Veal, lemon and caper casserole

PREPARATION TIME: 30 MINUTES | TOTAL COOKING TIME: 2 HOURS | SERVES 4–6

1 tablespoon olive oil

50 g (1¾ oz) butter

1 kg (2 lb 4 oz) stewing veal, cut into 4 cm (1½ inch) chunks

300 g (10½ oz) French shallots (eschalots)

3 leeks, white part only, cut into large chunks

2 garlic cloves, crushed

1 tablespoon plain (all-purpose) flour

500 ml (17 fl oz/2 cups) chicken stock

1 teaspoon grated lemon zest

80 ml (2½ fl oz/⅓ cup) lemon juice

2 bay leaves

2 tablespoons capers, drained and well rinsed

chopped flat-leaf (Italian) parsley, to serve

caperberries, to garnish (see NOTES)

1 Preheat the oven to 180°C (350°F/Gas 4). Heat the oil and half the butter in a large, heavy-based frying pan. Brown the veal in batches over medium–high heat, then transfer to a large casserole dish.

2 Blanch the shallots in boiling water for 30 seconds, then peel and add to the pan with the leek. Gently cook for 5 minutes, or until soft and golden. Add the garlic, cook for 1 minute, then transfer to the casserole dish.

3 Melt the remaining butter in the pan, add the flour and cook for 30 seconds. Remove from the heat, add the stock and stir until well combined. Return to the heat and cook, stirring, until the sauce begins to bubble.

4 Pour the sauce into the casserole dish and stir in the lemon zest, lemon juice and bay leaves. Cover and bake for 1–1½ hours, or until the veal is tender. During the last 20 minutes of cooking, remove the lid to allow the sauce to reduce a little.

5 Stir in the capers and season with salt and freshly cracked black pepper. Sprinkle with parsley and garnish with caperberries. Serve with steamed greens.

NOTES: *Caperberries are sold in jars of brine or vinegar in speciality stores.*

If possible, use tiny capers in this dish as they have a superb flavour, but regular capers can be used instead.

NUTRITION PER SERVE (6)
Protein 40 g; Fat 13 g; Carbohydrate 5 g; Dietary Fibre 2 g; Cholesterol 160 mg; 1300 kJ (300 Cal)

Add the leek and peeled shallots to the pan, and gently fry until soft and golden.

Remove the pan from the heat and stir in the stock, scraping up any brown sediment.

Eggplant parmigiana

PREPARATION TIME: 30 MINUTES | TOTAL COOKING TIME: 1 HOUR 10 MINUTES | SERVES 6–8

60 ml (2 fl oz/¼ cup) olive oil

1 onion, diced

2 garlic cloves, crushed

1.25 kg (2 lb 12 oz) tomatoes, peeled and chopped (see NOTE)

oil, for shallow-frying

1 kg (2 lb 4 oz) eggplants (aubergines), very thinly sliced

250 g (9 oz) bocconcini (fresh baby mozzarella cheese), sliced

185 g (6½ oz/1½ cups) finely grated cheddar cheese

2 very large handfuls basil leaves, torn

50 g (1¾ oz/½ cup) grated parmesan cheese

1   Heat the oil in a large frying pan over medium heat. Cook the onion until soft. Add the garlic and cook for 1 minute. Add the tomato and simmer for 15 minutes. Season with salt. Preheat the oven to 200°C (400°F/Gas 6).

2   Shallow-fry the eggplant in small batches for 3–4 minutes, or until golden brown. Drain on paper towels.

3   Place one-third of the eggplant slices in a 1.75 litre (61 fl oz/7 cup) ovenproof dish. Top with half the bocconcini and half the cheddar. Repeat the layers, finishing with a good layer of the eggplant.

4   Pour over the tomato mixture. Scatter with torn basil leaves, then the parmesan. Bake for 40 minutes and serve.

VARIATION: *If you prefer not to fry the eggplant, brush it lightly with oil and brown lightly under a hot grill.*

NOTE: *To peel the tomatoes, score a cross in the base. Put in a heatproof bowl and cover with boiling water. Leave for 30 seconds, then transfer to cold water and peel off the skin.*

Fry the onion and garlic in the oil, then add the chopped tomato.

Shallow-fry the eggplant in batches, then drain on paper towels.

NUTRITION PER SERVE (8)
Protein 17 g; Fat 25 g; Carbohydrate 7 g; Dietary Fibre 5 g; Cholesterol 40 mg; 1340 kJ (320 Cal)

Braised oxtail casserole

PREPARATION TIME: 15 MINUTES | TOTAL COOKING TIME: 2 HOURS 20 MINUTES | SERVES 6

60 ml (2 fl oz/¼ cup) oil
16 small pieces oxtail, about 1.5 kg (3 lb 5 oz)
6 baby potatoes, halved
1 large onion, chopped
2 carrots, chopped
250 g (9 oz) button mushrooms
2 tablespoons plain (all-purpose) flour
750 ml (26 fl oz/3 cups) beef stock
1 teaspoon dried marjoram leaves
2 tablespoons worcestershire sauce

1 Preheat the oven to 180°C (350°F/Gas 4). Heat 2 tablespoons of the oil in a saucepan over medium–high heat. Cook the oxtail quickly in small batches and until well browned. Place in a deep casserole dish and add the potato.

2 Heat the remaining oil in the pan. Cook the onion and carrot, stirring, over medium heat for 5 minutes. Transfer to the casserole dish. Add the mushrooms to the pan, and cook, stirring, for 5 minutes. Stir in the flour. Reduce the heat to low, and stir for 2 minutes.

3 Add the stock gradually, stirring until the liquid boils and thickens. Add the marjoram and worcestershire sauce. Pour into the casserole dish. Bake, covered, for 1½ hours. Stir, then bake, uncovered, for a further 30 minutes. Sprinkle with freshly ground black pepper and serve immediately.

Cook the oxtail pieces in small batches in the hot oil.

Cook the onion and carrot, stirring, for 5 minutes over medium heat.

NUTRITION PER SERVE
Protein 35 g; Fat 53 g; Carbohydrate 16 g; Dietary Fibre 3.5 g; Cholesterol 102 mg; 2825 kJ (675 Cal)

Duck with juniper berries

PREPARATION TIME: 35 MINUTES | TOTAL COOKING TIME: 2 HOURS | SERVES 4

1.8 kg (4 lb) duck

oil, for cooking

1 granny smith apple, peeled and thinly
    sliced

1 leek, (white part only), cut into large
    chunks

½ small red cabbage, shredded

2 bay leaves

2 thyme sprigs

6 juniper berries, lightly crushed

¼ teaspoon black peppercorns

375 ml (13 fl oz/1½ cups) chicken stock

250 ml (9 fl oz/1 cup) orange juice

50 g (1¾ oz) butter, chopped

2 tablespoons soft brown sugar

80 ml (2½ fl oz/⅓ cup) cider vinegar

1½ teaspoons cornflour (cornstarch)

chervil sprigs, to serve

1   Preheat the oven to 180°C (350°F/Gas 4).
Cut the duck in half by cutting down both sides
of the backbone and through the breastbone.
Discard the backbone. Cut each duck half into
four portions, removing any fat. Brown the
duck portions in a lightly oiled, heavy-based
frying pan over medium heat; remove the duck
and set aside.

2   Drain the frying pan of all but 1 tablespoon
of fat, reserving the excess. Cook the apple
until golden all over, then remove from the pan
and set aside. Add 1 tablespoon of the fat to the
pan and lightly brown the leek.

3   Add the cabbage, bay leaves, thyme sprigs,
juniper berries and peppercorns, and cook,
stirring, for 10 minutes, or until the cabbage
softens. Transfer to a large flameproof casserole
dish. Add the stock and orange juice and bring
to the boil. Add the duck, pressing gently into
the liquid, then cover and bake for 1½ hours.

4   Remove the duck and keep warm. Drain the
liquid into a saucepan. Simmer for 5 minutes,
or until reduced to 250 ml (9 fl oz/1 cup). Stir
in the butter, sugar and vinegar. Blend the
cornflour with 1 tablespoon water and stir into
the mixture until it boils and thickens.

5   Stir the apple and half the sauce into the
cabbage mixture, and season to taste. Spoon
onto a serving plate, top with the duck, drizzle
with the remaining sauce and garnish with
chervil. Serve immediately.

NUTRITION PER SERVE
Protein 50 g; Fat 30 g; Carbohydrate 25 g; Dietary
Fibre 4 g; Cholesterol 335 mg; 2250 kJ (540 Cal)

Remove the backbone and any excess fat from the
inside of the duck.

Add the duck portions to the cabbage mixture,
pressing them into the liquid.

Stir the butter, brown sugar and vinegar into the
reduced sauce.

Lamb shanks with garlic

PREPARATION TIME: 20 MINUTES | TOTAL COOKING TIME: 1 HOUR 30 MINUTES | SERVES 6

6 large lamb shanks
1 tablespoon oil
2 leeks, sliced
1 rosemary sprig
250 ml (9 fl oz/1 cup) dry white wine
1 garlic bulb
oil, for brushing

1   Preheat the oven to 180°C (350°F/Gas 4). Season the lamb shanks. Heat the oil in a frying pan over medium–high heat. Cook the lamb shanks quickly in batches until well browned. Drain on paper towels, then place the shanks in a casserole dish.

2   Cook the leek in the frying pan over medium–high heat, stirring, until tender. Add to the lamb shanks with the rosemary and wine.

3   Cut the garlic horizontally through the centre. Brush the cut surfaces with a little oil. Place cut side up in the casserole dish, but not covered by liquid. Bake, covered, for 1 hour. Remove the lid and bake for a further 15 minutes. Discard the rosemary. Serve with steamed vegetables and crusty bread on which to spread the roasted garlic.

NUTRITION PER SERVE
Protein 33 g; Fat 18 g; Carbohydrate 2 g; Dietary Fibre 2 g; Cholesterol 101 mg; 1350 kJ (320 Cal)

Cook the shanks quickly in batches in the oil in a frying pan.

Cook the leek in the frying pan, stirring, until the leek is tender.

Place the cut garlic bulb on top of the lamb shanks and leek.

Creamy potato casserole

PREPARATION TIME: 20 MINUTES | TOTAL COOKING TIME: 40 MINUTES | SERVES 4–6

750 g (1 lb 10 oz) all-purpose potatoes (see NOTES)
1 onion
125 g (4½ oz/1 cup) grated cheddar cheese
375 ml (13 fl oz/1½ cups) cream
2 teaspoons chicken stock powder (see NOTES)

1 Preheat the oven to 180°C (350°F/Gas 4). Peel the potatoes and thinly slice them. Peel the onion and slice it into rings.

2 Arrange a layer of overlapping potato slices in the base of a large casserole dish. Top the potato slices with a layer of the onion rings. Divide the grated cheese in half and set aside one half to use as a topping. Sprinkle a little of the remaining grated cheese over the onion rings. Continue layering in this order until all the potato and the onion have been used, finishing with a little of the grated cheese.

3 Pour the cream into a small jug, add the chicken stock powder and whisk gently until the mixture is thoroughly combined. Carefully pour the cream mixture over the layered potato and onion slices, and sprinkle the top with the reserved grated cheese. Bake the casserole, uncovered, for 40 minutes, or until the potato is tender, the cheese has melted and the top is golden brown.

NOTES: *Waxy or all-purpose potatoes are best to use in this recipe because they hold their shape better when slow-cooked.*

If you have a mandolin, use it to cut the potatoes into very thin slices. If not, make sure you use a very sharp knife.

If you prefer, you can use different types of stock, including vegetable, to vary the flavour.

NUTRITION PER SERVE (6)
Protein 9 g; Fat 35 g; Carbohydrate 15 g; Dietary Fibre 2 g; Cholesterol 100 mg; 1635 kJ (390 Cal)

Sprinkle a little of the grated cheese over each layer of onion rings.

Pour the cream and chicken stock powder mixture over the potato and onion.

Beef, potato and capsicum casserole

PREPARATION TIME: 35 MINUTES | TOTAL COOKING TIME: 2 HOURS 20 MINUTES | SERVES 4–6

300 g (10½ oz) French shallots (eschalots)
2 tablespoons olive oil
1 kg (2 lb 4 oz) gravy beef, cut into 4 cm
   (1½ inch) cubes
4 garlic cloves, crushed
3 teaspoons paprika
1 teaspoon fennel seeds
½ teaspoon ground cumin
1 tablespoon plain (all-purpose) flour
125 ml (4 fl oz/½ cup) red wine
2 tablespoons brandy
½ teaspoon dried thyme
½ teaspoon dried oregano
1 bay leaf
375 ml (13 fl oz/1½ cups) beef stock
1 tablespoon honey
400 g (14 oz) potatoes, cut into large chunks
2 red capsicums (peppers), chopped
125 g (4½ oz/½ cup) sour cream, to serve
snipped chives, to serve

1   Preheat the oven to 180°C (350°F/Gas 4). Place the shallots in a bowl, cover with boiling water and leave for 30 seconds. Drain and peel.

2   Heat the oil in a large heavy-based saucepan, then brown the meat in batches over medium–high heat, and transfer to a large casserole dish.

3   Add the shallots to the saucepan and cook over medium heat until soft and golden. Add the garlic, paprika, fennel seeds and cumin; cook until fragrant.

4   Add the flour, cook for 30 seconds, then remove from the heat. Stir in the red wine and brandy. Return to the heat and add the thyme, oregano, bay leaf and stock. Stir until the mixture bubbles, then add to the meat.

5   Cover and bake for 1½ hours, then add the honey, potato and capsicum. Cook, uncovered, for 30 minutes, or until the potato is tender. Season to taste. Serve with a dollop of sour cream and a sprinkling of chives.

NUTRITION PER SERVE (6)
Protein 40 g; Fat 20 g; Carbohydrate 30 g; Dietary Fibre 3 g; Cholesterol 140 mg; 1790 kJ (430 Cal)

Drain the blanched shallots, then carefully peel off the skin.

Brown the meat in batches in the hot oil over medium–high heat.

Add the red wine and brandy to the spice mixture, and stir well.

Tomato chicken casserole

PREPARATION TIME: 45 MINUTES | TOTAL COOKING TIME: 1 HOUR 20 MINUTES | SERVES 4

1.5 kg (3 lb 5 oz) chicken pieces
40 g (1½ oz) butter
1 tablespoon oil
1 large onion, chopped
2 garlic cloves, chopped
1 small green capsicum (pepper), chopped
150 g (5½ oz) mushrooms, thickly sliced
1 tablespoon plain (all-purpose) flour
250 ml (9 fl oz/1 cup) white wine
1 tablespoon white wine vinegar
4 tomatoes, peeled, seeded and chopped
2 tablespoons tomato paste (concentrated
    purée)
90 g (3¼ oz/½ cup) small black olives
2 large handfuls flat-leaf (Italian) parsley,
    chopped

1   Preheat the oven to 180°C (350°F/Gas 4).
Remove the excess fat from the chicken pieces
and pat dry with paper towels. Heat 2 teaspoons
of the butter and 2 teaspoons of the oil in a large
flameproof casserole dish. Cook half the chicken
over high heat until browned all over, then set
aside. Heat another 2 teaspoons of the butter
and the remaining oil, and cook the remaining
chicken. Set aside.

2   Heat the remaining butter in the casserole
dish and cook the onion and garlic for 2–3
minutes over medium–high heat. Add the
capsicum and mushroom, and cook, stirring,
for 3 minutes. Stir in the flour and cook for
1 minute. Add the wine, vinegar, tomato and
tomato paste, and cook, stirring, for 2 minutes,
or until slightly thickened.

3   Return the chicken to the casserole dish and
make sure it is covered by the tomato and onion
mixture. Place in the oven and cook, covered, for
1 hour, or until the chicken is tender. Stir in the
olives and parsley. Season with salt and freshly
cracked black pepper, and serve with pasta.

Score a cross in the base of the tomatoes, soak in boiling water for 30 seconds, then drain and peel.

Cook the chicken in batches over high heat until browned all over.

NUTRITION PER SERVE
Protein 55 g; Fat 15 g; Carbohydrate 9.5 g; Dietary
Fibre 5 g; Cholesterol 125 mg; 1675 kJ (401 Cal)

Fish and macaroni casserole

PREPARATION TIME: 20 MINUTES | TOTAL COOKING TIME: 55 MINUTES | SERVES 4

155 g (5½ oz/1 cup) macaroni pasta

30 g (1 oz) butter

1 onion, chopped

500 g (1 lb 2 oz) white fish fillets, cut into 2 cm (¾ inch) cubes (see NOTE)

1 tablespoon chopped thyme

100 g (3½ oz) button mushrooms, sliced

½ teaspoon hot English mustard

1 tablespoon plain (all-purpose) flour

250 ml (9 fl oz/1 cup) chicken stock

125 ml (4 fl oz/½ cup) cream

125 g (4½ oz/½ cup) sour cream

80 g (2¾ oz/1 cup) fresh breadcrumbs

125 g (4½ oz/1 cup) grated cheddar cheese

50 g (1¾ oz/½ cup) grated parmesan cheese

2 tablespoons chopped flat-leaf (Italian) parsley

1 Preheat the oven to 180°C (350°F/Gas 4). Cook the macaroni in a large saucepan of rapidly boiling water until just *al dente*. Drain and set aside.

2 Heat the butter in a heavy-based saucepan over medium heat. Cook the onion for 3 minutes, or until golden. Add the fish, thyme and mushrooms. Cook for 5 minutes, or until the fish is tender. Remove from the pan and keep warm.

3 Stir the mustard and flour into the pan. Add the stock and cream gradually, stirring over medium heat for 3 minutes, or until sauce boils and thickens. Boil for 1 minute, then remove from heat. Stir in sour cream.

4 Transfer the mixture to a large bowl, and stir in the macaroni, and fish and mushroom mixture. Spoon into a large ovenproof dish. Combine the breadcrumbs, cheeses and parsley. Sprinkle over the macaroni mixture. Bake for 30 minutes, or until golden, and serve.

NOTE: *If you prefer, you can use a drained tin of tuna instead of the fresh fish.*

NUTRITION PER SERVE
Protein 49 g; Fat 50 g; Carbohydrate 46 g; Dietary Fibre 3.5 g; Cholesterol 217 mg; 3465 kJ (830 Cal)

Cook the macaroni in a large saucepan of boiling water until just tender.

Add the fish, thyme and mushrooms to the pan, and cook.

Lamb and bean casserole

PREPARATION TIME: 25 MINUTES + OVERNIGHT SOAKING | TOTAL COOKING TIME: 2 HOURS 15 MINUTES | SERVES 6

300 g (10½ oz/1½ cups) borlotti (cranberry) beans or red kidney beans
1 kg (2 lb 4 oz) boned leg of lamb
1½ tablespoons olive oil
2 bacon slices, rind removed, chopped
1 large onion, chopped
2 garlic cloves, crushed
1 large carrot, chopped
500 ml (17 fl oz/2 cups) dry red wine
1 tablespoon tomato paste (concentrated purée)
375 ml (13 fl oz/1½ cups) beef stock
2 large rosemary sprigs
2 thyme sprigs
small thyme sprigs, extra, to garnish

1 Put the beans in a bowl and cover with plenty of water. Leave to soak overnight, then drain well.

2 Preheat the oven to 160°C (315°F/Gas 2–3). Trim any excess fat from the lamb and cut the lamb into 3 cm (1¼ inch) pieces.

3 Heat 1 tablespoon of the oil in a large flameproof casserole dish. Add half the meat and toss over medium–high heat for 2 minutes, or until browned. Remove from the dish and repeat with the remaining lamb. Remove from the dish.

4 Heat the remaining olive oil in the casserole dish and add the bacon and onion. Cook over medium heat for 3 minutes, or until the onion is translucent. Add the garlic and carrot, and cook for 1 minute, or until aromatic.

5 Return the meat and any juices to the casserole dish, increase the heat to high and add the wine. Bring to the boil and cook for 2 minutes. Add the beans, tomato paste, stock, rosemary sprigs and thyme sprigs, return to the boil, then cover, place in the oven and cook for 2 hours, or until the meat is tender. Stir occasionally during cooking. Skim off any excess fat, remove the sprigs of herbs. Season and garnish with extra thyme sprigs to serve.

NUTRITION PER SERVE
Protein 50 g; Fat 10 g; Carbohydrate 48 g; Dietary Fibre 9 g; Cholesterol 117 mg; 2367 kJ (565 Cal)

Remove any excess fat from the lamb, then cut it into large pieces.

Heat the oil, then add the lamb and toss until it is browned all over.

Return the meat and juices to the casserole dish, add the wine and bring to the boil.

Spiced beef

PREPARATION TIME: 20 MINUTES I TOTAL COOKING TIME: 1 HOUR 40 MINUTES I SERVES 4–6

60 g (2¼ oz/⅓ cup) soft brown sugar
1 teaspoon ground cinnamon
1 teaspoon ground nutmeg
1 teaspoon ground cardamom
1 teaspoon ground black pepper
1.5 kg (3 lb 5 oz) piece fresh silverside,
   trimmed
1 orange, quartered
1 large onion, quartered
60 ml (2 fl oz/¼ cup) red wine vinegar

1   Preheat the oven to 160°C (315°F/Gas 2–3). Combine the sugar, cinnamon, nutmeg, cardamom and pepper in a small bowl. Rub the mixture all over the meat, pressing it on firmly with your fingers. Place the meat in a deep casserole dish.

2   Place the orange and onion around the meat, and pour in the vinegar combined with 250 ml (9 fl oz/1 cup) water. Bake, covered, for 1–1½ hours, or until the meat is tender.

3   Remove the meat from the dish, cover and set aside. Remove the orange pieces from the cooking liquid. Strain the remaining cooking liquid into a shallow saucepan and cook, uncovered, for 10 minutes, or until reduced by half. The meat can be served warm or cold, accompanied by the sauce. Serve with mash and green beans.

NOTES: *To serve the silverside cold, refrigerate it overnight in the cooking liquid before draining.*

A whole piece of rump or topside steak may be used in place of the fresh silverside.

Use your fingers to press the spice mixture over the silverside.

Pour the combined vinegar and water over the beef, orange and onion.

NUTRITION PER SERVE (6)
Protein 56 g; Fat 5.5 g; Carbohydrate 10 g; Dietary Fibre 0.5 g; Cholesterol 168 mg; 1325 kJ (315 Cal)

Chicken and cauliflower casserole

PREPARATION TIME: 20 MINUTES | TOTAL COOKING TIME: 1 HOUR | SERVES 6

30 g (1 oz) butter

4 boneless, skinless chicken breast, cut into
    3 cm (1¼ inch) cubes

6 spring onions (scallions), sliced

2 garlic cloves, crushed

2 tablespoons plain (all-purpose) flour

375 ml (13 fl oz/1½ cups) chicken stock

2 teaspoons dijon mustard

280 g (10 oz) cauliflower, cut into florets

1 kg (2 lb 4 oz) potatoes, quartered

2 tablespoons full-cream (whole) milk

60 g (2¼ oz) butter, extra

2 eggs

30 g (1 oz/⅓ cup) flaked toasted almonds

1   Preheat the oven to 180°C (350°F/Gas 4).
Heat half the butter in a large frying pan and
cook the chicken in batches until browned and
cooked through. Remove from the pan. In the
same pan, melt the remaining butter and cook
the spring onion and garlic for 2 minutes. Stir
in the flour and mix well. Pour in the stock
and cook, stirring, until the mixture boils and
thickens. Add the mustard and then stir in the
chicken. Season well with salt and pepper.

2   Meanwhile, steam or microwave the
cauliflower until just tender, taking care not to
overcook it. Refresh the cauliflower in iced water
and drain well.

3   Boil the potato in salted water for 15–20
minutes, or until tender. Drain and mash well
with the milk, extra butter and eggs. Put the
cauliflower in a 2.5 litre (87 fl oz/10 cup)
ovenproof dish and pour in the chicken mixture.
Pipe or spoon the mashed potato over the
top. Sprinkle with the almonds and bake for
25 minutes, or until the top is browned and
cooked through. Serve straight from the dish.

NUTRITION PER SERVE
Protein 25 g; Fat 20 g; Carbohydrate 25 g; Dietary
Fibre 5.5 g; Cholesterol 135 mg; 1610 kJ (385 Cal)

Use a large sharp knife to cut the chicken breasts
into cubes.

Add the chicken to the pan and cook in batches
until browned.

Tuna and white bean casserole

PREPARATION TIME: 40 MINUTES + OVERNIGHT SOAKING | TOTAL COOKING TIME: 3 HOURS | SERVES 6

400 g (14 oz/2 cups) dried cannellini beans
60 ml (2 fl oz/¼ cup) olive oil
2 red onions, chopped
2 garlic cloves, crushed
1 teaspoon ground coriander
1 teaspoon finely grated lemon zest
2 teaspoons chopped thyme
500 ml (17 fl oz/2 cups) white wine
500 ml (17 fl oz/2 cups) fish stock
480 g (1 lb 1 oz) tin tuna in brine, drained
1 bunch basil, leaves only
4 large ripe tomatoes, cut into 1 cm (½ inch)
   slices

TOPPING
40 g (1½ oz/½ cup) fresh breadcrumbs
1 garlic clove, crushed
30 g (1 oz/¾ cup) finely chopped flat-leaf
   (Italian) parsley
30 g (1 oz) butter, melted

1 Soak the beans in water overnight, then drain and set aside.

2 Heat the oil in a large, heavy-based saucepan. Add the onion, garlic, coriander, lemon zest and thyme. Cook over medium heat for 10–15 minutes, or until the onion is softened. Add the beans and cook for 10 minutes.

3 Add the wine and stock. Cover and cook over low heat for 2 hours, until the beans are tender but not mashed.

4 Preheat the oven to 210°C (415°F/Gas 6–7). Transfer the bean mixture to a large casserole dish. Top with the tuna and basil leaves. Arrange the tomato slices over the basil.

5 To make the topping, combine the breadcrumbs, garlic and parsley. Sprinkle over the tomato. Drizzle with the butter. Bake for 30 minutes, or until golden and serve.

NUTRITION PER SERVE
Protein 32 g; Fat 16 g; Carbohydrate 36 g; Dietary Fibre 16 g; Cholesterol 41 mg; 1920 kJ (459 Cal)

Add the drained cannellini beans to the onion mixture in the pan.

Add the wine and stock to the bean mixture, and cook for 2 hours.

Arrange the tuna over the bean mixture in the casserole dish.

Lamb shanks in tomato sauce on polenta

PREPARATION TIME: 10 MINUTES | TOTAL COOKING TIME: 2 HOURS 30 MINUTES | SERVES 4

2 tablespoons olive oil
1 large red onion, sliced
4 French-trimmed lamb shanks
(about 250 g/9 oz each) (see NOTE)
2 garlic cloves, crushed
400 g (14 oz) tin chopped tomatoes
125 ml (4 fl oz/½ cup) red wine
2 teaspoons chopped rosemary
150 g (5½ oz/1 cup) instant polenta
50 g (1¾ oz) butter
50 g (1¾ oz/½ cup) grated parmesan cheese
rosemary, extra, to garnish

1   Preheat the oven to 160°C (315°F/Gas 2–3). Heat the oil in a 4 litre (140 fl oz/16 cup) flameproof casserole dish over medium heat and sauté the onion for 3–4 minutes, or until softening and becoming transparent. Add the lamb shanks and cook for 2–3 minutes, or until lightly browned. Add the garlic, tomato and wine, then bring to the boil and cook for 3–4 minutes. Stir in the rosemary. Season with ¼ teaspoon each of salt and pepper.

2   Cover and bake for 2 hours. Remove the lid, return to the oven and simmer for a further 15 minutes, or until the lamb just starts to fall off the bone. Check periodically that the sauce is not too dry, adding water if needed.

3   About 20 minutes before serving, bring 1 litre (35 fl oz/4 cups) water to the boil in a saucepan. Add the polenta in a thin stream, whisking continuously, then reduce the heat to very low. Simmer for 8–10 minutes, or until thick and coming away from the side of pan. Stir in the butter and parmesan. To serve, spoon the polenta onto serving plates, top with the shanks and tomato sauce. Top with rosemary.

NOTE: *French-trimmed lamb shanks are lamb shanks with the meat scraped back to make a neat lamb 'drumstick'. If these are unavailable, you can use regular lamb shanks instead.*

Check periodically that the sauce is not too dry, adding water if needed.

Add the polenta to the water in a very thin stream, whisking continuously.

NUTRITION PER SERVE
Protein 39 g; Fat 36.5 g; Carbohydrate 31 g; Dietary Fibre 3 g; Cholesterol 137 mg; 2615 kJ (625 Cal)

Mexican chicken casserole

PREPARATION TIME: 15 MINUTES | TOTAL COOKING TIME: 1 HOUR | SERVES 4

165 g (5¾ oz/¾ cup) short-grain rice
300 g (10½ oz) tin red kidney beans, drained
    and thoroughly rinsed
3½ tablespoons chopped coriander (cilantro)
    leaves
1 tablespoon oil
600 g (1 lb 5 oz) boneless, skinless chicken
    thighs
2 x 200 g (7 oz) jars spicy taco sauce
250 g (9 oz/2 cups) grated cheddar cheese
125 g (4½ oz/½ cup) sour cream

1   Preheat the oven to 180°C (350°F/Gas 4). Lightly grease a 7 cm (2¾ inch) deep, 21 cm (8¼ inch) round casserole dish. Bring a large saucepan of water to the boil, add the rice and cook for 10–12 minutes, stirring occasionally. Drain and set aside.

2   In the prepared dish, combine the beans and 1½ tablespoons of the coriander, then add the rice and toss together. Lightly press the mixture so the beans are mixed into the rice and the mixture is flat.

3   Heat the oil in a large frying pan over medium–high heat. Sauté the chicken thighs for 3 minutes, then turn over. Add the spicy taco sauce, and cook for a further 3 minutes.

4   To assemble, spread half the cheese over the rice. Arrange the chicken and sauce on top in a star shape, sprinkle with 1½ tablespoons of the coriander, then sprinkle with the remaining cheese. Cover with foil.

5   Bake for 35–40 minutes, or until the mixture is bubbling and the cheese is melted and slightly browned—remove the foil for the last 5 minutes of cooking. Cut into four servings with a knife and scoop out carefully, keeping the layers intact. Serve sprinkled with the remaining coriander and sour cream.

NUTRITION PER SERVE
Protein 52 g; Fat 50 g; Carbohydrate 66 g; Dietary Fibre 6 g; Cholesterol 235 mg; 3825 kJ (915 Cal)

Arrange the chicken thighs and sauce on top of the cheese in a star shape.

Bake the casserole until it is bubbling and the cheese is melted.

Beef casserole with caraway dumplings

PREPARATION TIME: 1 HOUR | TOTAL COOKING TIME: 1 HOUR 30 MINUTES | SERVES 6

1.5 kg (3 lb 5 oz) round or topside steak, trimmed and cut into 3 cm (1¼ inch) cubes
60 g (2¼ oz/½ cup) plain (all-purpose) flour
¼ teaspoon freshly ground black pepper
80 ml (2½ fl oz/⅓ cup) olive oil
1 garlic clove, crushed
2 onions, sliced
1 teaspoon sweet paprika
½ teaspoon ground cinnamon
80 ml (2½ fl oz/⅓ cup) red wine
125 ml (4 fl oz/½ cup) beef stock
½ teaspoon mixed dried herbs
160 g (5½ oz/⅔ cup) tomato pasta sauce
3 large red capsicums (peppers)

DUMPLINGS
185 g (6½ oz/1½ cups) self-raising flour
65 g (2¼ oz) butter
125 ml (4 fl oz/½ cup) full-cream (whole) milk
1 teaspoon caraway seeds
1 tablespoon full-cream (whole) milk, extra

NUTRITION PER SERVE
Protein 61 g; Fat 31 g; Carbohydrate 40 g; Dietary Fibre 2.5 g; Cholesterol 176 mg; 2880 kJ (685 Cal)

1 Preheat the oven to 180°C (350°F/Gas 4). Toss the meat lightly in the combined flour and pepper, and shake off any excess.

2 Heat 2 tablespoons of the oil in a heavy-based saucepan. Cook the meat in batches over medium–high heat until browned. Drain on paper towels.

3 Heat the remaining oil in the saucepan. Cook the garlic and onion over medium heat, stirring, for 2 minutes, or until soft. Return the meat to the pan with the spices, wine, stock, mixed herbs and pasta sauce. Bring to the boil, then remove from the heat and transfer to a deep casserole dish. Bake, covered, for 45 minutes. Remove from the oven and uncover. Increase the oven to 240°C (475°F/Gas 8).

4 Halve the capsicums lengthways and remove the seeds. Grill (broil), skin side up, under a hot grill (broiled) for 10 minutes, or until the skin blackens. Remove, place in a sealable plastic bag and cool. Peel off the skins. Cut the capsicum into 2 cm (¾ inch) wide strips. Arrange over the meat.

5 To make the dumplings, process flour and butter in a food processor for 10 seconds, or until fine and crumbly. Add all milk and process for 10 seconds, until a soft dough is formed. Turn out onto a floured surface. Add caraway seeds and knead for 1 minute until smooth. Press dough out to a 1 cm (½ inch) thick round. Cut 4 cm (1½ inch) rounds using a cutter. Top casserole with dumplings and brush with milk. Return to oven, uncovered, for 15 minutes, or until dumplings are puffed and golden.

Return the meat to the pan with the spices, wine, stock, mixed herbs and tomato pasta sauce.

Carefully peel the blackened skin from the grilled capsicum pieces.

After pressing the dough out flat, cut into rounds with a fluted cutter.

Creamy fish casserole

PREPARATION TIME: 10 MINUTES | TOTAL COOKING TIME: 1 HOUR | SERVES 4

2 large potatoes, chopped
60 ml (2 fl oz/¼ cup) full-cream (whole) milk
    or cream
1 egg
60 g (2¼ oz) butter
60 g (2¼ oz/½ cup) grated cheddar cheese
800 g (1 lb 12 oz) white fish fillets, cut into
    large chunks (see NOTE)
375 ml (13 fl oz/1½ cups) full-cream (whole)
    milk, extra
1 onion, finely chopped
1 garlic clove, crushed
2 tablespoons plain (all-purpose) flour
2 tablespoons lemon juice
2 teaspoons grated lemon zest
1 tablespoon chopped dill

1 Preheat the oven to 180°C (350°F/Gas 4).
Boil or steam the potato for 8 minutes, or until
tender. Drain and mash with the milk or cream,
egg and half the butter. Mix in half the cheese,
then set aside.

2 Put the fish in a shallow frying pan and
cover with the extra milk. Bring to the boil, then
reduce the heat and simmer for 2–3 minutes,
or until the fish flakes easily. Drain the fish
well, reserving the milk, and place in a 1.5 litre
(52 fl oz/6 cup) ovenproof dish.

3 Melt the remaining butter over medium heat
in a saucepan and cook the onion and garlic
for 2 minutes. Stir in the flour and cook for
1 minute, or until golden. Remove from the heat
and gradually stir in the reserved milk. Return to
the heat and stir constantly until the sauce boils
and thickens. Reduce the heat and simmer for
2 minutes. Add the lemon juice, lemon zest and
dill, and season. Mix with the fish, cover with the
potato and sprinkle with the remaining cheese.
Bake for 35 minutes, or until golden.

NOTE: *You could use ling, perch, hake or snapper.*

Cook the fish in the simmering milk until it flakes
easily when tested.

Stir the flour into the onion and garlic, and cook
until golden.

NUTRITION PER SERVE
Protein 54 g; Fat 29 g; Carbohydrate 24 g; Dietary
Fibre 2.5 g; Cholesterol 253 mg; 2390 kJ (570 Cal)

Lancashire hotpot

PREPARATION TIME: 20 MINUTES I TOTAL COOKING TIME: 2 HOURS I SERVES 8

8 lamb forequarter chops
4 lamb kidneys
30 g (1 oz/¼ cup) plain (all-purpose) flour
50 g (1¾ oz) butter
4 potatoes, thinly sliced
2 large brown onions, sliced
1 large carrot, chopped
435 ml (15¼ fl oz/1¾ cups) beef or vegetable
   stock
2 teaspoons chopped thyme
1 bay leaf
melted butter, extra

1   Preheat the oven to 160°C (315°F/Gas 2–3), and grease a large casserole dish. Trim the chops of excess fat and sinew, then remove and discard the cores from the kidneys. Cut kidneys into quarters. Toss the chops and kidneys in the flour, shaking off and reserving the excess. Heat the butter in a frying pan and brown the chops quickly on both sides. Remove the chops from the pan and brown the kidneys.

2   Layer half the potato slices in the base of the casserole dish and top with the chops and the kidneys.

3   Add the onion and carrot to the pan, and cook until the carrot begins to brown. Layer on top of the chops and kidneys. Sprinkle the reserved flour over the base of the pan and fry, stirring, until dark brown. Gradually pour in the stock and bring to the boil, stirring. Season well, and add the thyme and bay leaf. Reduce the heat and simmer for 10 minutes. Pour into the casserole dish.

4   Layer the remaining potato over the meat and vegetables. Cover and bake for 1¼ hours. Increase the oven temperature to 180°C (350°F/Gas 4), brush the potato with the extra melted butter and cook, uncovered, for 20 minutes, or until the potato is brown. Season and serve.

Remove the cores from the kidneys and then cut the kidneys into quarters.

Cover the base with potato slices, then add the chops and kidneys.

NUTRITION PER SERVE
Protein 38 g; Fat 11 g; Carbohydrate 13 g; Dietary Fibre 2 g; Cholesterol 175 mg; 1285 kJ (305 Cal)

Pork sausage and soya bean casserole

PREPARATION TIME: 25 MINUTES + AT LEAST 8 HOURS SOAKING | TOTAL COOKING TIME: 4 HOURS | SERVES 4

325 g (11½ oz/1¾ cups) dried soya beans
8 thin pork sausages
2 tablespoons soya bean oil, or oil
1 red onion, chopped
4 garlic cloves, chopped
1 large carrot, diced
1 celery stalk, diced
2 x 415 g (14¾ oz) tins chopped tomatoes
1 tablespoon tomato paste (concentrated
    purée)
250 ml (9 fl oz/1 cup) white wine
2 thyme sprigs
1 teaspoon dried oregano
1 tablespoon oregano, chopped
thyme sprigs, extra, to garnish

1 Soak the soya beans in cold water for at least 8 hours. Drain well. Place in a large saucepan with enough fresh water to cover. Bring to the boil, then reduce the heat and slowly simmer for 1¼–2 hours—keep the beans covered with water during cooking; drain.

2 Meanwhile prick the sausages all over. Cook in a frying pan, turning, for 10 minutes, or until browned. Drain on paper towels.

3 Heat the oil in a 3.5 litre (122 fl oz/14 cup) flameproof casserole dish over medium heat. Cook the onion and garlic for 3–5 minutes, or until softened. Add the carrot and celery. Cook, stirring, for 5 minutes. Stir in the tomato, tomato paste, wine, thyme sprigs and dried oregano, and bring to the boil. Reduce the heat and simmer, stirring often, for 10 minutes, or until reduced and thickened slightly.

4 Preheat the oven to 160°C (315°F/Gas 2–3). Add the sausages, beans and 250 ml (9 fl oz/1 cup) water to the casserole dish. Bake, covered, for 2 hours. Stir occasionally, adding more water to keep the beans covered.

5 Return the casserole dish to the stove, skim off any fat, then reduce the liquid until thickened slightly. Remove the thyme and stir in the chopped oregano. Garnish with extra thyme sprigs and serve.

NUTRITION PER SERVE
Protein 46 g; Fat 58 g; Carbohydrate 20 g; Dietary Fibre 23 g; Cholesterol 93 mg; 3479 kJ (830 Cal)

Drain the soaked and cooked soya beans well in a colander.

Cook the sausages in a frying pan, turning frequently, until brown all over.

Simmer the tomato mixture until reduced and thickened slightly.

Curries

Thai beef and peanut curry

PREPARATION TIME: 30 MINUTES + 5 MINUTES SOAKING | TOTAL COOKING TIME: 1 HOUR 30 MINUTES | SERVES 4–6

CURRY PASTE
8–10 large dried red chillies
6 red Asian shallots (eschalots), chopped
6 garlic cloves, chopped
1 teaspoon ground coriander
1 tablespoon ground cumin
1 teaspoon white pepper
2 lemongrass stems (white part only), bruised
    and sliced
1 tablespoon chopped fresh galangal
6 coriander (cilantro) roots
2 teaspoons shrimp paste
2 tablespoons roasted peanuts
peanut oil, if needed

1 tablespoon peanut oil
400 ml (14 fl oz) tin coconut cream (do not
    shake the tin)
1 kg (2 lb 4 oz) round or blade steak, thinly
    sliced
400 ml (14 fl oz) tin coconut milk
4 makrut (kaffir lime) leaves, whole
90 g (3¼ oz/⅓ cup) crunchy peanut butter
60 ml (2 fl oz/¼ cup) lime juice
2½ tablespoons fish sauce
3–4 tablespoons grated palm sugar (jaggery)
    or soft brown sugar
Thai basil leaves, to garnish
1 tablespoon chopped peanuts, extra, to
    garnish (optional)

1 To make the curry paste, soak the chillies in boiling water for 5 minutes, or until soft. Remove the stem and seeds, then chop. Place all the curry paste ingredients in a food processor and process to a smooth paste. Add a little peanut oil if it is too thick.

2 Place the oil and the thick cream from the top of the coconut cream (reserving the rest) in a large saucepan over high heat. Add 6–8 tablespoons of the curry paste and cook, stirring, for 5 minutes, or until fragrant. Cook for 5–10 minutes, or until the coconut cream splits and becomes oily.

3 Add the beef, the reserved coconut cream, the coconut milk, makrut leaves and peanut butter, and cook for 8 minutes, or until the beef just starts to change colour. Reduce the heat and simmer for 1 hour, or until the beef is tender.

4 Stir in the lime juice, fish sauce and palm sugar, and transfer to a serving dish. Garnish with the Thai basil leaves, and extra peanuts, if desired, and serve immediately.

NUTRITION PER SERVE (6)
Protein 45 g; Fat 35 g; Carbohydrate 16.3 g; Dietary Fibre 5.6 g; Cholesterol 95 mg; 2384 kJ (569 Cal)

Place all the curry paste ingredients in a food processor and process until smooth.

Cook the coconut cream and curry paste until it splits and becomes oily.

Thai duck and pineapple curry

PREPARATION TIME: 10 MINUTES | TOTAL COOKING TIME: 15 MINUTES | SERVES 4–6

1 tablespoon peanut oil

8 spring onions (scallions), sliced on the
   diagonal into 3 cm (1¼ inch) lengths

2 garlic cloves, crushed

2–4 tablespoons Thai red curry paste (see page
   251)

750 g (1 lb 10 oz) Chinese roast duck,
   chopped

400 ml (14 fl oz) tin coconut milk

450 g (1 lb) tin pineapple pieces in syrup,
   drained

3 makrut (kaffir lime) leaves

1 large handful coriander (cilantro) leaves,
   chopped, plus extra leaves, to garnish

2 tablespoons chopped mint, plus extra leaves,
   to garnish

1   Heat a wok until very hot, add the peanut
oil and swirl to coat the side. Add the spring
onion, garlic and red curry paste, and stir-fry for
1 minute, or until fragrant.

2   Add the roast duck, coconut milk, pineapple
pieces, makrut leaves, and half each of the
coriander and mint. Bring to the boil, then
reduce the heat and simmer for 10 minutes, or
until the duck is heated through and the sauce
has thickened slightly. Stir in the remaining fresh
herbs. Garnish with extra coriander and mint
leaves and serve with steamed jasmine rice.

NUTRITION PER SERVE (6)
Protein 24 g; Fat 25 g; Carbohydrate 4 g; Dietary
Fibre 2 g; Cholesterol 140 mg; 1415 kJ (340 Cal)

Heat a wok until very hot, add the peanut oil and
swirl to coat.

Stir-fry the spring onion, garlic and red curry paste
until fragrant.

Simmer until the duck is heated through and the
sauce has thickened slightly.

Crab curry

PREPARATION TIME: 25 MINUTES | TOTAL COOKING TIME: 20 MINUTES | SERVES 6

4 raw large blue swimmer or mud crabs
1 tablespoon oil
1 large onion, finely chopped
2 garlic cloves, crushed
1 lemongrass stem (white part only), finely
    chopped
1 teaspoon sambal oelek (South-East Asian
    chilli paste)
1 teaspoon ground cumin
1 teaspoon ground turmeric
1 teaspoon ground coriander
270 ml (9½ fl oz) coconut cream
500 ml (17 fl oz/2 cups) chicken stock
1 large handful basil leaves

1 Pull back the apron and remove the top shell from the crabs. Remove the intestines and grey feathery gills. Cut each crab into four pieces. Use a cracker to crack the claws open; this will make it easier to eat later and will also allow the flavours to get into the crabmeat.

2 Heat the oil in a large saucepan or wok. Add the onion, garlic, lemongrass and sambal oelek, and cook for 2–3 minutes, or until softened.

3 Add the cumin, turmeric, coriander and ½ teaspoon salt, and cook for a further 2 minutes, or until fragrant.

4 Stir in the coconut cream and stock. Bring to the boil, then reduce the heat, add the crab pieces and cook, stirring occasionally, for 10 minutes, or until the liquid has reduced and thickened slightly and the crabs are cooked. Scatter the basil leaves over the crab and serve with rice.

NUTRITION PER SERVE
Protein 0.5 g; Fat 7 g; Carbohydrate 1.5 g; Dietary
Fibre 0.5 g; Cholesterol 20 mg; 290 kJ (70 Cal)

Pull back the apron and remove the top shell from the crabs.

Remove the intestines and grey feathery gills from the crabs.

Pork and tamarind curry

PREPARATION TIME: 20 MINUTES | TOTAL COOKING TIME: 1 HOUR 50 MINUTES | SERVES 6

80 ml (2½ fl oz/⅓ cup) oil

2 onions, thickly sliced

4 large garlic cloves, crushed

3 tablespoons Sri Lankan curry powder
(see page 250)

1 tablespoon grated fresh ginger

10 dried curry leaves or 5 fresh curry leaves

2 teaspoons chilli powder

¼ teaspoon fenugreek seeds

1.25 kg (2 lb 12 oz) lean pork shoulder,
cubed

1 lemongrass stem (white part only), finely
chopped

2 tablespoons tamarind purée

4 cardamom pods, crushed

400 ml (14 fl oz) tin coconut cream

CUCUMBER SAMBAL

1–2 large cucumbers, halved, seeded and
finely chopped

500 g (1 lb 2 oz/2 cups) plain yoghurt

2 tablespoons coriander (cilantro) leaves,
finely chopped

1 tablespoon lemon juice

2 garlic cloves, crushed

1 Heat the oil in a heavy-based Dutch oven or deep, lidded frying pan. Add the onion, garlic, curry powder, ginger, curry leaves, chilli powder, fenugreek seeds and 1 teaspoon salt, and cook, stirring, over medium heat for 5 minutes.

2 Add the pork, lemongrass, tamarind purée, cardamom and 375 ml (13 fl oz/1½ cups) hot water, then reduce the heat and simmer, covered, for 1 hour.

3 Stir in the coconut cream and simmer on a low heat, uncovered, for 40–45 minutes, or until the sauce has reduced and become thick and creamy.

4 To make the cucumber sambal, place the cucumber in a bowl and stir in the yoghurt, coriander, lemon juice and garlic. Season to taste with salt and pepper.

5 Serve the curry with the cucumber sambal, steamed basmati rice and chapattis.

NUTRITION PER SERVE
Protein 55 g; Fat 30 g; Carbohydrate 9.5 g; Dietary Fibre 3 g; Cholesterol 110 mg; 2260 kJ (540 Cal)

Halve the cucumber, remove the seeds and finely chop the flesh.

Cook the onion, garlic and spices in a heavy-based frying pan.

Simmer the curry until the sauce has reduced and become thick and creamy.

Chu chee seafood

PREPARATION TIME: 30 MINUTES | TOTAL COOKING TIME: 20 MINUTES | SERVES 4

2 x 270 ml (9½ fl oz) tins coconut cream (do
  not shake the tins)
3 tablespoons chu chee curry paste (see page
  251)
500 g (1 lb 2 oz) scallops, roe removed
500 g (1 lb 2 oz) raw king prawns, peeled and
  deveined, leaving the tails intact
2–3 tablespoons fish sauce
2–3 tablespoons grated palm sugar (jaggery) or
  soft brown sugar
8 makrut (kaffir lime) leaves, finely shredded
2 red chillies, thinly sliced
2 large handfuls Thai basil leaves

1   Place 250 ml (9 fl oz/1 cup) of the thick
coconut cream from the top of the tins in a
wok. Heat until just boiling, then stir in the
curry paste, reduce the heat and simmer for
10 minutes, or until fragrant and the oil just
begins to separate.

2   Stir in the remaining coconut cream, the
scallops and prawns, and cook for 5 minutes,
or until tender. Add the fish sauce, palm sugar,
makrut leaves and chilli, and cook for 1 minute.
Stir in half of the basil and garnish with the
remaining leaves before serving.

NUTRITION PER SERVE
Protein 44 g; Fat 30 g; Carbohydrate 23 g; Dietary
Fibre 3 g; Cholesterol 230 mg; 2253 kJ (538 Cal)

Carefully remove the thick coconut cream from the
top of the tins.

Stir in the curry paste and simmer until the oil
begins to separate.

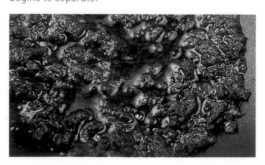

Stir in the remaining cream, the scallops and
prawns, and simmer until tender.

Green tofu curry

PREPARATION TIME: 20 MINUTES | TOTAL COOKING TIME: 20 MINUTES | SERVES 6

CURRY PASTE
10 small green chillies
50 g (1¾ oz) red Asian shallots (eschalots)
2 garlic cloves
4 large handfuls finely chopped coriander
 (cilantro) stems and roots
1 lemongrass stem (white part only), chopped
2 tablespoons grated fresh galangal
1 tablespoon ground coriander
1 teaspoon ground cumin
1 teaspoon black peppercorns
½ teaspoon ground turmeric
1 tablespoon lime juice

2 tablespoons oil
1 onion, sliced
400 ml (14 fl oz) tin coconut cream
4–5 makrut (kaffir lime) leaves, torn
500 g (1 lb 2 oz) firm tofu, cut into 2 cm
 (¾ inch) cubes
1 tablespoon lime juice
1 tablespoon shredded Thai basil

1 To make the curry paste, place all the ingredients in a food processor and process until it is smooth.

2 Heat the oil in a frying pan, add the onion and cook for 5 minutes, or until soft. Add 4 tablespoons curry paste (or more for a stronger flavour) and cook, stirring, for 2 minutes. Stir in the coconut cream and 250 ml (9 fl oz/1 cup) water, and season with salt. Bring to the boil and add the makrut leaves and tofu. Reduce the heat and simmer for 8 minutes, stirring often. Stir in the lime juice and Thai basil, and serve.

HINT: *The recipe for the curry paste makes 1 cup, but you will only need ⅓ cup. Freeze the remaining paste in two portions to use at a later date.*

Place the curry paste ingredients in a food processor and process until smooth.

Cook the onion slices for 5 minutes, or until they are soft.

NUTRITION PER SERVE
Protein 3.5 g; Fat 25 g; Carbohydrate 3 g; Dietary
Fibre 1.5 g; Cholesterol 0 mg; 1020 kJ (242 Cal)

Chicken kapitan

PREPARATION TIME: 35 MINUTES | TOTAL COOKING TIME: 1 HOUR 20 MINUTES | SERVES 4–6

1 teaspoon small dried shrimp
80 ml (2½ fl oz/⅓ cup) oil
6–8 red chillies, seeded and finely chopped
4 garlic cloves, finely chopped
3 lemongrass stems (white part only),
    finely chopped
2 teaspoons ground turmeric
10 macadamia nuts
2 large onions, chopped
250 ml (9 fl oz/1 cup) coconut milk
1.5 kg (3 lb 5 oz) chicken, cut into 8 pieces
125 ml (4 fl oz/½ cup) coconut cream
2 tablespoons lime juice
lime wedges, to serve

1   Put the shrimp in a frying pan and dry-fry (no oil) over a low heat, shaking the pan regularly, for 3 minutes, or until the shrimp are dark orange and are giving off a strong aroma. Transfer to a mortar and pound with a pestle until finely ground. Alternatively, you may process in a food processor.

2   Place half of the oil, the chilli, garlic, lemongrass, turmeric and nuts in a food processor, and process in short bursts until very finely chopped, regularly scraping down the side of the bowl.

3   Heat the remaining oil in a wok or frying pan, add the onion and ¼ teaspoon salt, and cook, stirring regularly, over low heat for 8 minutes, or until golden.

4   Add the spice mixture and shrimp, and stir for 5 minutes. If the mixture begins to stick, add 2 tablespoons of the coconut milk. It is important to cook the mixture thoroughly to develop the flavours.

5   Add the chicken to the wok and cook, stirring, for 5 minutes, or until beginning to brown. Stir in the remaining coconut milk and 250 ml (9 fl oz/1 cup) water, and bring to the boil. Reduce the heat and simmer for 50 minutes, or until the chicken is cooked and the sauce has thickened slightly. Add the coconut cream and bring the mixture back to the boil, stirring constantly. Add the lime juice and serve immediately with rice and lime wedges.

NUTRITION PER SERVE (6)
Protein 58 g; Fat 30 g; Carbohydrate 4 g; Dietary
Fibre 2 g; Cholesterol 125 mg; 2211 kJ (528 Cal)

Dry-fry the shrimp over low heat until they turn dark orange and fragrant.

Place the shrimp in a mortar and pound with a pestle until finely ground.

Simmer until the chicken is cooked and the sauce has thickened slightly.

Lamb neck curry

PREPARATION TIME: 30 MINUTES I TOTAL COOKING TIME: 1 HOUR 40 MINUTES I SERVES 4–6

1 tablespoon oil
8 best lamb neck chops (see NOTE)
2 onions, sliced
3 garlic cloves, finely chopped
2 teaspoons finely chopped fresh ginger
1 small green chilli, seeded and finely chopped
½ teaspoon ground cumin
1 teaspoon ground fennel
1½ teaspoons ground turmeric
1½ teaspoons chilli powder
2 teaspoons garam masala
1 star anise
1 cinnamon stick
5 curry leaves
2 bay leaves
500 ml (17 fl oz/2 cups) beef stock
8 tomatoes, peeled and quartered
coriander (cilantro) leaves, to garnish

1   Heat the oil in a large frying pan and cook the lamb in batches for 5–8 minutes, or until browned. Place the chops in a large saucepan.

2   Add the onion to the frying pan and cook, stirring frequently, for 5 minutes, or until soft and browned. Stir in the garlic, ginger and chilli, and cook for 1 minute. Then stir in the cumin, fennel, turmeric, chilli powder, garam masala, star anise, cinnamon stick, curry leaves and bay leaves, and cook, stirring to prevent sticking, for a further 1 minute.

3   Add 2 tablespoons cold water to the frying pan, mix well, and then add the beef stock. Bring to the boil, then pour over the lamb. Stir in the tomato, reduce the heat and simmer, covered, for 1¼ hours. Garnish with coriander and serve with jasmine rice.

NOTE: *Best lamb neck chops come from the meat just under the shoulder and are sweeter, leaner and meatier than lamb neck.*

Cook the lamb neck chops in batches in a large frying pan until browned.

Stir the spices to prevent them from sticking to the base of the pan.

NUTRITION PER SERVE (6)
Protein 17 g; Fat 7 g; Carbohydrate; 5 g; Dietary Fibre 5 g; Cholesterol 48 mg; 658 kJ (157 Cal)

Indonesian vegetable and coconut curry

PREPARATION TIME: 20 MINUTES | TOTAL COOKING TIME: 35 MINUTES | SERVES 6

CURRY PASTE
5 candlenuts or macadamia nuts
75 g (2½ oz) red Asian shallots (eschalots)
2 garlic cloves
2 teaspoons sambal oelek (South-East Asian chilli paste)
¼ teaspoon ground turmeric
1 teaspoon grated fresh galangal
1 tablespoon peanut butter

2 tablespoons oil
1 onion, sliced
400 ml (14 fl oz) tin coconut cream
200 g (7 oz) carrots, cut into matchsticks
200 g (7 oz) snake (yard-long) beans, trimmed, cut into 7 cm (2¾ inch) lengths
300 g (10½ oz) Chinese cabbage, roughly shredded
100 g (3½ oz) fresh shiitake mushrooms
¼ teaspoon sugar

1 To make the curry paste, place the candlenuts, shallots, garlic, sambal oelek, turmeric, galangal and peanut butter in a food processor, and process to a smooth paste.

2 Heat the oil in a large saucepan over low heat. Cook the curry paste, stirring, for 5 minutes, or until fragrant. Add the onion and cook for 5 minutes. Stir in 60 ml (2 fl oz/¼ cup) coconut cream and cook, stirring constantly, for 2 minutes, or until thickened. Add the carrot and beans, and cook over high heat for 3 minutes. Stir in the cabbage, mushrooms and 250 ml (9 fl oz/1 cup) water. Cook over high heat for 8–10 minutes, or until the vegetables are nearly cooked.

3 Stir in the remaining coconut cream and the sugar, and season with salt. Bring to the boil, stirring constantly, then reduce the heat and simmer for 8–10 minutes, to allow the flavours to develop. Serve hot.

NUTRITION PER SERVE
Protein 6 g; Fat 24.4 g; Carbohydrate 10 g; Dietary Fibre 5.6 g; Cholesterol 0 mg; 1211 kJ (289 Cal)

Process the curry paste ingredients together to a smooth paste.

Add the coconut cream and cook, stirring, until the sauce has thickened.

Lamb and spinach curry

PREPARATION TIME: 30 MINUTES | TOTAL COOKING TIME: 2 HOURS 20 MINUTES | SERVES 6

1 kg (2 lb 4 oz) English spinach
125 ml (4 fl oz/½ cup) oil
1.5 kg (3 lb 5 oz) boned leg of lamb, cut into
    3 cm (1¼ inch) cubes (see NOTE)
2 red onions, finely chopped
6 garlic cloves, crushed
1½ tablespoons grated fresh ginger
2 bay leaves
2 tablespoons ground coriander
1 tablespoon ground cumin
1 teaspoon ground turmeric
2 large vine-ripened tomatoes, peeled,
    seeded and chopped
2–3 small green chillies, seeded and finely
    chopped
100 g (3½ oz) Greek yoghurt
1 cinnamon stick
2 teaspoons garam masala
coriander (cilantro) leaves, to garnish

1 Preheat the oven to 170°C (325°F/ Gas 3). Trim the spinach and quickly blanch in simmering water. Drain, cool slightly and squeeze to remove any excess moisture, then process in a food processor until smooth.

2 Heat half the oil in a large saucepan. Add the lamb pieces in batches and cook over high heat for 4–5 minutes, or until browned. Remove the lamb from the pan.

3 Heat the remaining oil in the saucepan. Add the onion and cook, stirring frequently, for 10 minutes, or until golden brown but not burnt. Add the garlic, ginger and bay leaves, and cook, stirring, for 3 more minutes.

4 Add the spices and cook, stirring, for 2 minutes, or until fragrant. Add the tomato and chilli, and stir over low heat for 5 minutes, or until the tomato is thick and pulpy. Remove from the heat and cool for 5 minutes. Transfer to a 4 litre (140 fl oz/16 cup) casserole dish and stir in the yoghurt.

5 Add the meat to the dish and add the cinnamon stick and 1 teaspoon salt. Bake, covered, for 1 hour and then uncovered for a further 15 minutes. Stir in the spinach and garam masala, and cook, stirring occasionally, for 15 minutes, or until the meat is tender. Remove the bay leaves and cinnamon stick, garnish with coriander and serve with rice.

NOTE: *Ask your butcher to bone and cut the lamb for you. A 2.2 kg (4 lb 15 oz) leg will yield about 1.5 kg (3 lb 5 oz) meat.*

NUTRITION PER SERVE
Protein 60 g; Fat 30 g; Carbohydrate 5 g; Dietary Fibre 6.5 g; Cholesterol 170 mg; 2240 kJ (533 Cal)

Squeeze the blanched, cooled spinach to remove any excess moisture.

Process the cooked spinach in a food processor until it becomes smooth.

Stir in the tomato and chilli over low heat until the tomato is thick and pulpy.

Pork vindaloo

PREPARATION TIME: 20 MINUTES | TOTAL COOKING TIME: 2 HOURS | SERVES 4

60 ml (2 fl oz/¼ cup) oil
1 kg (2 lb 4 oz) pork fillets, cut into bite-sized
    pieces
2 onions, finely chopped
4 garlic cloves, finely chopped
1 tablespoon finely chopped fresh ginger
1 tablespoon garam masala
2 teaspoons brown mustard seeds
4 tablespoons vindaloo paste (see page 250)
plain yoghurt, to serve

1 Heat the oil in a saucepan, add the pork in small batches and cook over medium heat for 5–7 minutes, or until browned. Remove meat from the pan.

2 Add the onion, garlic, ginger, garam masala and mustard seeds to the saucepan, and cook, stirring, for 5 minutes, or until the onion is soft.

3 Return all the meat to the pan, add the vindaloo paste and cook, stirring, for 2 minutes. Add 625 ml (21½ fl oz/2½ cups) water and bring to the boil. Reduce the heat and simmer, covered, for 1½ hours, or until the meat is tender. Serve with a dollop of yoghurt, boiled rice and naan bread, if desired.

Trim the pork of any excess fat or sinew and cut into cubes.

Cook the pork in small batches over medium heat until browned.

NUTRITION PER SERVE
Protein 58 g; Fat 20 g; Carbohydrate 4 g; Dietary
Fibre 2 g; Cholesterol 125 mg; 1806 kJ (430 Cal)

Madras beef curry

PREPARATION TIME: 20 MINUTES | TOTAL COOKING TIME: 1 HOUR 45 MINUTES | SERVES 4

1 tablespoon oil or ghee

1 onion, chopped

3–4 tablespoons Madras curry paste (see page 250)

1 kg (2 lb 4 oz) skirt or chuck steak, trimmed of fat and cut into 2.5 cm (1 inch) cubes

60 g (2¼ oz/¼ cup) tomato paste (concentrated purée)

250 ml (9 fl oz/1 cup) beef stock

coriander (cilantro) sprigs, to garnish

1   Heat the oil in a large frying pan, add the onion and cook over medium heat for 10 minutes, or until browned. Add the curry paste and stir for 1 minute, or until fragrant. Then add the meat and cook, stirring, until coated with the curry paste.

2   Stir in the tomato paste and stock. Reduce the heat and simmer, covered, for 1¼ hours, Add more stock or water if necessary. Simmer uncovered for 15 minutes, or until the meat is tender. Garnish with coriander and serve with steamed rice.

NUTRITION PER SERVE
Protein 53 g; Fat 15 g; Carbohydrate 4.5 g; Dietary Fibre 1.5 g; Cholesterol 170 mg; 1514 kJ (362 Cal)

Trim the meat of any excess fat or sinew and cut it into cubes.

Cook the onion in a large frying pan over medium heat until browned.

Add the meat to the pan and stir to thoroughly coat in the curry paste.

Cheese and pea curry

PREPARATION TIME: 30 MINUTES + 30 MINUTES DRAINING + 4 HOURS SETTING | TOTAL COOKING TIME: 40 MINUTES | SERVES 6

PANEER
2 litres (70 fl oz/8 cups) full-cream (whole)
    milk
80 ml (2½ fl oz/⅓ cup) lemon juice

CURRY PASTE
2 large onions, chopped
3 garlic cloves
1 teaspoon grated fresh ginger
1 teaspoon cumin seeds
3 dried red chillies
1 teaspoon cardamom seeds
4 cloves
1 teaspoon fennel seeds
2 pieces cassia bark

oil, for deep-frying
500 g (1 lb 2 oz) frozen peas
2 tablespoons oil
400 g (14 oz) tomato paste (concentrated
    purée)
1 tablespoon garam masala
1 teaspoon ground coriander
¼ teaspoon ground turmeric
1 tablespoon cream
coriander (cilantro) leaves, to garnish

1 To make the paneer, place the milk in a large saucepan, bring to the boil, stir in the lemon juice and turn off the heat. Stir the mixture for 1–2 seconds as it curdles. Place in a colander and leave for 30 minutes for the whey to drain off. Place the paneer curds on a clean, flat surface, cover with a plate, weigh down and leave for at least 4 hours.

2 To make the curry paste, place all the ingredients in a spice grinder or food processor, and grind to a smooth paste.

3 Cut the solid paneer into 2 cm (¾ inch) cubes. Fill a deep heavy-based saucepan one-third full of oil and heat to 180°C (350°F), or until a cube of bread browns in 15 seconds. Cook the paneer in batches for 2–3 minutes, or until golden. Drain on paper towels.

4 Cook the peas in a saucepan of boiling water for 3 minutes, or until tender. Drain.

5 Heat the oil in a large saucepan, add the curry paste and cook over medium heat for 4 minutes, or until fragrant. Add the tomato paste, spices, cream and 125 ml (4 fl oz/½ cup) water. Season with salt, and simmer over medium heat for 5 minutes. Add the paneer and peas, and cook for 3 minutes. Garnish with coriander leaves, and serve hot.

NUTRITION PER SERVE
Protein 18 g; Fat 28 g; Carbohydrate 27 g; Dietary
Fibre 7 g; Cholesterol 50 mg; 1788 kJ (427 Cal)

Boil the milk and lemon juice, and stir for a few seconds as the milk curdles.

Cover the paneer curds with a plate, weigh it down and leave it to set.

Deep-fry the paneer cubes in batches until golden brown, then drain on paper towels.

Nonya chicken curry

PREPARATION TIME: 20 MINUTES | TOTAL COOKING TIME: 35 MINUTES | SERVES 4

CURRY PASTE
2 red onions, chopped
4 small red chillies, seeded and sliced
4 garlic cloves, sliced
2 lemongrass stems (white part only), sliced
3 cm x 2 cm (1¼ inch x ¾ inch) piece fresh
    galangal, sliced
8 makrut (kaffir lime) leaves, roughly chopped
1 teaspoon ground turmeric
½ teaspoon shrimp paste, roasted (see NOTE)

2 tablespoons oil
750 g (1 lb 10 oz) chicken thigh fillets, cut into
    bite-sized pieces
400 ml (14 fl oz) tin coconut milk
3 tablespoons tamarind purée
1 tablespoon fish sauce
3 makrut (kaffir lime) leaves, finely shredded,
    to garnish

1   To make the curry paste, place all the
ingredients in a food processor or blender and
process to a thick paste.

2   Heat a wok or large saucepan over high heat,
add the oil and swirl to coat the side. Add the
curry paste and cook, stirring occasionally, over
low heat for 8–10 minutes, or until fragrant.
Add the chicken and stir-fry with the paste for
2–3 minutes.

3   Add the coconut milk, tamarind purée
and fish sauce to the wok, and simmer, stirring
occasionally, for 15–20 minutes, or until the
chicken is tender. Garnish with the makrut
leaves. Serve with rice and steamed bok choy
(pak choy).

NOTE: *To dry-roast the shrimp paste, wrap it
in foil and place it under a hot grill (broiler) for
1 minute.*

Trim the chicken of any excess fat or sinew and cut
into bite-sized pieces.

Add the chicken to the wok and stir-fry with the
curry paste.

NUTRITION PER SERVE
Protein 45 g; Fat 35 g; Carbohydrate 7.5 g; Dietary
Fibre 3.5 g; Cholesterol 94 mg; 2175 kJ (520 Cal)

Beef and lentil curry

PREPARATION TIME: 45 MINUTES + 10 MINUTES SOAKING | TOTAL COOKING TIME: 1 HOUR 50 MINUTES | SERVES 6

3–4 small dried red chillies

60 ml (2 fl oz/¼ cup) oil

2 red onions, cut into thin wedges

4 garlic cloves, finely chopped

1 tablespoon grated fresh ginger

1 tablespoon garam masala

3 cardamom pods, lightly crushed

1 cinnamon stick

2 teaspoons ground turmeric

750 g (1 lb 10 oz) chuck steak, cut into cubes

400 g (14 oz) tin chopped tomatoes

95 g (3¼ oz/½ cup) brown or green lentils

125 g (4½ oz/½ cup) red lentils

200 g (7 oz) pumpkin (winter squash), diced

150 g (5½ oz) eggplant (aubergine), diced

125 g (4½ oz) baby English spinach

1 tablespoon tamarind purée

2 tablespoons grated palm sugar (jaggery) or
soft brown sugar

1 Soak the chillies in boiling water for
10 minutes, then drain and finely chop.

2 Heat the oil in a large saucepan. Add the
onion and cook, stirring, over medium heat
for 5 minutes, or until soft. Add the garlic and
ginger, and cook for a further 2 minutes.

3 Add the chilli, garam masala, cardamom
pods, cinnamon, turmeric and ½ teaspoon black
pepper. Cook, stirring, for 2 minutes, or until
fragrant. Add beef and stir constantly for 3–4
minutes, or until meat is coated in spices.

4 Add the tomato, lentils, 1 teaspoon salt and
750 ml (26 fl oz/3 cups) water. Simmer, covered,
for 1 hour until tender. Stir often to prevent
burning. Add extra water, if needed.

5 Add the pumpkin and eggplant to pan, and
cook, covered, for 20 minutes, or until tender.
Stir in the spinach, tamarind and palm sugar,
and cook for a further 10 minutes.

NUTRITION PER SERVE
Protein 34 g; Fat 14 g; Carbohydrate 22 g; Dietary
Fibre 6.5 g; Cholesterol 84 mg; 1452 kJ (347 Cal)

Lightly crush the cardamom pods with the back of
a heavy knife.

Add the beef to the pan and stir to coat with
the spices.

Spicy prawns

PREPARATION TIME: 30 MINUTES + 15 MINUTES STANDING | TOTAL COOKING TIME: 1 HOUR 20 MINUTES | SERVES 4–6

1 kg (2 lb 4 oz) raw prawns (shrimp), peeled and deveined, leaving the tails intact (reserve shells and heads)

1 teaspoon ground turmeric

60 ml (2 fl oz/¼ cup) oil

2 onions, finely chopped

4–6 garlic cloves, finely chopped

1–2 small green chillies, seeded and chopped

2 teaspoons ground cumin

2 teaspoons ground coriander

1 teaspoon paprika

90 g (3¼ oz/⅓ cup) plain yoghurt

80 ml (2½ fl oz/⅓ cup) thick (double/heavy) cream

2 large handfuls coriander (cilantro) leaves, chopped

1 Bring 1 litre (35 fl oz/4 cups) water to the boil in a large saucepan. Add the reserved prawn shells and heads, reduce the heat and simmer for 25-30 minutes. Skim any scum that forms on the surface during cooking with a skimmer or slotted spoon. Drain, discard the shells and heads, and return the liquid to the pan. You will need 750 ml (26 fl oz/3 cups) liquid. Make up with water, if necessary. Add the turmeric and peeled prawns, and cook for 1 minute, or until the prawns just turn pink. Remove the prawns and set the stock aside.

2 Heat the oil in a large saucepan. Cook the onion on low–medium heat, stirring, for 8 minutes, or until light golden brown. Take care not to burn the onion. Add the garlic and chilli, cook for 2 minutes, then add the cumin, coriander and paprika, and cook, stirring, for 2–3 minutes, or until it becomes fragrant.

3 Gradually add the reserved prawn stock, bring to the boil and cook, stirring occasionally, for 35 minutes, or until the mixture has reduced by half and thickened.

4 Remove from the heat and stir in the yoghurt. Add the prawns and stir over low heat for 2–3 minutes, or until the prawns are warmed through, but do now allow the mixture to boil. Stir in the cream and coriander leaves. Cover and leave to stand for 15 minutes to allow the flavours to infuse. Reheat gently and serve with rice.

NOTE: *You can also remove the prawn tails, if you prefer.*

NUTRITION PER SERVE (6)
Protein 35 g; Fat 17 g; Carbohydrate 3 g; Dietary Fibre 1 g; Cholesterol 270 mg; 1293 kJ (310 Cal)

Skim any scum on the surface with a skimmer or a slotted spoon.

Boil the mixture, stirring occasionally, until it has reduced by half and thickened.

Green chicken curry

PREPARATION TIME: 40 MINUTES | TOTAL COOKING TIME: 30 MINUTES | SERVES 4–6

500 ml (17 fl oz/2 cups) coconut cream (do not shake the tin—see NOTE)

4 tablespoons Thai green curry paste (see page 251)

2 tablespoons grated palm sugar (jaggery) or soft brown sugar

2 tablespoons fish sauce

4 makrut (kaffir lime) leaves, finely shredded

1 kg (2 lb 4 oz) boneless, skinless chicken thigh or breasts, cut into thick strips

200 g (7 oz) bamboo shoots, trimmed and cut into thick strips

100 g (3½ oz) snake (yard-long) beans, trimmed and cut into 5 cm (2 inch) lengths

1 handful basil leaves

1 Place 125 ml (4 fl oz/½ cup) of the thick coconut cream from the top of the tin in a wok, and bring to the boil. Add the curry paste, then reduce the heat and simmer for 15 minutes, or until fragrant and the oil starts to separate from the cream. Add the palm sugar, fish sauce and makrut leaves to the pan.

2 Stir in the remaining coconut cream and the chicken, bamboo shoots and beans, and simmer for 15 minutes, or until the chicken is tender. Stir in the basil and serve with rice.

NOTE: *Do not shake the tin of coconut cream because good-quality coconut cream has a layer of very thick cream at the top that has separated from the rest of the cream. This has a higher fat content, which causes it to split or separate more readily than the rest of the coconut cream.*

Lift off the thick cream from the top of the tin of coconut cream.

Simmer the coconut cream and curry paste until the oil separates.

NUTRITION PER SERVE (6)
Protein 40 g; Fat 22 g; Carbohydrate 11 g; Dietary Fibre 2 g; Cholesterol 85 mg; 1698 kJ (405 Cal)

Massaman beef curry

PREPARATION TIME: 30 MINUTES I TOTAL COOKING TIME: 1 HOUR 45 MINUTES I SERVES 4

1 tablespoon tamarind pulp

2 tablespoons oil

750 g (1 lb 10 oz) lean stewing beef, cubed

500 ml (17 fl oz/2 cups) coconut milk

4 cardamom pods, bruised

500 ml (17 fl oz/2 cups) coconut cream

2–3 tablespoons Massaman curry paste (see page 251)

8 baby onions, peeled (see NOTE)

8 baby potatoes, peeled and quartered (see NOTE)

2 tablespoons fish sauce

2 tablespoons grated palm sugar (jaggery) or soft brown sugar

80 g (2¾ oz/½ cup) unsalted peanuts, roasted and ground

coriander (cilantro) leaves, to garnish

1 Place the tamarind pulp and ½ cup (125 ml/ 4 fl oz) boiling water in a bowl and set aside to cool. When cool, mash the pulp to dissolve in the water, then strain and reserve the liquid. Discard the pulp.

2 Heat the oil in a wok or a large saucepan and cook the beef in batches over high heat for 5 minutes, or until browned. Reduce the heat, add the coconut milk and cardamom, and simmer for 1 hour, or until the beef is tender. Remove the beef, strain and reserve the meat and also the cooking liquid separately.

3 Heat the coconut cream in the wok and stir in the curry paste. Cook for 5 minutes, or until the oil starts to separate from the cream.

4 Add the onions, potatoes, fish sauce, palm sugar, peanuts, beef mixture, reserved cooking liquid and tamarind water, and simmer for 25–30 minutes. Serve with coriander and rice.

NOTE: *Use small onions and potatoes, about 20–30 g (¾–1 oz) each.*

NUTRITION PER SERVE
Protein 52 g; Fat 77 g; Carbohydrate 35 g; Dietary Fibre 7.5 g; Cholesterol 115 mg; 4324 kJ (1033 Cal)

Mash the tamarind pulp with a fork, then strain and reserve the liquid.

Cook the beef in batches over high heat until well browned.

Chicken curry with apricots

PREPARATION TIME: 40 MINUTES + 1 HOUR SOAKING | TOTAL COOKING TIME: 1 HOUR 15 MINUTES | SERVES 6–8

18 dried apricots

1 tablespoon ghee or oil

2 x 1.5 kg (3 lb 5 oz) chickens, cut into pieces

3 onions, thinly sliced

1 teaspoon grated fresh ginger

3 garlic cloves, crushed

3 large green chillies, seeded and finely chopped

1 teaspoon cumin seeds

1 teaspoon chilli powder

½ teaspoon ground turmeric

4 cardamom pods, bruised

4 large tomatoes, peeled and cut into eighths (see NOTE on page 80)

NUTRITION PER SERVE (8)
Protein 44 g; Fat 6.5 g; Carbohydrate 6.5 g; Dietary Fibre 2.5 g; Cholesterol 100 mg; 1105 kJ (264 Cal)

1 Soak the dried apricots in 250 ml (9 fl oz/ 1 cup) hot water for 1 hour.

2 Melt the ghee in a large saucepan, add the chicken in batches and cook over high heat for 5–6 minutes, or until browned. Remove from the pan. Add the onion and cook, stirring often, for 10 minutes, or until the onion has softened and turned golden brown.

3 Add the ginger, garlic and chopped chilli, and cook, stirring, for 2 minutes. Stir in the cumin seeds, chilli powder and ground turmeric, and cook for a further 1 minute.

4 Return the chicken to the pan, add the cardamom, tomato and apricots, with any remaining liquid, and mix well. Simmer, covered, for 35 minutes, or until the chicken is tender.

5 Remove the chicken, cover and keep warm. Bring the liquid to the boil and boil rapidly, uncovered, for 5 minutes, or until it has thickened slightly. To serve, spoon the liquid over the chicken. Serve with steamed rice mixed with raisins, grated carrot and toasted flaked almonds.

Cook the chicken pieces over high heat, in batches, until browned.

Cook the onion for 10 minutes, or until soft and golden brown.

Boil rapidly for 5 minutes, or until the mixture thickens slightly.

Thai beef and pumpkin curry

PREPARATION TIME: 20 MINUTES | TOTAL COOKING TIME: 1 HOUR 30 MINUTES | SERVES 6

2 tablespoons oil

750 g (1 lb 10 oz) blade steak, thinly sliced

4 tablespoons Massaman curry paste (see page 251)

2 garlic cloves, finely chopped

1 onion, sliced lengthways

6 curry leaves, torn

750 ml (26 fl oz/3 cups) coconut milk

450 g (1 lb) butternut pumpkin (squash), roughly diced

2 tablespoons chopped unsalted peanuts

1 tablespoon grated palm sugar (jaggery) or soft brown sugar

2 tablespoons tamarind purée

2 tablespoons fish sauce

curry leaves, extra, to garnish

1   Heat a wok or frying pan over high heat. Add the oil and swirl to coat the side. Add the meat in batches and cook for 5 minutes, or until browned. Remove the meat from the wok.

2   Add the curry paste, garlic, onion and curry leaves to the wok, and stir to coat. Return the meat to the wok and cook, stirring, over medium heat for 2 minutes.

3   Add the coconut milk to the wok, then reduce the heat to low and gently simmer for 45 minutes. Add the pumpkin and simmer for 25–30 minutes, or until the meat and the pumpkin are tender and the sauce has thickened.

4   Stir in the peanuts, palm sugar, tamarind purée and fish sauce, and simmer for 1 minute. Garnish with curry leaves and season with cracked black pepper. Serve with steamed rice.

Cut the meat across the grain and at an angle into thin slices.

Add the meat to the wok and cook in small batches until browned.

NUTRITION PER SERVE
Protein 33 g; Fat 43 g; Carbohydrate 16 g; Dietary Fibre 4.5 g; Cholesterol 66 mg; 2403 kJ (574 Cal)

Chu chee tofu

PREPARATION TIME: 20 MINUTES | TOTAL COOKING TIME: 15 MINUTES | SERVES 6

CURRY PASTE
10 small red chillies
50 g (1¾ oz) red Asian shallots (eschalots), peeled
1 tablespoon finely chopped coriander (cilantro) stem and root
1 lemongrass stem (white part only), chopped
2 tablespoons grated fresh galangal
2 garlic cloves
1 tablespoon ground coriander
1 teaspoon ground cumin
1 teaspoon black peppercorns
½ teaspoon ground turmeric
1 tablespoon lime juice

1 tablespoon oil
1 onion, finely chopped
500 ml (17 fl oz/2 cups) coconut milk
200 g (7 oz) fried tofu puffs, halved on the diagonal
coriander (cilantro) sprigs, to garnish

1 To make the curry paste, place all the ingredients in a food processor or spice grinder and process until smooth.

2 Heat the oil in a large saucepan, add the onion and cook over medium heat for 4–5 minutes, or until it starts to brown. Add 3 tablespoons of the curry paste and cook, stirring, for 2 minutes.

3 Stir in the coconut milk and 125 ml (4 fl oz/½ cup) water, and season with salt. Bring slowly to the boil, stirring constantly. Add the tofu puffs, then reduce the heat and simmer, stirring frequently, for 5 minutes, or until the sauce thickens slightly. Garnish with the coriander sprigs.

NUTRITION PER SERVE
Protein 5.6 g; Fat 23 g; Carbohydrate 7.5 g; Dietary Fibre 3.3 g; Cholesterol 0.3 mg; 1081 kJ (234 Cal)

Grind all the ingredients for the curry paste in a food processor or spice grinder until smooth.

Cook the onion over medium heat until it is just starting to brown.

Fish koftas in tomato curry sauce

PREPARATION TIME: 40 MINUTES | TOTAL COOKING TIME: 30 MINUTES | SERVES 6

750 g (1 lb 10 oz) firm fish fillets, such as
    snapper or ling, roughly chopped
1 onion, chopped
2–3 garlic cloves, chopped
1 tablespoon grated fresh ginger
2 large handfuls coriander (cilantro) leaves
1 teaspoon garam masala
¼ teaspoon chilli powder
1 egg, lightly beaten

TOMATO CURRY SAUCE
2 tablespoons oil
1 large onion, finely chopped
3–4 garlic cloves, finely chopped
1 tablespoon grated fresh ginger
1 teaspoon ground turmeric
1 teaspoon ground cumin
1 teaspoon ground coriander
½ teaspoon garam masala
¼ teaspoon chilli powder
2 x 400 g (14 oz) tins chopped tomatoes
2 large handfuls coriander (cilantro) leaves,
    chopped, plus extra, to garnish

oil, for shallow-frying

NUTRITION PER SERVE
Protein 30 g; Fat 15 g; Carbohydrate 7 g; Dietary
Fibre 3 g; Cholesterol 118 mg; 1145 kJ (273 Cal)

1 Place the fish in a food processor and process until smooth. Add the onion, garlic, ginger, coriander leaves, garam masala, chilli powder and egg, and process using the pulse button until well combined. Using wetted hands, form 1 tablespoon of the mixture into a ball. Repeat with the remaining mixture.

2 To make the tomato curry sauce, heat the oil in a large saucepan, add the onion, garlic and ginger, and cook, stirring frequently, over medium heat for 8 minutes, or until lightly golden.

3 Add the spices and cook, stirring, for 2 minutes, or until aromatic. Add the tomato and 250 ml (9 fl oz/1 cup) water, then reduce the heat and simmer, stirring frequently, for 15 minutes, or until the sauce has reduced and thickened.

4 Meanwhile, heat 2 cm (¾ inch) of the oil in a large frying pan. Add the fish koftas in three to four batches and cook for 3 minutes, or until browned all over. Drain on paper towels.

5 Add the koftas to the sauce and simmer over low heat for 5 minutes, or until cooked through. Gently fold in the coriander, season with salt. Serve with steamed rice and warm naan bread. Garnish with coriander.

NOTE: *The fish mixture is quite moist. Wetting your hands will stop the mixture from sticking to them.*

Using wetted hands, form tablespoons of the mixture into balls.

Cook the onion, garlic and ginger over medium heat until lightly golden.

Lamb korma

PREPARATION TIME: 30 MINUTES + 1 HOUR MARINATING | TOTAL COOKING TIME: 1 HOUR 10 MINUTES | SERVES 4–6

2 kg (4 lb 8 oz) leg of lamb, boned
1 onion, chopped
2 teaspoons grated fresh ginger
3 garlic cloves
2 teaspoons ground coriander
2 teaspoons ground cumin
1 teaspoon cardamom seeds
large pinch cayenne pepper
2 tablespoons ghee or oil
1 onion, extra, sliced
2½ tablespoons tomato paste (concentrated purée)
125 g (4½ oz/½ cup) plain yoghurt
125 ml (4 fl oz/½ cup) coconut cream
55 g (2 oz/½ cup) ground almonds
toasted slivered almonds, to serve

1   Trim any excess fat or sinew from the lamb, cut it into 3 cm (1¼ inch) cubes and place in a large bowl.

2   Place the chopped onion, ginger, garlic, coriander, cumin, cardamom seeds, cayenne pepper and ½ teaspoon salt in a food processor. Process the ingredients until they form a smooth paste. Add the spice mixture to the cubed lamb and mix well to coat the lamb in the spices. Leave to marinate for 1 hour.

3   Heat the ghee in a large saucepan, add the sliced onion and cook, stirring, over low heat for 7 minutes, or until the onion is soft. Add the lamb and spice mixture, and cook, stirring constantly, for 8–10 minutes, or until the lamb changes colour. Stir in the tomato paste, yoghurt, coconut cream and ground almonds.

4   Reduce the heat and simmer the curry, covered, stirring occasionally, for 50 minutes, or until the meat is tender. Add a little water if the mixture becomes too dry. Season the curry with salt and pepper, and garnish with the toasted slivered almonds. Serve with steamed rice.

Trim any excess fat or sinew from the lamb and cut it into cubes.

Process the spice mixture in a food processor until it forms a smooth paste.

NUTRITION PER SERVE (6)
Protein 80 g; Fat 23 g; Carbohydrate 5 g; Dietary Fibre 2 g; Cholesterol 240 mg; 2280 kJ (545 Cal)

Dhal

PREPARATION TIME: 15 MINUTES | TOTAL COOKING TIME: 35 MINUTES | SERVES 4–6

200 g (7 oz) red lentils
4 cm (1½ inch) piece fresh ginger, cut into
    3 slices
½ teaspoon ground turmeric
1 tablespoon ghee or oil
2 garlic cloves, crushed
1 onion, finely chopped
½ teaspoon yellow mustard seeds
pinch asafoetida (optional)
1 teaspoon cumin seeds
1 teaspoon ground coriander
2 green chillies, halved lengthways
2 tablespoons lemon juice
1 tablespoon chopped coriander (cilantro)
    leaves

1 Place the lentils and 750 ml (26 fl oz/3 cups) water in a saucepan, and bring to the boil. Reduce the heat, add the ginger and turmeric, and simmer, covered, for 20 minutes, or until the lentils are tender. Stir occasionally to prevent the lentils sticking to the pan. Remove the ginger and stir in ½ teaspoon salt.

2 Heat the ghee in a frying pan, add the garlic, onion and mustard seeds, and cook over medium heat for 5 minutes, or until the onion is golden. Add the asafoetida, cumin seeds, ground coriander and chillies, and cook for 2 minutes.

3 Add the onion mixture to the lentils and stir gently to combine. Add 125 ml (4 fl oz/½ cup) water, reduce the heat to low and cook for 5 minutes. Stir in the lemon juice, and season. Sprinkle with the coriander. Serve as a side dish with Indian curries.

NUTRITION PER SERVE (6)
Protein 8.5 g; Fat 3.5 g; Carbohydrate 13 g; Dietary Fibre 5 g; Cholesterol 8 mg; 505 kJ (120 Cal)

Add the ginger and turmeric to the lentils, and cook until the lentils are tender.

Cook the garlic, onion and mustard seeds until the onion is golden.

Vietnamese chicken curry

PREPARATION TIME: 30 MINUTES + OVERNIGHT REFRIGERATION | TOTAL COOKING TIME: 1 HOUR 10 MINUTES | SERVES 6

4 large chicken leg quarters (leg and thigh pieces)

1 tablespoon general-purpose Indian curry powder (see page 250)

1 teaspoon caster (superfine) sugar

80 ml (2½ fl oz/⅓ cup) oil

500 g (1 lb 2 oz) orange sweet potato, cut into 3 cm (1¼ inch) cubes

1 large onion, cut into thin wedges

4 garlic cloves, chopped

1 lemongrass stem (white part only), finely chopped

2 bay leaves

1 large carrot, cut into 1 cm (½ inch) pieces on the diagonal

400 ml (14 fl oz) tin coconut milk

1 Remove the skin and any excess fat from the chicken. Pat dry with paper towels and cut each piece into 3 even pieces, making 12 pieces. Place the curry powder, sugar, ½ teaspoon black pepper and 2 teaspoons salt in a bowl, and mix well. Rub the curry mixture into the chicken pieces. Place the chicken on a plate, cover with plastic wrap and put in the refrigerator overnight.

2 Heat the oil in a large saucepan. Add the sweet potato and cook over medium heat for 3 minutes, or until lightly golden. Remove with a slotted spoon.

3 Remove all but 2 tablespoons of the oil from the pan. Add the onion and cook, stirring, for 5 minutes. Then add the garlic, lemongrass and bay leaves, and cook for 2 minutes.

4 Add the chicken and cook, stirring, over medium heat for 5 minutes, or until the chicken is well coated in the mixture and starting to change colour. Add 250 ml (9 fl oz/1 cup) water and simmer, covered, for 20 minutes. Stir once or twice.

5 Stir in the carrot, sweet potato and coconut milk, and simmer on a low heat, uncovered, stirring occasionally, for 30 minutes, or until the chicken is cooked and tender. Be careful not to break up the sweet potato cubes. Serve with steamed rice or rice stick noodles.

NUTRITION PER SERVE
Protein 26 g; Fat 30 g; Carbohydrate 17 g; Dietary Fibre 3.5 g; Cholesterol 50 mg; 1787 kJ (427 Cal)

Remove the skin and any excess fat from the chicken pieces.

Using a large knife, cut each chicken leg quarter into three even pieces.

Rub the curry and spice mixture all over each of the chicken pieces.

Coconut seafood and tofu curry

PREPARATION TIME: 30 MINUTES | TOTAL COOKING TIME: 30 MINUTES | SERVES 4

2 tablespoons soya bean oil, or cooking oil
500 g (1 lb 2 oz) firm white fish (ling, perch),
    cut into 2 cm (¾ inch) cubes
250 g (9 oz) raw prawns (shrimp), peeled and
    deveined, leaving the tails intact
2 x 400 ml (14 fl oz) tins coconut milk
1 tablespoon Thai red curry paste (page 251)
4 fresh or 8 dried makrut (kaffir lime) leaves
2 tablespoons fish sauce
2 tablespoons finely chopped lemongrass
    (white part only)
2 garlic cloves, crushed
1 tablespoon finely chopped fresh galangal
1 tablespoon shaved palm sugar (jaggery) or
    soft brown sugar
300 g (10½ oz) silken firm tofu, cut into
    1.5 cm (⅝ inch) cubes
125 g (4½ oz/½ cup) bamboo shoots, trimmed
    and cut into matchsticks
1 large red chilli, thinly sliced
2 teaspoons lime juice
spring onions (scallions), chopped, to garnish
coriander (cilantro) leaves, to garnish

1   Heat the oil in a large frying pan or wok over medium heat. Sear fish and prawns for 1 minute on each side. Remove the seafood from the pan.

2   Place 60 ml (2 fl oz/¼ cup) of the coconut milk and the curry paste in the frying pan, and cook over medium heat for 2 minutes, or until fragrant and the oil separates. Add the remaining coconut milk, makrut leaves, fish sauce, lemongrass, garlic, galangal, palm sugar and 1 teaspoon salt. Cook over low heat for 15 minutes.

3   Add the tofu, bamboo shoots and chilli. Simmer for a further 3–5 minutes. Return to medium heat, add the seafood and lime juice, and cook for a further 3 minutes, or until the seafood is just cooked. Serve with steamed rice and garnish with the spring onion and coriander.

NUTRITION PER SERVE
Protein 50 g; Fat 58 g; Carbohydrate 15 g; Dietary
Fibre 4 g; Cholesterol 180 mg; 3201 kJ (765 Cal)

Peel the prawns, remove the veins and keep the tails intact.

Cook the coconut milk and the curry paste until the oil separates.

Vegetable curry

PREPARATION TIME: 20 MINUTES | TOTAL COOKING TIME: 30 MINUTES | SERVES 6

250 g (9 oz) potatoes, cut into 2 cm (¾ inch) cubes
250 g (9 oz) pumpkin (winter squash), cut into 2 cm (¾ inch) cubes
200 g (7 oz) cauliflower, broken into florets
150 g (5½ oz) yellow squash, quartered
2 tablespoons oil
2 onions, chopped
3 tablespoons general purpose Indian curry powder (see page 250)
400 g (14 oz) tin chopped tomatoes
250 ml (9 fl oz/1 cup) vegetable stock
150 g (5½ oz) green beans, trimmed and cut into 4 cm (1½ inch) lengths
90 g (3¼ oz/⅓ cup) plain yoghurt
40 g (1½ oz/⅓ cup) sultanas (golden raisins)

1 Cook the potato and pumpkin in a saucepan of boiling water for 6 minutes, then remove. Add the cauliflower and squash, cook for 4 minutes, then remove.

2 Heat the oil in a large saucepan, add the onion and cook, stirring, over medium heat for 8 minutes, or until starting to brown.

3 Add the curry powder and stir for 1 minute, or until fragrant. Stir in the tomato and vegetable stock, and combine well.

4 Add the chopped potato, pumpkin, cauliflower and squash, and cook for 5 minutes, then add the beans and cook for a further 2–3 minutes, or until the vegetables are tender.

5 Add the yoghurt and sultanas, and stir to combine. Simmer for 3 minutes, or until thickened slightly. Season to taste with salt and black pepper, and serve with chapattis.

Cook the onion over medium heat until it is just starting to brown.

Add the beans and cook until the vegetables are just tender.

NUTRITION PER SERVE
Protein 7 g; Fat 8.5 g; Carbohydrate 20 g; Dietary Fibre 7 g; Cholesterol 2.5 mg; 805 kJ (192 Cal)

Duck and coconut curry

PREPARATION TIME: 20 MINUTES | TOTAL COOKING TIME: 1 HOUR 15 MINUTES | SERVES 6

CURRY PASTE
1 red onion, chopped
2 garlic cloves
2 coriander (cilantro) roots, chopped
2 teaspoons chopped fresh ginger
1½ teaspoons coriander seeds, dry-roasted and ground
1 teaspoon cardamom seeds, dry-roasted and ground
1 teaspoon fenugreek seeds, dry-roasted and ground
1 teaspoon brown mustard seeds, dry-roasted and ground
10 black peppercorns, ground
2 teaspoons garam masala
¼ teaspoon ground turmeric
2 teaspoons tamarind purée

6–8 boneless, skinless duck breasts
1 red onion, sliced
125 ml (4 fl oz/½ cup) white vinegar
500 ml (17 fl oz/2 cups) coconut milk
2 tablespoons coriander (cilantro) leaves

1 To make the curry paste, place all the ingredients in a food processor and process to a thick paste. Put aside.

2 Trim any excess fat from the duck breasts, then place, skin side down, in a large saucepan and cook over medium heat for 10 minutes, or until the skin is brown and any remaining fat has melted. Turn the fillets over and cook for 5 minutes, or until tender. Remove and drain on paper towels.

3 Reserve 1 tablespoon duck fat, discarding the remaining fat. Add the onion and cook for 5 minutes, then add the curry paste and stir over low heat for 10 minutes, or until fragrant.

4 Return the duck to the pan and stir to coat with the paste. Stir in the vinegar, coconut milk, 1 teaspoon salt and 125 ml (4 fl oz/½ cup) water. Simmer, covered, for 45 minutes, or until the duck breasts are tender. Stir in the coriander just prior to serving. Serve with steamed rice and naan bread.

NUTRITION PER SERVE
Protein 55 g; Fat 33 g; Carbohydrate 5.5 g; Dietary Fibre 2.5 g; Cholesterol 323 mg; 2256 kJ (540 Cal)

Place the curry paste ingredients in a food processor and process to a thick paste.

Use a sharp knife to trim any excess fat from the duck breasts.

Cook the duck, skin side down, until the skin is brown and the fat has melted.

Red beef and eggplant curry

PREPARATION TIME: 40 MINUTES | TOTAL COOKING TIME: 1 HOUR 30 MINUTES | SERVES 4

250 ml (9 fl oz) tin coconut cream (do not shake the tin)

2 tablespoons Thai red curry paste (see page 251)

500 g (1 lb 2 oz) round or topside steak, cut into strips (see NOTE)

2 tablespoons fish sauce

1 tablespoon grated palm sugar (jaggery) or soft brown sugar

5 makrut (kaffir lime) leaves, halved

500 ml (17 fl oz/2 cups) coconut milk

8 Thai eggplants (aubergines), halved

2 tablespoons finely shredded Thai basil leaves

1 Place the thick coconut cream from the top of the tin in a wok and bring to the boil. Boil for 10 minutes, or until the oil starts to separate. Add the curry paste and simmer, stirring to prevent it sticking to the bottom, for 5 minutes, or until fragrant.

2 Add the meat and cook, stirring, for 3–5 minutes, or until it changes colour. Add the fish sauce, palm sugar, makrut leaves, coconut milk and remaining coconut cream, and simmer for 1 hour, or until the meat is tender and the sauce has slightly thickened.

3 Add the eggplant and cook for 10 minutes, or until tender. If the sauce is too thick, add a little water. Stir in half the shredded basil leaves. Garnish with the remaining basil leaves and serve with steamed rice.

NOTE: *Cut the meat into 5 x 5 x 2 cm (2 x 2 x ¾ inch) pieces, then cut across the grain at a 45° angle into 5 mm (¼ inch) thick slices.*

Boil the thick coconut cream until the oil separates from the cream.

Cook until the meat is tender and the sauce has slightly thickened.

NUTRITION PER SERVE
Protein 30 g; Fat 43 g; Carbohydrate 10 g; Dietary Fibre 5 g; Cholesterol 85 mg; 2276 kJ (544 Cal)

Jungle curry prawns

PREPARATION TIME: 30 MINUTES + 10 MINUTES SOAKING | TOTAL COOKING TIME: 15 MINUTES | SERVES 6

CURRY PASTE
10–12 dried red chillies
4 red Asian shallots (eschalots), chopped
4 garlic cloves, sliced
1 lemongrass stem (white part only), sliced
1 tablespoon finely chopped fresh galangal
2 small coriander (cilantro) roots, chopped
1 tablespoon finely chopped fresh ginger
1 tablespoon shrimp paste, dry-roasted
60 ml (2 fl oz/¼ cup) oil

1 tablespoon oil
1 garlic clove, crushed
40 g (1½ oz/¼ cup) ground candlenuts
1 tablespoon fish sauce
300 ml (10½ fl oz) fish stock
1 tablespoon whisky
600 g (1 lb 5 oz) raw prawns (shrimp), peeled
    and deveined, leaving the tails intact
1 small carrot, slivered
200 g (7 oz) snake (yard-long) beans, trimmed
    and cut into 2 cm (¾ inch) lengths
50 g (1¾ oz) bamboo shoots
3 makrut (kaffir lime) leaves, crushed
basil leaves, to garnish

1 To make the curry paste, soak the chillies in 250 ml (9 fl oz/1 cup) boiling water for 10 minutes, then drain and place in a food processor with the remaining curry paste ingredients. Season with salt and white pepper, and process to a smooth paste.

2 Heat a wok over medium heat, add the oil and stir to coat the side. Add 3 tablespoons of the curry paste and the garlic, and cook, stirring constantly, for 5 minutes, or until fragrant. Stir in the candlenuts, fish sauce, stock, whisky, prawns, vegetables and makrut leaves, and bring to the boil. Reduce the heat and simmer for 5 minutes, or until cooked through. Garnish with the basil and serve with steamed rice.

NUTRITION PER SERVE
Protein 23 g; Fat 15 g; Carbohydrate 3 g; Dietary Fibre 2.5 g; Cholesterol 150 mg; 990 kJ (235 Cal)

Place all the curry paste ingredients in a food processor and process to a smooth paste.

Cook the curry paste and crushed garlic in a wok until fragrant.

Potato curry

PREPARATION TIME: 20 MINUTES | TOTAL COOKING TIME: 35 MINUTES | SERVES 6

CURRY PASTE
4 cardamom pods
1 teaspoon grated fresh ginger
2 garlic cloves
6 small red chillies
1 teaspoon cumin seeds
40 g (1½ oz/¼ cup) raw cashew nut pieces
1 tablespoon white poppy seeds (khus)
    (see NOTE)
1 cinnamon stick
6 cloves

1 kg (2 lb 4 oz) potatoes, cubed
2 onions, roughly chopped
2 tablespoons oil
½ teaspoon ground turmeric
1 teaspoon besan (chickpea flour)
250 g (9 oz/1 cup) plain yoghurt
coriander (cilantro) leaves, to garnish

1 To make the curry paste, lightly crush the cardamom pods with the flat side of a heavy knife. Remove the seeds, discarding the pods. Place the seeds and the remaining curry paste ingredients in a food processor, and process to a smooth paste.

2 Bring a large saucepan of lightly salted water to the boil. Add the potato and cook for 5–6 minutes, or until just tender. Drain.

3 Place the onion in a food processor and process in short bursts until it is finely ground but not puréed. Heat the oil in a large saucepan, add the ground onion and cook over low heat for 5 minutes. Add the curry paste and cook, stirring, for a further 5 minutes, or until fragrant. Stir in the potato, turmeric, salt to taste and 250 ml (9 fl oz/1 cup) water.

4 Reduce the heat and simmer, tightly covered, for 10 minutes, or until the potato is cooked but not breaking up and the sauce has thickened slightly.

5 Combine the besan with the yoghurt, add to the potato mixture and cook, stirring, over low heat for 5 minutes, or until thickened again. Garnish with the coriander leaves.

NOTE: *White poppy seeds (khus) should not be mistaken for black and do not yield opium. They are off-white, odourless and flavourless until roasted when they have a slight sesame aroma and flavour. If they are not available, replace the poppy seeds with sesame seeds.*

NUTRITION PER SERVE
Protein 7.5 g; Fat 11 g; Carbohydrate 27 g; Dietary Fibre 3.5 g; Cholesterol 6.5 mg; 1010 kJ (240 Cal)

Lightly crush the cardamom pods with the flat side of a heavy knife.

Add the curry paste to the onion and cook until the mixture is fragrant.

Simmer until the potato is cooked but not breaking up, and the sauce has thickened slightly.

Lamb rogan josh

PREPARATION TIME: 25 MINUTES | TOTAL COOKING TIME: 1 HOUR 45 MINUTES | SERVES 4–6

1 tablespoon ghee or oil
2 onions, chopped
125 g (4½ oz/½ cup) plain yoghurt
1 teaspoon chilli powder
1 tablespoon ground coriander
2 teaspoons ground cumin
1 teaspoon ground cardamom
½ teaspoon ground cloves
1 teaspoon ground turmeric
3 garlic cloves, crushed
1 tablespoon grated fresh ginger
400 g (14 oz) tin chopped tomatoes
1 kg (2 lb 4 oz) boned leg of lamb, cut into
    2.5 cm (1 inch) cubes
30 g (1 oz/¼ cup) slivered almonds
1 teaspoon garam masala
coriander (cilantro) leaves, to garnish

1   Heat the ghee in a large saucepan, add the onion and cook, stirring, for 5 minutes, or until soft. Stir in the yoghurt, chilli powder, coriander, cumin, cardamom, cloves, turmeric, garlic and ginger. Add the tomato and 1 teaspoon salt, and simmer for 5 minutes.

2   Add the lamb and stir until coated. Cover and cook over low heat, stirring occasionally, for 1–1½ hours, or until the lamb is tender. Uncover and simmer until the liquid thickens.

3   Meanwhile, toast the almonds in a dry frying pan over medium heat for 3–4 minutes, shaking the pan gently, until the nuts are golden brown. Remove from the pan at once to prevent them from burning.

4   Add the garam masala to the curry and mix through well. Sprinkle the slivered almonds and coriander leaves over the top. Serve with steamed rice and chapattis.

Cook the onion in the ghee for 5 minutes, or until the onion is soft.

Remove the lid and simmer the curry until the liquid thickens.

NUTRITION PER SERVE (6)
Protein 40 g; Fat 13 g; Carbohydrate 5.5 g; Dietary Fibre 2 g; Cholesterol 122 mg; 1236 kJ (295 Cal)

Chickpea curry

PREPARATION TIME: 10 MINUTES | OVERNIGHT SOAKING | TOTAL COOKING TIME: 1 HOUR 15 MINUTES | SERVES 6

220 g (7¾ oz/1 cup) dried chickpeas
2 tablespoons oil
2 onions, finely chopped
2 large ripe tomatoes, chopped
½ teaspoon ground coriander
1 teaspoon ground cumin
1 teaspoon chilli powder
¼ teaspoon ground turmeric
1 tablespoon channa (chole) masala (see
    NOTE)
20 g (¾ oz) ghee or butter
1 small white onion, thinly sliced
fresh mint and coriander (cilantro) leaves,
    to garnish

1 Place the chickpeas in a bowl, cover with water and leave to soak overnight. Drain, rinse and place in a large saucepan. Cover with plenty of water and bring to the boil, then reduce the heat and simmer for 40 minutes, or until soft. Drain and set aside.

2 Heat the oil in a large saucepan, add the onion and cook over medium heat for 15 minutes, or until golden brown. Add the tomato, ground coriander and cumin, chilli powder, turmeric, channa (chole) masala and 500 ml (17 fl oz/2 cups) cold water, and cook for 10 minutes, or until the tomato is soft. Add the chickpeas, season well with salt and cook for 7–10 minutes, or until the sauce thickens. Transfer to a serving dish. Place the ghee or butter on top and allow to melt before serving. Garnish with the sliced onion, mint and coriander leaves.

NOTE: *Channa (chole) masala is a spice blend specifically used in this dish. It is available at Indian grocery stores. Garam masala (see page 250 for a recipe) can be used as a substitute, but this will alter the final flavour.*

NUTRITION PER SERVE
Protein 8 g; Fat 11 g; Carbohydrate 17 g; Dietary
Fibre 6 g; Cholesterol 8.5 mg; 835 kJ (200 Cal)

Cook the onion in a large saucepan until it is golden brown.

Add the drained chickpeas and cook until the sauce has thickened.

Balinese seafood curry

PREPARATION TIME: 20 MINUTES + 20 MINUTES MARINATING | TOTAL COOKING TIME: 20 MINUTES | SERVES 6

CURRY PASTE
2 tomatoes, peeled, seeded and roughly
  chopped
5 small red chillies, seeded and chopped
5 garlic cloves, chopped
2 lemongrass stems (white part only), sliced
1 tablespoon coriander seeds, dry-roasted
  and ground
1 teaspoon shrimp powder, dry-roasted
  (see NOTE)
1 tablespoon ground almonds
¼ teaspoon ground nutmeg
1 teaspoon ground turmeric
3 tablespoons tamarind purée

1 tablespoon lime juice
250 g (9 oz) swordfish, cut into 3 cm
  (1¼ inch) cubes
60 ml (2 fl oz/¼ cup) oil
2 red onions, chopped
2 small red chillies, seeded and sliced
400 g (14 oz) raw prawns (shrimp), peeled
  and deveined, leaving the tails intact
250 g (9 oz) squid tubes, cut into 1 cm
  (½ inch) rings
125 ml (4 fl oz/½ cup) fish stock
Thai basil leaves, shredded, to garnish

1   To make the curry paste, place all the ingredients in a blender or food processor, and blend to a thick paste.

2   Place the lime juice in a bowl and season with salt and freshly ground black pepper. Add the swordfish, toss to coat well and leave to marinate for 20 minutes.

3   Heat the oil in a saucepan or wok, add the onion, sliced red chilli and curry paste, and cook, stirring occasionally, over low heat for 10 minutes, or until fragrant.

4   Add the swordfish and prawns, and stir to coat in the curry paste mixture. Cook for 3 minutes, or until the prawns just turn pink, then add the squid and cook for 1 minute.

5   Add the stock and bring to the boil, then reduce the heat and simmer for 2 minutes, or until the seafood is cooked and tender. Season to taste with salt and freshly ground black pepper. Garnish with the shredded Thai basil leaves and serve.

NOTE: *If you cannot purchase shrimp powder, place some dried baby shrimp in a mortar and pestle and grind to a fine powder. Alternatively, you can place them in the small bowl of a food processor and process to a fine powder.*

NUTRITION PER SERVE
Protein 30 g; Fat 14 g; Carbohydrate 3.5 g; Dietary Fibre 2 g; Cholesterol 210 mg; 1100 kJ (263 Cal)

Remove the seeds from the chillies, and roughly chop the flesh.

Peel and devein the raw prawns, leaving the tails intact.

Using a sharp knife, cut the cleaned squid tubes into rings.

Beef rendang

PREPARATION TIME: 20 MINUTES I TOTAL COOKING TIME: 2 HOURS 30 MINUTES I SERVES 6

2 onions, roughly chopped
2 garlic cloves, crushed
400 ml (14 fl oz) tin coconut milk
2 teaspoons ground coriander seeds
½ teaspoon ground fennel seeds
2 teaspoons ground cumin seeds
¼ teaspoon ground cloves
1.5 kg (3 lb 5 oz) chuck steak, cut into 3 cm (1¼ inch) cubes
4–6 small fresh red chillies, chopped
1 tablespoon lemon juice
1 lemongrass stem (white part only), bruised, cut lengthways
2 teaspoons grated palm sugar (jaggery) or soft brown sugar
coriander (cilantro) sprigs, to garnish

1   Place the onion and garlic in a food processor, and process until smooth, adding water, if necessary.

2   Place the coconut milk in a large saucepan and bring to the boil, then reduce the heat to medium and cook, stirring occasionally, for 15 minutes, or until the milk has reduced by half and the oil has separated. Do not allow the milk to brown.

3   Add the coriander seeds, fennel, cumin and cloves to the pan, and stir for 1 minute. Add the meat and cook for 2 minutes, or until it changes colour. Add the onion mixture, chilli, lemon juice, lemongrass and palm sugar. Cook, covered, over medium heat for 2 hours, or until the liquid has reduced and the mixture has thickened. Stir frequently to prevent it sticking to the bottom of the pan.

4   Uncover and continue cooking until the oil from the coconut milk begins to emerge again, letting the curry develop. Be careful that it does not burn. The curry is cooked when it is brown and dry. Serve with rice and coriander sprigs.

Process the onion and garlic in a food processor until smooth.

Cook the coconut milk over medium heat until reduced and the oil has separated.

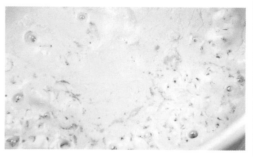

NUTRITION PER SERVE
Protein 53 g; Fat 20 g; Carbohydrate 5.5 g; Dietary Fibre 1.5 g; Cholesterol 168 mg; 1775 kJ (424 Cal)

Yellow vegetable curry

PREPARATION TIME: 20 MINUTES | TOTAL COOKING TIME: 50 MINUTES | SERVES 6

60 ml (2 fl oz/¼ cup) oil

1 onion, finely chopped

2 tablespoons Thai yellow curry paste (see page 250)

250 g (9 oz) potato, diced

200 g (7 oz) zucchini (courgettes), diced

150 g (5½ oz) red capsicum pepper, diced

100 g (3½ oz) green beans, trimmed

50 g (1¾ oz) bamboo shoots, trimmed and sliced

250 ml (9 fl oz/1 cup) vegetable stock

400 ml (14 fl oz) tin coconut cream

Thai basil leaves, to garnish

1 Heat the oil in a large saucepan, add the onion and cook over medium heat for 4–5 minutes, or until softened. Add the curry paste and cook, stirring, for 2 minutes, or until fragrant.

2 Add all the vegetables and cook, stirring, over high heat for 2 minutes. Pour in the stock, reduce the heat to medium and cook, covered, for 15–20 minutes, or until the vegetables are tender. Cook, uncovered, over high heat for 5–10 minutes, or until the sauce has reduced slightly.

3 Stir in the coconut cream, and season with salt. Bring to the boil, stirring frequently, then reduce the heat and simmer for 5 minutes. Garnish with the Thai basil leaves.

NUTRITION PER SERVE
Protein 4 g; Fat 24 g; Carbohydrate 12 g; Dietary Fibre 3.7 g; Cholesterol 0.5 mg; 1196 kJ (286 Cal)

Heat the oil in a saucepan, add the onion and cook until turning golden.

Add the curry paste to the pan and cook until the mixture is fragrant.

Cook the curry over high heat until the sauce has reduced slightly.

Massaman vegetable curry

PREPARATION TIME: 25 MINUTES | TOTAL COOKING TIME: 45 MINUTES | SERVES 4–6

CURRY PASTE

1 tablespoon oil

1 teaspoon coriander seeds

1 teaspoon cumin seeds

8 cloves

½ teaspoon fennel seeds

seeds from 4 cardamom pods

6 red Asian shallots (eschalots), chopped

3 garlic cloves, chopped

1 teaspoon finely chopped lemongrass stems
  (white part only)

1 teaspoon finely chopped fresh galangal

4 large dried red chillies

1 teaspoon ground nutmeg

1 teaspoon white pepper

1 tablespoon oil

250 g (9 oz) baby onions

500 g (1 lb 2 oz) small new potatoes

300 g (10½ oz) carrots, cut into 3 cm
  (1¼ inch) pieces

225 g (8 oz) tin whole champignons, drained

1 cinnamon stick

1 makrut (kaffir lime) leaf

1 bay leaf

250 ml (9 fl oz/1 cup) coconut cream

1 tablespoon lime juice

3 teaspoons grated palm sugar (jaggery) or
  soft brown sugar

1 tablespoon shredded Thai basil leaves

1 tablespoon roasted peanuts

1   To make the curry paste, heat the oil in a frying pan over low heat, add the coriander seeds, cumin seeds, cloves, fennel seeds and cardamom seeds, and cook for 1–2 minutes, or until fragrant. Place in a food processor and add the shallots, garlic, lemongrass, galangal, chillies, nutmeg and white pepper. Process until smooth, adding a little water as necessary.

2   Heat the oil in a large saucepan, add the curry paste and cook, stirring, over medium heat for 2 minutes, or until fragrant. Add the vegetables, cinnamon stick, makrut leaf and bay leaf. Season with salt. Add enough water to cover—about 500 ml (17 fl oz/2 cups)—and bring to the boil. Reduce the heat and simmer, covered, stirring frequently, for 30–35 minutes, or until the vegetables are cooked. Stir in the coconut cream and cook, uncovered, for 4 minutes, stirring frequently, until thickened slightly. Stir in the lime juice, palm sugar and shredded Thai basil. Add a little water if the sauce is too dry. Season with freshly ground black pepper and garnish with the peanuts.

NUTRITION PER SERVE (6)
Protein 6.3 g; Fat 17 g; Carbohydrate 22.4 g; Dietary Fibre 6.7 g; Cholesterol 0 mg; 1156 kJ (276 Cal)

Process the curry paste ingredients in a food processor until smooth.

Stir in the coconut cream and cook, stirring frequently, until thickened slightly.

Goan fish curry

PREPARATION TIME: 20 MINUTES I TOTAL COOKING TIME: 35 MINUTES I SERVES 6

60 ml (2 fl oz/¼ cup) oil
1 large onion, finely chopped
4–5 garlic cloves, chopped
2 teaspoons grated fresh ginger
4–6 small dried red chillies
1 tablespoon coriander seeds
2 teaspoons cumin seeds
1 teaspoon ground turmeric
¼ teaspoon chilli powder
30 g (1 oz/⅓ cup) desiccated coconut
270 ml (9½ fl oz) coconut milk
2 tomatoes, peeled and chopped
2 tablespoons tamarind purée
1 tablespoon white vinegar
6 curry leaves
1 kg (2 lb 4 oz) boneless, skinless firm fish
    fillets, such as flake or ling, cut into 8 cm
    (3 inch) pieces
coriander (cilantro) leaves, to garnish

1   Heat the oil in a large saucepan. Add the onion and cook, stirring, over low heat for 10 minutes, or until softened. Add the garlic and ginger, and cook for a further 2 minutes.

2   Place the chillies, coriander seeds, cumin seeds, turmeric, chilli powder and coconut in a frying pan, and dry-fry (no oil), stirring constantly, over medium heat for 2 minutes, or until aromatic. Place in a food processor and finely grind.

3   Add the spice mixture, coconut milk, tomato, tamarind purée, vinegar and curry leaves to the onion mixture. Stir to mix thoroughly, add 250 ml (9 fl oz/1 cup) water and simmer for 10 minutes, or until mixture has softened and just thickened. Stir frequently to prevent sticking.

4   Add the fish and cook, covered, over low heat for 10 minutes, or until cooked through. Stir gently once or twice during cooking and add water if needed. Garnish with coriander and serve with rice and pappadums.

Dry-fry the dried chillies, spices and desiccated coconut until fragrant.

Simmer until the tomato has softened and the mixture has thickened slightly.

NUTRITION PER SERVE
Protein 37 g; Fat 27 g; Carbohydrate 4 g; Dietary Fibre 3 g; Cholesterol 117 mg; 1685 kJ (400 Cal)

Balti chicken

PREPARATION TIME: 25 MINUTES | TOTAL COOKING TIME: 1 HOUR | SERVES 6

1 kg (2 lb 4 oz) chicken thigh fillets
80 ml (2½ fl oz/⅓ cup) oil
1 large red onion, finely chopped
4–5 garlic cloves, finely chopped
1 tablespoon grated fresh ginger
2 teaspoons ground cumin
2 teaspoons ground coriander
1 teaspoon ground turmeric
½ teaspoon chilli powder
425 g (15 oz) tin chopped tomatoes
1 green capsicum (pepper), cut into 3 cm
    (1¼ inch) cubes
1–2 small green chillies, seeded and finely
    chopped
1 very large handful chopped coriander
    (cilantro) leaves
2 spring onions (scallions), chopped to garnish

1 Remove any excess fat or sinew from the chicken thigh fillets and cut into 4–5 pieces.

2 Heat a large wok over high heat, add the oil and swirl to coat the side. Add the onion and stir-fry over medium heat for 5 minutes, or until softened but not browned. Add the garlic and ginger, and stir-fry for 3 minutes.

3 Add the spices, 1 teaspoon salt and 60 ml (2 fl oz/¼ cup) water. Increase heat to high and stir-fry for 2 minutes, or until mixture thickens.

4 Add the tomato and 250 ml (9 fl oz/1 cup) water and cook, stirring often, for a further 10 minutes, or until the mixture is thick and pulpy and the oil comes to the surface.

5 Add the chicken to the wok, reduce the heat and simmer, stirring often, for 15 minutes. Add the capsicum and chilli, and simmer for 25 minutes, or until the chicken is tender. Add a little water if the mixture is too thick. Stir in the coriander and garnish with the spring onion. Serve with rice.

NUTRITION PER SERVE
Protein 40 g; Fat 17 g; Carbohydrate 5 g; Dietary
Fibre 2 g; Cholesterol 83 mg; 1370 kJ (327 Cal)

Add the spices, salt and water to the wok, and cook until thickened.

Cook, stirring, until the mixture thickens and the oil comes to the surface.

Stews

Corned beef

PREPARATION TIME: 5 MINUTES | TOTAL COOKING TIME: 1 HOUR 40 MINUTES | SERVES 6–8

1 tablespoon oil

1.5 kg (3 lb 5 oz) piece corned silverside, trimmed

1 tablespoon white vinegar

1 tablespoon soft brown sugar

4 cloves

4 black peppercorns

2 bay leaves

1 garlic clove, crushed

1 large parsley sprig

4 carrots

4 potatoes

6 small onions

ONION SAUCE

30 g (1 oz) butter

2 white onions, chopped

2 tablespoons plain (all-purpose) flour

330ml (11¼ fl oz/1⅓ cups) full-cream (whole) milk

HORSERADISH CREAM

60 ml (2 fl oz/¼ cup) horseradish relish

1 tablespoon white vinegar

125 ml (4 fl oz/½ cup) cream

NUTRITION PER SERVE (8)
Protein 37 g; Fat 13 g; Carbohydrate 19 g; Dietary Fibre 2.5 g; Cholesterol 111 mg; 1425 kJ (340 Cal)

1 Heat the oil in a deep, heavy-based saucepan. Cook the meat over medium–high heat, turning until well browned all over. Remove the pan from the heat and add the vinegar, sugar, cloves, peppercorns, bay leaves, garlic and parsley sprig.

2 Pour over enough water to cover. Cover and return to the heat, reduce the heat and bring slowly to a simmering point. Then simmer for a further 30 minutes.

3 Cut the carrots and potatoes into large pieces and add to the pan with the onions. Simmer, covered, for 1 hour, or until tender. Remove the vegetables and keep warm. Reserve 125 ml (4 fl oz/½ cup) of the cooking liquid.

4 Meanwhile to make the onion sauce, heat the butter in a small saucepan. Cook the onion gently for 10 minutes, or until soft but not browned. Transfer the onion to a bowl. Add the flour to the pan and stir over low heat for 2 minutes, or until the flour is lightly golden. Gradually add the milk and the reserved cooking liquid, and stir until the sauce boils and thickens. Boil for 1 minute, then remove from the heat and stir in the onion. Season to taste.

5 To make the horseradish cream, combine all of the ingredients in a bowl until smooth.

6 Drain the meat from the pan, discarding the remaining liquid and spices. Slice the meat, and serve it with the vegetables, onion sauce and horseradish cream. Garnish with bay leaves if desired.

Add the vinegar, sugar, cloves, peppercorns, bay leaves, garlic and parsley to the meat.

Remove the sauce from the heat and stir in the cooked onion.

Creamy veal with mushrooms

PREPARATION TIME: 20 MINUTES I TOTAL COOKING TIME: 25 MINUTES I SERVES 4

750 g (1 lb 10 oz) veal steaks, cut into 1 cm
    (½ inch) strips
30 g (1 oz/¼ cup) plain (all-purpose) flour
30 g (1 oz) butter
1 garlic clove, crushed
1 tablespoon dijon mustard
250 ml (9 fl oz/1 cup) cream
125 ml (4 fl oz/½ cup) white wine
1 tablespoon chopped fresh thyme
250 ml (9 fl oz/1 cup) chicken stock
375 g (13 oz) button mushrooms, halved

1   Toss the meat in the flour (inside a plastic
bag prevents mess), shaking off the excess. Heat
the butter and garlic in a large frying pan. Add
the meat and cook quickly in small batches
over medium heat until well browned. Drain
thoroughly on paper towels.

2   Brown the mushrooms in the pan and add
the mustard, cream, wine, thyme and stock.
Bring to the boil, then reduce the heat and
simmer, covered, for 10–15 minutes, stirring
occasionally, until the sauce thickens.

3   Add the veal and cook for a further
3–5 minutes, or until the meat is tender and
warmed through. Delicious served with pasta
and steamed vegetables.

Toss the veal strips in the flour, shaking off any
excess flour.

NUTRITION PER SERVE
Protein 47 g; Fat 38 g; Carbohydrate 8.5 g; Dietary
Fibre 3 g; Cholesterol 258 mg; 2425 kJ (580 Cal)

Chicken Marsala

PREPARATION TIME: 20 MINUTES | TOTAL COOKING TIME: 1 HOUR 15 MINUTES | SERVES 4

60 ml (2 fl oz/¼ cup) olive oil
3 leeks (white part only), thinly sliced
1 teaspoon finely chopped rosemary
3 bay leaves, torn
1 kg (2 lb 4 oz) chicken pieces
seasoned plain (all-purpose) flour
1 large eggplant (aubergine), cut into cubes
2 zucchini (courgettes), roughly chopped
125 ml (4 fl oz/½ cup) (see NOTE) Marsala
300 ml (10½ fl oz) chicken stock
500 g (1 lb 2 oz/2 cups) tomato paste
    (concentrated purée)
200 g (7 oz) button mushrooms, halved

1 Heat the oil in a large heavy-based saucepan. Fry the leek, rosemary and bay leaves over low heat for 5 minutes, or until soft, stirring occasionally. Remove with a slotted spoon, leaving as much oil in the pan as possible.

2 Toss the chicken pieces in the seasoned flour. Add the chicken to the pan and brown well in batches over medium heat. Return all the chicken to the pan with the leek mixture.

3 Add the eggplant and zucchini, and cook, stirring, for 2–3 minutes, or until softened, turning the chicken over. Add the Marsala and stock, and cook for 15 minutes over medium–high heat.

4 Add the tomato paste and season well with salt and pepper. Bring to the boil, turning the chicken pieces in the sauce. Reduce the heat to a very gentle simmer, then cover and cook for 35 minutes. Add the mushrooms and cook, uncovered, for 5 minutes.

NOTE: *Marsala is a famous Italian fortified wine. It has a smoky, rich flavour and ranges from dry to sweet.*

NUTRITION PER SERVE
Protein 63 g; Fat 20 g; Carbohydrate 13 g; Dietary Fibre 9 g; Cholesterol 125 mg; 2200 kJ (530 Cal)

Remove the softened leeks and herbs from the pan with a slotted spoon.

Add the chopped eggplant and zucchini to the chicken and leek mixture.

Steak and kidney stew

PREPARATION TIME: 35 MINUTES I TOTAL COOKING TIME: 2 HOURS 30 MINUTES I SERVES 4–6

1 kg (2 lb 4 oz) chuck steak, trimmed
8 lamb kidneys
60 ml (2 fl oz/¼ cup) oil
1 bacon slice, rind removed, cut into long,
    thin strips
40 g (1½ oz) butter
1 large onion, chopped
300 g (10½ oz) button mushrooms, halved
250 ml (9 fl oz/1 cup) Muscat
2–3 garlic cloves, crushed
¼ teaspoon ground allspice
½ teaspoon paprika
2 teaspoons coriander seeds, lightly crushed
1 tablespoon wholegrain mustard
250 ml (9 fl oz/1 cup) beef stock
2–3 tablespoons soft brown sugar
1–2 teaspoons thyme leaves
1–2 teaspoons rosemary chopped

1 Cut the steak into 2–3 cm (1 inch) cubes. Cut the kidneys in half, remove the core and any fat, then slice them in half again.

2 Heat 1 teaspoon of the oil in a large heavy-based saucepan. Add the bacon and cook over medium heat until just crisp. Remove and then set aside.

3 Heat 2 tablespoons of the oil and 30 g (1 oz) of the butter in the pan. Brown the steak cubes in batches, then set aside.

4 Add the onion to the pan and cook for 3 minutes, or until soft and golden. Add the mushrooms and cook, stirring, for 3 minutes, until starting to brown. Stir in half the Muscat and simmer for 3–4 minutes. Remove and set to the side.

5 Add the remaining oil and butter to the pan. Stir in the garlic, allspice, paprika and coriander seeds, and cook for 1 minute. Add the kidney and cook until just starting to brown. Stir in the mustard and remaining Muscat, and simmer for 2 minutes.

6 Stir in the bacon, steak, and onion and mushroom mixture. Stir in the stock, bring to the boil, then reduce the heat, cover and simmer for 1 hour. Add the sugar. Simmer, covered, for 40 minutes, then uncovered for 20 minutes, stirring in the herbs during the last 10 minutes.

NUTRITION PER SERVE (6)
Protein 40 g; Fat 20 g; Carbohydrate 15 g; Dietary Fibre 2 g; Cholesterol 155 mg; 1830 kJ (440 Cal)

Halve the kidneys and remove the cores and fat. Slice in half again.

Add half the Muscat to the onion and mushrooms, and simmer for 3–4 minutes.

Add the kidney to the pan-fried spices and cook until just starting to brown.

Pork and coriander stew

PREPARATION TIME: 15 MINUTES + OVERNIGHT MARINATING I TOTAL COOKING TIME: 1 HOUR 20 MINUTES I SERVES 4–6

1½ tablespoons coriander seeds
800 g (1 lb 12 oz) pork fillet, cut into 2 cm
    (¾ inch) cubes
1 tablespoon plain (all-purpose) flour
60 ml (2 fl oz/¼ cup) olive oil
1 large onion, thinly sliced
375 ml (13 fl oz/1½ cups) red wine
250 ml (9 fl oz/1 cup) chicken stock
1 teaspoon sugar
fresh coriander (cilantro) sprigs, to garnish

1 Crush the coriander seeds in a mortar with a pestle. Combine the pork, seeds and ½ teaspoon cracked pepper. Cover and marinate overnight in the refrigerator.

2 Combine the flour and pork, and toss to coat. Heat 2 tablespoons of the oil in a saucepan and cook the pork in batches over high heat. Remove.

3 Heat the remaining oil, add the onion and cook over medium heat for 2–3 minutes, or until golden. Return the meat to the pan, add the wine, stock and sugar. Season. Bring to the boil, then reduce the heat and simmer, covered, for 1 hour.

4 Remove the meat. Return the pan to the heat and boil over high heat for 3–5 minutes, or until the liquid reduces and thickens. Pour over the meat and garnish with coriander. Serve with boiled potatoes.

NUTRITION PER SERVE (6)
Protein 30 g; Fat 12 g; Carbohydrate 2.5 g; Dietary Fibre 0 g; Cholesterol 65 mg; 1180 kJ (282 Cal)

Coat the pork fillet pieces with the ground coriander seeds and cracked pepper.

Heat some oil in a saucepan and cook the pork in batches until brown.

Remove the cooked meat from the pan, cover and keep warm.

Stuffed squid stew

PREPARATION TIME: 50 MINUTES | TOTAL COOKING TIME: 50 MINUTES | SERVES 4

100 ml (3½ fl oz) olive oil
1 large onion, finely chopped
2 garlic cloves, crushed
80 g (2¾ oz/1 cup) fresh breadcrumbs
1 egg, lightly beaten
60 g (2¼ oz) kefalotyri cheese, grated
60 g (2¼ oz) haloumi cheese, grated
4 large or 8 small squid (1 kg/2 lb 4 oz),
    cleaned (see NOTE)
1 small onion, finely chopped, extra
2 garlic cloves, crushed, extra
500 g (1 lb 2 oz) firm ripe tomatoes, peeled
    and diced
150 ml (5 fl oz) red wine
1 tablespoon chopped oregano
1 tablespoon chopped flat-leaf (Italian) parsley

1   Heat 2 tablespoons of the oil in a frying pan, add the onion and cook over medium heat for 3 minutes. Remove. Combine with the garlic, breadcrumbs, egg and cheeses. Season.

2   Pat the squid tubes dry with paper towels and, using a teaspoon, fill them three-quarters full with the stuffing. Do not pack them too tightly or the stuffing mixture will swell and burst out during cooking. Secure the ends with wooden toothpicks.

3   Heat the remaining oil in a large frying pan, add the squid and cook for 1–2 minutes on all sides. Remove. Add the extra onion and cook over medium heat for 3 minutes, or until soft, then add the extra garlic and cook for a further 1 minute. Stir in the tomato and wine, and simmer for 10 minutes, or until thick and pulpy, then stir in the oregano and parsley. Return the squid to the pan and cook, covered, for 20–25 minutes, or until tender. Serve warm with the tomato sauce or cool with a salad.

NOTE: *Ask the fishmonger to clean the squid. Or, discard the tentacles and cartilage. Rinse the tubes under running water and pull off the skin.*

NUTRITION PER SERVE
Protein 57 g; Fat 35 g; Carbohydrate 30 g; Dietary Fibre 4 g; Cholesterol 558 mg; 2890 kJ (690 Cal)

Fill the squid tubes three-quarters full with the stuffing mixture.

Cook the stuffed squid tubes in a frying pan on all sides.

Turkey osso bucco

PREPARATION TIME: 25 MINUTES + THAWING | TOTAL COOKING TIME: 1 HOUR 30 MINUTES | SERVES 4–6

3 red capsicums (peppers)

2 kg (4 lb 8 oz) turkey hindquarters (legs with thighs), chopped (see NOTE)

seasoned plain (all-purpose) flour

60 ml (2 fl oz/¼ cup) olive oil

60 g (2¼ oz) butter

185 ml (6 fl oz/¾ cup) chicken stock

¼ teaspoon dried chilli flakes

4 sage leaves, chopped, or
    ½ teaspoon dried sage

2 garlic cloves, crushed

1 teaspoon finely grated lemon zest

150 g (5½ oz) sliced pancetta, or thinly sliced bacon

1 rosemary sprig

2 tablespoons chopped flat-leaf (Italian) parsley

1 Preheat the grill (broiler) to high. Cut the capsicums in half, then remove the seeds and membranes. Place the capsicum halves skin side up under the grill and cook for 5–8 minutes, or until the skin blackens and blisters. Transfer to a plastic bag, seal and allow to cool, then peel away the blackened skin. Cut the flesh into thick slices.

2 Pat the turkey pieces with paper towels to remove excess moisture, then coat well in the seasoned flour, dusting off any excess.

3 Heat the oil and butter in a large saucepan. Brown the turkey pieces in batches over medium–high heat, then drain the pan of oil.

4 Pour the chicken stock into the pan and stir well, scraping the base and side of the pan to mix in all the pan juices. Add the chilli flakes, sage, garlic and lemon zest, and cook, stirring, for 1 minute.

5 Return all the turkey pieces to the pan. Cover with the grilled capsicum slices, then layer the pancetta over the top to completely cover. Add the rosemary sprig, cover the pan and cook over low heat for 1 hour, or until the turkey is succulent, yet not falling off the bone.

6 Discard the rosemary and transfer the pancetta, capsicum slices and turkey pieces to a serving plate. Cover and keep warm. To thicken the sauce, place it over high heat and simmer for 3–4 minutes. Stir in the parsley, spoon the sauce around the turkey to serve.

NOTE: *Ask your butcher or poulterer to saw the turkey into 1.5–2 cm (¾ inch) pieces for you.*

NUTRITION PER SERVE (6)
Protein 65 g; Fat 55 g; Carbohydrate 5 g; Dietary Fibre 2 g; Cholesterol 345 mg; 4265 kJ (1020 Cal)

Place the grilled capsicum halves in a plastic bag, seal and allow to cool.

Coat the thawed turkey pieces in the seasoned flour., dusting off the excess.

In batches, brown the turkey in the hot oil and butter over medium–high heat.

Italian sausage and chickpea stew

PREPARATION TIME: 15 MINUTES | TOTAL COOKING TIME: 45 MINUTES | SERVES 4

2 large red capsicums (peppers)
1 tablespoon olive oil
2 large red onions, cut into thick wedges
2 garlic cloves, finely chopped
600 g (1 lb 5 oz) Italian-style thin pork sausages
300 g (10½ oz) chickpeas, drained
150 g (5½ oz) flat mushrooms, thickly sliced
125 ml (4 fl oz/½ cup) dry white wine
2 bay leaves
2 teaspoons chopped rosemary
400 g (14 oz) tin chopped tomatoes

1 Cut the capsicums into large pieces, removing the seeds and membrane. Place skin side up, under a hot grill (broiler) until the skin blackens and blisters. Allow to cool in a sealed plastic bag. Peel away the skin, and slice diagonally into thick strips.

2 Meanwhile, heat the oil in a large non-stick frying pan. Add the onion and garlic, and stir over medium heat for 6 minutes, or until the onion is soft and browned. Remove the onion from the pan and set aside. Add the sausages to the same pan. Cook over medium heat, turning occasionally, for 8 minutes, or until the sausages are browned. Remove the sausages from the pan, allow to cool and slice diagonally into 3 cm (1¼ inch) pieces.

3 Combine the capsicum slices, onion, sausage pieces, chickpeas and mushrooms in the frying pan, and cook over medium–high heat.

4 Add the wine, bay leaves and rosemary to the pan. Bring to the boil, then reduce the heat to low and simmer for 3 minutes. Stir in the tomato and simmer for 20 minutes, or until the sauce has thickened slightly. Remove the bay leaves and season to taste with sugar, salt and cracked black pepper. Delicious served with fettuccine, noodles, grilled ciabatta bread, mashed potato, soft polenta or parmesan cheese shavings.

Grill the capsicums under a hot grill until the skin blackens and blisters.

Remove the skin from the cooked capsicums and slice them into thin strips.

NUTRITION PER SERVE
Protein 20 g; Fat 25 g; Carbohydrate 25 g; Dietary Fibre 9.5 g; Cholesterol 50 mg; 1695 kJ (405 Cal)

Chicken with feta and olives

PREPARATION TIME: 15 MINUTES I TOTAL COOKING TIME: 1 HOUR I SERVES 4

2 tablespoons oil
8 chicken pieces (1.2 kg/2 lb 10 oz)
1 onion, chopped
25 g (1 oz) oregano, leaves picked
2 tablespoons tomato paste (concentrated purée)
2 x 400 g (14 oz) tins chopped tomatoes
150 g (5½ oz) black olives
150 g (5½ oz) feta, crumbled, to serve

1 Heat half the oil in a saucepan and cook the chicken pieces, in batches, for 3–4 minutes, or until golden. Remove from the pan and set aside.

2 In the same saucepan, heat the remaining oil and cook the onion and half the oregano leaves for 3 minutes, or until the onion is softened. Add the tomato paste to the onion mixture and stir for 2 minutes, then add the tomato and the chicken pieces.

3 Simmer, covered, for 40–50 minutes, or until the chicken is cooked through. Add the olives and remaining oregano leaves. To serve, spoon into bowls and top with the crumbled feta.

NUTRITION PER SERVE
Protein 50 g; Fat 28 g; Carbohydrate 11 g; Dietary Fibre 5 g; Cholesterol 165 mg; 2110 kJ (505 Cal)

Cook the chicken pieces in the hot oil until they are golden brown.

Cook the onion and half the oregano leaves until the onion is soft.

Add the olives and remaining oregano leaves to the chicken pieces.

Catalan fish stew

PREPARATION TIME: 30 MINUTES | TOTAL COOKING TIME: 40 MINUTES | SERVES 6–8

300 g (10½ oz) red mullet fillets

400 g (14 oz) firm white fish fillets

300 g (10½ oz) cleaned squid

1.5 litres (52 fl oz/6 cups) fish stock

80 ml (2½ fl oz/⅓ cup) olive oil

1 onion, chopped

6 garlic cloves, chopped

1 small red chilli, chopped

1 teaspoon paprika

pinch saffron threads

150 ml (5 fl oz) white wine

425 g (15 oz) tin chopped tomatoes

16 raw prawns (shrimp), peeled and deveined, leaving the tails intact

2 tablespoons brandy

24 black mussels, scrubbed and hairy beards removed

1 tablespoon chopped flat leaf (Italian) parsley

PICADA

2 tablespoons olive oil

2 slices day-old bread, cubed

2 garlic cloves

5 blanched almonds, toasted

2 tablespoons chopped flat-leaf (Italian) parsley

NUTRITION PER SERVE (8)
Protein 26 g; Fat 18 g; Carbohydrate 5 g; Dietary
Fibre 1.5 g; Cholesterol 136 mg; 1275 kJ (305 Cal)

1 Cut the fish and squid into 4 cm (1½ inch) pieces and set aside. Place the stock in a large saucepan, bring to the boil and boil for 15 minutes, or until reduced by half.

2 To make the picada, heat the oil in a frying pan, add the bread and cook, stirring, for 2–3 minutes, or until golden, adding the garlic at the last minute. Place the almonds, bread, garlic and parsley in a food processor and process, adding a little of the stock to make a smooth paste.

3 Heat 2 tablespoons of the oil in a large saucepan, add the onion, garlic, chilli and paprika, and cook, stirring, for 1 minute. Add the saffron, wine, tomato and stock. Bring to the boil, then reduce the heat and simmer.

4 Heat the remaining oil in a frying pan and quickly fry the fish and squid for 3–5 minutes. Remove from the pan. Add the prawns, cook for 1 minute and then pour in the brandy. Carefully ignite the brandy with a match and let the flames burn down. Remove from the pan.

5 Add the mussels to the stock and simmer, covered, for 2–3 minutes, or until opened. Discard any that do not open. Add all the seafood and the picada to the pan, stirring until the sauce has thickened and the seafood has cooked through. Season to taste, sprinkle with the parsley, and serve.

Quickly cook the fish and calamari in the oil in a frying pan.

Add the mussels to the stock and simmer for 2–3 minutes or until they open.

Braised beef in red wine

PREPARATION TIME: 10 MINUTES I TOTAL COOKING TIME: 2 HOURS I SERVES 6

30 g (1 oz/¼ cup) plain (all-purpose) flour
¼ teaspoon ground black pepper
1 kg (2 lb 4 oz) lean round or chuck steak, cut
    into 3 cm (1¼ inch) cubes
1 tablespoon oil
15 g (½ oz) butter
12 baby onions
250 ml (9 fl oz/1 cup) beef stock
250 ml (9 fl oz/1 cup) red wine
2 tablespoons tomato paste (concentrated
    purée)
1 tablespoon French mustard
1 bay leaf
¼ teaspoon mixed dried herbs
1 tablespoon chopped flat-leaf (Italian)
    parsley, to garnish

1 Combine the flour and pepper. Toss the meat
in the seasoned flour, shaking off the excess.

2 Heat the oil and butter in a heavy-based
saucepan. Cook the meat quickly in batches over
medium–high heat until well browned. Remove
and drain on paper towels.

3 Add the onions to the saucepan and cook
over medium heat until softened. Return the
meat to the pan, add the stock, wine, tomato
paste, mustard and herbs. Bring to the boil,
reduce the heat and cook, covered, for 1½ hours,
or until the meat is tender, stirring occasionally.

NUTRITION PER SERVE
Protein 37 g; Fat 10 g; Carbohydrate 7.5 g; Dietary
Fibre 1.5 g; Cholesterol 110 mg; 1235 kJ (295 Cal)

Toss the meat in the seasoned flour, shaking off the
excess.

Cook the meat in batches until well browned, then
drain on paper towels.

Stir in the stock, wine, tomato paste, mustard and
herbs, then simmer until the meat is tender.

Chicken with balsamic vinegar

PREPARATION TIME: 5 MINUTES | TOTAL COOKING TIME: 50 MINUTES | SERVES 4

2 tablespoons olive oil
8 chicken pieces
125 ml (4 fl oz/½ cup) chicken stock
125 ml (4 fl oz/½ cup) dry white wine
125 ml (4 fl oz/½ cup) balsamic vinegar
   (see NOTE)
40 g (1½ oz) chilled butter

1 Heat the oil in a large flameproof casserole dish over medium heat and cook the chicken, in batches, for 7–8 minutes, or until browned. Pour off any excess fat.

2 Add the stock, bring to the boil, then reduce the heat and simmer, covered, for 30 minutes, or until the chicken is cooked through.

3 Add the white wine and vinegar and increase the heat to high. Boil for 1 minute, or until the liquid has thickened. Remove from the heat, stir in the butter until melted, and season. Spoon the sauce over the chicken to serve, accompanied by roast potatoes and salad.

NOTE: *Use a good-quality balsamic vinegar, as the cheaper varieties can be too acidic.*

NUTRITION PER SERVE
Protein 40 g; Fat 25 g; Carbohydrate 0.5 g; Dietary Fibre 0 g; Cholesterol 165 mg; 1790 kJ (430 Cal)

Cook the chicken pieces in batches until they are browned all over.

Simmer the chicken and stock, covered, until the chicken is cooked through.

Remove the pan from the heat and stir in the butter until melted.

Lamb hotpot with rice noodles

PREPARATION TIME: 20 MINUTES + 2 HOURS MARINATING | TOTAL COOKING TIME: 2 HOURS | SERVES 4

2 garlic cloves, crushed

2 teaspoons grated fresh ginger

1 teaspoon Chinese five-spice

¼ teaspoon ground white pepper

2 tablespoons Chinese rice wine

1 teaspoon sugar

1 kg (2 lb 4 oz) boneless lamb shoulder, trimmed and cut into 3 cm (1¼ inch) pieces

30 g (1 oz) whole dried Chinese mushrooms

1 tablespoon peanut oil

1 large onion, cut into wedges

2 cm (¾ inch) piece fresh ginger, cut into matchsticks

1 teaspoon sichuan peppercorns, crushed or ground

2 tablespoons sweet bean paste

1 teaspoon black peppercorns, ground and toasted

500 ml (17 fl oz/2 cups) chicken stock

60 ml (2 fl oz/¼ cup) oyster sauce

2 star anise

60 ml (2 fl oz/¼ cup) Chinese rice wine, extra

80 g (2¾ oz) tin sliced bamboo shoots, drained

100 g (3½ oz) tin water chestnuts, drained and sliced

400 g (14 oz) fresh rice noodles, cut into 2 cm (¾ inch) wide strips

1 spring onion (scallion), sliced on the diagonal

1 Combine the garlic, grated ginger, five-spice, white pepper, rice wine, sugar and 1 teaspoon salt in a large bowl. Add the lamb and toss to coat. Cover and marinate for 2 hours.

2 Meanwhile, soak the mushrooms in boiling water for 20 minutes. Drain. Discard the stems.

3 Heat a wok over high heat, add the oil and swirl to coat. Stir-fry the onion, ginger and sichuan peppercorns for 2 minutes. Cook the lamb in three batches, stir-frying for 2–3 minutes each batch, or until starting to brown. Return all the lamb to the wok. Stir in the bean paste and black peppercorns, and cook for 3 minutes, or until the lamb is brown.

4 Add the stock and transfer to a 2 litre (70 fl oz/8 cup) flameproof clay pot or casserole dish. Stir in the oyster sauce, star anise and extra rice wine and simmer, covered, over low heat for 1½ hours, or until the lamb is tender. Stir in the bamboo shoots and water chestnuts, and cook for 20 minutes. Add the mushrooms.

5 Cover the noodles with boiling water and gently separate. Drain and rinse the noodles, then add to the hotpot, stirring for 1–2 minutes, or until heated through. Serve sprinkled with spring onion.

NUTRITION PER SERVE
Protein 58 g; Fat 21 g; Carbohydrate 57 g; Dietary Fibre 4 g; Cholesterol 168 mg; 2805 kJ (670 Cal)

Stir the bean paste and peppercorns into the lamb and onion mixture.

Stir the bamboo shoots and water chestnuts into the hotpot.

Sichuan chicken

PREPARATION TIME: 10 MINUTES I TOTAL COOKING TIME: 30 MINUTES I SERVES 4

¼ teaspoon Chinese five-spice
750 g (1 lb 10 oz) boneless, skinless chicken
    thighs, halved
2 tablespoons peanut oil
1 tablespoon fresh ginger, cut into matchsticks
1 teaspoon sichuan peppercorns, crushed
1 teaspoon chilli bean paste (toban djan)
2 tablespoons light soy sauce
1 tablespoon Chinese rice wine
250 g (9 oz/1¼ cups) jasmine rice
600 g (1 lb 5 oz) baby bok choy (pak choy),
    leaves separated

1   Sprinkle the five-spice powder over the
halved chicken fillets. Heat a wok until very hot,
add half the oil and swirl to coat the side. Add
the chicken pieces and cook for 2 minutes each
side, or until browned. Remove from the wok.

2   Reduce the heat to medium. Add the ginger
to the wok and cook for 30 seconds. Add the
crushed sichuan peppercorns and chilli bean
paste. Return the chicken pieces to the wok, add
the soy sauce, wine and 125 ml (4 fl oz/½ cup)
water, then simmer for 15–20 minutes, or until
the chicken is cooked through.

3   Meanwhile, bring a saucepan of water to
the boil. Add the rice and cook for 12 minutes,
stirring occasionally. Drain well.

4   Heat the remaining peanut oil in a saucepan.
Add the baby bok choy and toss gently for
1 minute, or until the leaves wilt and the stems
are tender. Serve with the chicken and rice.

Sprinkle the chinese five spice powder over the
chicken pieces.

Add the soy sauce, wine and water to the
browned chicken.

NUTRITION PER SERVE
Protein 42 g; Fat 24 g; Carbohydrate 52 g; Dietary
Fibre 2.5 g; Cholesterol 163 mg; 2465 kJ (590 Cal)

Japanese-style sukiyaki

PREPARATION TIME: 10 MINUTES | TOTAL COOKING TIME: 10 MINUTES | SERVES 4

SAUCE

½–1 teaspoon dashi granules

80 ml (2½ fl oz/⅓ cup) soy sauce

2 tablespoons sake (dry rice wine)

2 tablespoons mirin (sweet rice wine)

1 tablespoon caster (superfine) sugar

300 g (10½ oz) shirataki noodles

50 g (1¾ oz) lard

5 large spring onions (scallions), cut into 1 cm (½ inch) slices on the diagonal

16 fresh shiitake mushrooms, cut into smaller pieces if large

800 g (1 lb 12 oz) rump steak, thinly sliced across the grain

100 g (3½ oz) watercress, trimmed

4 eggs (optional)

1 To make the sauce, dissolve the dashi granules in 125 ml (4 fl oz/½ cup) water. Add the soy sauce, sake, mirin and sugar, and stir until combined.

2 Drain the noodles, then soak them in boiling water for 2 minutes. Rinse in cold water and drain well.

3 Melt the lard in a large frying pan over medium heat. Cook the spring onion, mushrooms and beef in batches, stirring, for 1–2 minutes each batch, or until just brown. Return the meat, spring onion and mushrooms to the pan, then add the sauce and watercress. Cook for 1 minute, or until heated through and the watercress has wilted—the sauce needs to just cover the ingredients but not drown them.

4 To serve, divide the noodles among four serving bowls and spoon the sauce evenly over the top. If desired, crack an egg into each bowl and break up through the sauce using chopsticks until it partially cooks.

Rinse the noodles well in a colander, under cold running water.

Add the sauce and watercress, and cook briefly until the watercress has just wilted.

NUTRITION PER SERVE
Protein 54 g; Fat 28 g; Carbohydrate 46 g; Dietary Fibre 5 g; Cholesterol 342 mg; 2755 kJ (660 Cal)

Lentil bhujia stew

PREPARATION TIME: 30 MINUTES + OVERNIGHT SOAKING + 30 MINUTES REFRIGERATION | TOTAL COOKING TIME: 1 HOUR 10 MINUTES | SERVES 4–6

370 g (13 oz/2 cups) green or brown lentils
1 large onion, grated
1 large potato, grated
1 teaspoon ground cumin
1 teaspoon ground coriander
1 teaspoon ground turmeric
90 g (3¼ oz/¾ cup) plain (all-purpose) flour
oil, for shallow-frying
2 garlic cloves, crushed
1 tablespoon grated fresh ginger
250 g (9 oz/1 cup) tomato paste
    (concentrated purée)
500 ml (17 fl oz/2 cups) vegetable stock
250 ml (9 fl oz/1 cup) cream
200 g (7 oz) green beans, trimmed, tailed and
    cut in half
2 carrots, sliced
2 hard-boiled eggs, chopped
rosemary sprigs, to garnish

1 Soak the lentils overnight in cold water. Drain well. Squeeze the excess moisture from the lentils, onion and potato using a tea towel (dish towel). Place them in a bowl with the ground spices and flour; mix well and leave for 10 minutes. With floured hands, shape the mixture into walnut-sized balls and place on a foil-lined tray. Cover and refrigerate for 30 minutes.

2 Heat 2 cm (¾ inch) of oil in a heavy-based frying pan. Cook the balls in batches over high heat until golden brown. Drain balls by placing on paper towels.

3 Heat 2 tablespoons of oil in a saucepan and gently fry the garlic and ginger for 2 minutes. Stir in the tomato paste, stock and cream. Bring to the boil, then reduce the heat and simmer for 10 minutes. Add the beans, lentil balls and carrot. Cook, covered, for 30 minutes, stirring twice. Add the egg and cook for 10 minutes. Garnish with rosemary to serve.

VARIATION: *Split peas can be used in this recipe in place of the lentils. Soak them in cold water overnight, then drain well before using.*

NUTRITION PER SERVE (6)
Protein 23 g; Fat 30 g; Carbohydrate 45 g; Dietary Fibre 13 g; Cholesterol 125 mg; 2290 kJ (550 Cal)

Shape the lentil mixture into walnut-sized balls, and place on a foil-lined tray.

Fry the lentil balls in oil in batches over high heat, until golden brown.

Add the beans, lentil balls and carrot to the simmering sauce.

Spicy vegetable stew with dhal

PREPARATION TIME: 25 MINUTES + 2 HOURS SOAKING | TOTAL COOKING TIME: 1 HOUR 35 MINUTES | SERVES 4–6

DHAL

165 g (5¾ oz/¾ cup) yellow split peas
5 cm (2 inch) piece fresh ginger, grated
2–3 garlic cloves, crushed
1 red chilli, seeded and chopped
2 tablespoons oil
1 teaspoon yellow mustard seeds
1 teaspoon cumin seeds
1 teaspoon ground cumin
½ teaspoon garam masala
1 red onion, cut into thin wedges
3 tomatoes, peeled, seeded and chopped
3 slender eggplants (aubergines), cut into 2 cm
    (¾ inch) slices
2 carrots, cut into 2 cm (¾ inch) slices
¼ cauliflower, cut into florets
375 ml (13 fl oz/1½ cups) vegetable stock
2 small zucchini (courgettes), cut into 3 cm
    (1¼ inch) slices
80 g (2¾ oz/½ cup) frozen peas
1 large handful coriander (cilantro) leaves,
    plus extra, to garnish.

1 Put the split peas in a bowl, cover with water and soak for 2 hours. Drain. To make the dhal put the split peas in a large saucepan with the ginger, garlic, chilli and 750 ml (26 fl oz/3 cups) water. Bring to the boil, reduce the heat and simmer for 45 minutes, or until soft.

2 Heat the oil in a large saucepan. Cook the spices over medium heat for 30 seconds, or until fragrant. Add the onion and cook for a further 2 minutes, or until the onion is soft. Stir in the tomato, eggplant, carrot and cauliflower.

3 Add the dhal mixture and stock, mix together well and simmer, covered, for 45 minutes, or until the vegetables are tender. Stir occasionally. Add the zucchini and peas during the last 10 minutes of cooking. Stir in the coriander leaves, then garnish and serve.

Peel the skin from the tomatoes, then remove the seeds and chop.

Simmer the dal mixture for 45 minutes, or until the split peas are soft.

NUTRITION PER SERVE (6)
Protein 11 g; Fat 7 g; Carbohydrate 20 g; Dietary Fibre 8.5 g; Cholesterol 17 mg; 780 kJ (186 Cal)

Lamb tagine

PREPARATION TIME: 15 MINUTES + 1 HOUR MARINATING | TOTAL COOKING TIME: 1 HOUR 45 MINUTES | SERVES 6–8

1.5 kg (3 lb 5 oz) leg or shoulder of lamb, cut
    into 2.5 cm (1 inch) pieces
3 garlic cloves, chopped
80 ml (2½ fl oz/⅓ cup) olive oil
2 teaspoons ground cumin
1 teaspoon ground ginger
1 teaspoon ground turmeric
1 teaspoon paprika
½ teaspoon ground cinnamon
2 onions, thinly sliced
600 ml (21 fl oz) beef stock
¼ preserved lemon, pulp discarded, zest rinsed
    and cut into thin strips
425 g (15 oz) tin chickpeas, drained
35 g (1¼ oz) cracked green olives (see NOTE)
1 large handful chopped coriander (cilantro)
    leaves, plus extra to garnish

1 Place the lamb pieces in a non-metallic bowl, add the garlic, 2 tablespoons of the oil and the ground cumin, ginger, turmeric, paprika, cinnamon, and ½ teaspoon ground black pepper and 1 teaspoon salt. Mix well to coat, then leave to marinate for 1 hour.

2 Heat the remaining oil in a large saucepan, add the lamb in batches and cook over high heat for 2–3 minutes, or until browned. Remove from the pan. Add the onion and cook for 2 minutes, then return the meat to the pan and add the beef stock. Reduce the heat and simmer, covered, for 1 hour.

3 Add the preserved lemon strips, drained chickpeas and olives, and cook, uncovered, for a further 30 minutes, or until the lamb is tender and the sauce has reduced and thickened. Stir in the coriander. Serve in bowls and garnish with extra coriander.

NOTE: *Cracked green olives are marinated in herbs and are available from specialty shops.*

NUTRITION PER SERVE (8)
Protein 50 g; Fat 20 g; Carbohydrate 11 g; Dietary Fibre 5.5 g; Cholesterol 124 mg; 1765 kJ (422 Cal)

Coat the lamb in the spice marinade, then leave to marinate for 1 hour.

Add the lemon strips, drained chickpeas and olives and cook, uncovered.

Moroccan seafood with coriander

PREPARATION TIME: 50 MINUTES | TOTAL COOKING TIME: 50 MINUTES | SERVES 6

2 tablespoons olive oil

2 red onions, roughly chopped

1 red capsicum (pepper), chopped

4 garlic cloves, crushed

2 teaspoons ground cumin

1 teaspoon ground coriander

2 teaspoons sweet paprika

½ teaspoon dried chilli flakes

250 ml (9 fl oz/1 cup) chicken or fish stock

425 g (15 oz) tin chopped tomatoes

80 ml (2½ fl oz/⅓ cup) orange juice

1 tablespoon sugar

40 g (1½ oz/⅓ cup) raisins

375 g (13 oz) baby new potatoes

500 g (1 lb 2 oz) baby octopus, cleaned

12 raw king prawns (shrimp), peeled and
deveined, leaving the tails intact

1 kg (2 lb 4 oz) thick white fish fillets, cut
into chunks

CORIANDER PUREE

2 very large handfuls coriander (cilantro)
leaves

2 tablespoons ground almonds

80 ml (2½ fl oz/⅓ cup) extra virgin olive oil

½ teaspoon ground cumin

1 teaspoon honey

1 Heat the olive oil in a large saucepan and then cook the onion over medium heat for about 5 minutes, or until soft. Add the capsicum and garlic, and cook for another minute. Add the cumin, coriander, paprika and chilli flakes, and cook until fragrant.

2 Pour in the stock, tomato, orange juice, sugar and raisins, and bring to the boil. Add the potatoes, reduce the heat to low and gently simmer for 20–30 minutes, or until the potatoes are just tender. Season to taste.

3 Use a small sharp knife to remove the octopus heads; slit the heads open and remove the gut. Grasp the body firmly and push the beak out with your index finger; remove and discard. Add the octopus, prawns and fish to the pan and cook, covered, for 10 minutes, or until the fish flakes when tested with a fork.

4 To make the coriander purée, place the coriander leaves and ground almonds in a food processor. With the motor running, drizzle in the oil and process until smooth, then add the cumin, honey and salt to taste. Process until well combined.

5 To serve, dish the stew onto serving plates and drizzle a spoonful of purée on top. Serve with couscous and a green leaf salad.

NUTRITION PER SERVE
Protein 60 g; Fat 30 g; Carbohydrate 25 g; Dietary Fibre 4 g; Cholesterol 175mg; 2415kJ (580cal)

Peel and devein the prawns, and cut the cleaned octopus into bite-sized pieces.

Process the coriander leaves and ground almonds, gradually drizzling in the oil.

Vegetable tagine

PREPARATION TIME: 20 MINUTES | TOTAL COOKING TIME: 1 HOUR | SERVES 4–6

2 tablespoons oil
2 onions, chopped
1 teaspoon ground ginger
2 teaspoons ground paprika
2 teaspoons ground cumin
1 cinnamon stick
pinch saffron threads
1.5 kg (3 lb 5 oz) vegetables, peeled and
    cut into large chunks (carrot, eggplant
    (aubergine), orange sweet potato, parsnip,
    potato, pumpkin (winter squash)
½ preserved lemon, rinsed, pith and flesh
    removed, thinly sliced
400 g (14 oz) tin chopped tomatoes
250 ml (9 fl oz/1 cup) vegetable stock
100 g (3½ oz) dried pears, halved
50 g (1¾ oz) pitted prunes
2 zucchini (courgettes), cut into large chunks
300 g (10½ oz) couscous
1 tablespoon olive oil
2 tablespoons chopped flat-leaf (Italian) parsley
50 g (1¾ oz/⅓ cup) blanched almonds

1   Preheat the oven to 180°C (350°F/Gas 4).
Heat the oil in a large flameproof dish, add the
onion and cook over medium heat for 5 minutes.
Add the spices and cook for 3 minutes.

2   Add the 1.5 kg chopped vegetables and
cook, stirring, until coated and the vegetables
soften. Add the lemon, tomato, stock, pears and
prunes. Cover, transfer to the oven and cook
for 30 minutes. Add the zucchini and cook for
15–20 minutes, or until the vegetables are tender.

3   Cover the couscous with the olive oil and
500 ml (17 fl oz/2 cups) boiling water, and stand
until all the water absorbs. Fluff with a fork.

4   Remove the cinnamon stick from the vegetables,
then stir in the parsley. Serve on a large platter
with the couscous on the bottom and the
vegetables on top. Sprinkle with almonds.

Cook the vegetables until they are coated in the spices and start to soften.

Once all the water has been absorbed, fluff the couscous with a fork.

NUTRITION PER SERVE (6)
Protein 15 g; Fat 15.4 g; Carbohydrate 80.5 g; Dietary
Fibre 10.6 g; Cholesterol 0 mg; 2260 kJ (540 Cal)

Chilli chicken with tacos

PREPARATION TIME: 10 MINUTES | TOTAL COOKING TIME: 45 MINUTES | SERVES 4

1 tablespoon olive oil

1 onion, finely chopped

500 g (1 lb 2 oz) minced (ground) chicken

1–2 teaspoons mild chilli powder

440 g (15½ oz) tin chopped tomatoes

2 tablespoons tomato paste (concentrated
purée)

1–2 teaspoons soft brown sugar

425 g (15 oz) tin red kidney beans, drained
and rinsed

taco shells, or corn chips, to serve

sour cream, to serve

1 Heat the oil in a large saucepan. Add the chopped onion and cook over medium heat for 3 minutes, or until soft. Increase the heat to high and add the chicken. Cook until the chicken has browned, breaking up any lumps with a wooden spoon.

2 Add the chilli powder to the chicken and cook for 1 minute. Stir in the tomato, tomato paste and 125 ml (4 fl oz/½ cup) water.

3 Bring to the boil, then reduce the heat and simmer for 30 minutes. Stir through the sugar to taste and the kidney beans. Season. Serve along with warmed corn chips or in taco shells with the sour cream.

NUTRITION PER SERVE
Protein 37 g; Fat 8.5 g; Carbohydrate 20 g; Dietary
Fibre 9 g; Cholesterol 60 mg; 1305 kJ (312 Cal)

Add the chicken to the onion and cook until browned, breaking up any lumps.

Stir the tomato, tomato paste and water into the chicken mixture.

After 30 minutes, stir in the sugar and drained kidney beans.

Beef pot roast

PREPARATION TIME: 15 MINUTES | TOTAL COOKING TIME: 3 HOURS 15 MINUTES | SERVES 6

300 g (10½ oz) baby brown onions
2 carrots
3 parsnips, peeled
40 g (1½ oz) butter
1–1.5 kg (2 lb 4 oz–3 lb 5 oz) eye of
    silverside, trimmed of fat (see NOTE)
60 ml (2 fl oz/¼ cup) dry red wine
1 large tomato, finely chopped
250 ml (9 fl oz/1 cup) beef stock
mild or hot English mustard, to serve

1 Put the onions in a heatproof bowl and cover with boiling water. Leave for 1 minute, then drain well. Allow them to cool, then peel off the skins.

2 Cut the carrots and parsnips in half lengthways, then into even-sized pieces. Heat half the butter in a large heavy-based saucepan that will tightly fit the meat (it will shrink during cooking), add the onions, carrot and parsnip, and cook, stirring, over medium–high heat until browned. Remove from the pan. Add the remaining butter to the pan and add the meat, browning well all over. Increase the heat to high and pour in the wine. Bring to the boil, then add the tomato and stock. Return to the boil, then reduce the heat to low, cover and simmer for 2 hours, turning once. Add the vegetables and simmer, covered, for 1 hour.

3 Remove the meat from the pan and put it on a board ready for carving. Cover with foil and leave it to stand while finishing the sauce.

4 Increase the heat to high and boil the pan juices with the vegetables for 10 minutes to reduce and thicken slightly. Skim off any excess fat, and taste before seasoning. Slice the meat and arrange on a serving platter or individual serving plates with the vegetables. Drizzle generously with the pan juices. Serve with mustard and pepper.

NUTRITION PER SERVE
Protein 60 g; Fat 10 g; Carbohydrate 95 g; Dietary
Fibre 3.5 g; Cholesterol 185 mg; 1690 kJ (405 Cal)

NOTE: *Eye of silverside is a tender, long-shaped cut of silverside that carves easily into serving-sized pieces. A regular piece of silverside or topside may be substituted.*

Put the baby brown onions in a bowl and cover with boiling water.

Add the butter and meat to the pan, and brown the meat well on all sides.

Add the vegetables to the meat, then cover and simmer for 1 hour.

Bean and capsicum stew

PREPARATION TIME: 20 MINUTES + SOAKING | TOTAL COOKING TIME: 1 HOUR 35 MINUTES | SERVES 4–6

200 g (7 oz/1 cup) dried haricot beans (see NOTE)

2 tablespoons olive oil

2 large garlic cloves, crushed

1 red onion, halved and cut into thin wedges

1 red capsicum (pepper), cut into 1.5 cm (⅝ inch) squares

1 green capsicum (pepper), cut into 1.5 cm (⅝ inch) squares

2 x 400 g (14 oz) tins chopped tomatoes

2 tablespoons tomato paste (concentrated purée)

500 ml (17 fl oz/2 cups) vegetable stock

2 tablespoons chopped basil

125 g (4½ oz/⅔ cup) Kalamata olives, pitted

1–2 teaspoons soft brown sugar

basil leaves, to garnish

1 Put the beans in a large bowl, cover with cold water and soak overnight. Rinse well, then transfer to a saucepan, cover with cold water and cook for 45 minutes, or until just tender. Drain.

2 Heat the oil in a large saucepan. Cook the garlic and onion wedges over medium heat for 2–3 minutes, or until the onion is soft. Add the red and green capsicum, and cook for a further 5 minutes.

3 Stir in the tomato, tomato paste, stock and beans. Simmer, covered, for 40 minutes, or until the beans are cooked through. Stir in the basil, olives and sugar. Season with salt and pepper, garnish with basil leaves. Serve piping hot with crusty bread.

NOTE: *200 g (1 cup) of dried haricot beans /'yields about 2½ cups cooked beans. You can use 2½ cups tinned haricot or borlotti (cranberry) beans if you prefer.*

Cook the garlic, onion wedges and capsicum in a large saucepan.

Simmer the mixture for 40 minutes, or until the beans are cooked through.

NUTRITION PER SERVE (6)
Protein 10 g; Fat 8 g; Carbohydrate 27 g; Dietary Fibre 9 g; Cholesterol 0 mg; 965 kJ (231 Cal)

Veal goulash

PREPARATION TIME: 25 MINUTES | TOTAL COOKING TIME: 2 HOURS | SERVES 4

500 g (1 lb 2 oz) veal, cut into 2.5 cm
    (1 inch) pieces
2 tablespoons plain (all-purpose) flour
2 tablespoons olive oil
2 onions, thinly sliced
2 garlic cloves, finely chopped
1 tablespoon sweet paprika
1 teaspoon ground cumin
440 g (15½ oz) tin chopped tomatoes
2 carrots, sliced
½ red capsicum (pepper), chopped
½ green capsicum (pepper), chopped
250 ml (9 fl oz/1 cup) beef stock
125 ml (4 fl oz/½ cup) red wine
125 g (4½ oz/½ cup) sour cream
chopped flat-leaf (Italian) parsley, to garnish

1   Put the veal and flour in a plastic bag and shake to coat the veal with the flour. Shake off any excess. Heat 1 tablespoon of the oil in a large, deep heavy-based saucepan over medium heat. Brown the meat well in batches, then remove the meat and set aside.

2   Add the remaining oil to the pan. Cook the onion, garlic, paprika and cumin for 5 minutes, stirring frequently. Return the meat and any juices to the pan with the tomato, carrot and capsicum. Cover and cook for 10 minutes.

3   Add the stock and wine, and season with salt and pepper. Stir well, then cover and simmer over very low heat for 1½ hours. Stir in half the sour cream, season with more salt and pepper if needed and serve garnished with parsley and the remaining sour cream if desired. Delicious served with buttered boiled small potatoes or noodles.

NOTE: *If you prefer your sauce to be a little thicker, cook, uncovered, for 5 minutes over high heat before adding the sour cream.*

Remove any excess fat, then cut the veal into 2.5 cm (1 inch) pieces.

Put the veal and flour in a plastic bag and shake to coat well.

NUTRITION PER SERVE
Protein 30 g; Fat 25 g; Carbohydrate 15 g; Dietary Fibre 4.5 g; Cholesterol 144 mg; 1790 kJ (430 Cal)

Beef stroganoff

PREPARATION TIME: 25 MINUTES I TOTAL COOKING TIME: 30 MINUTES I SERVES 6

1 kg (2 lb 4 oz) piece rump steak, trimmed
40 g (1½ oz/⅓ cup) plain (all-purpose) flour
¼ teaspoon ground black pepper
60 ml (2 fl oz/¼ cup) olive oil
1 large onion, chopped
500 g (1 lb 2 oz) baby mushrooms
1 tablespoon sweet paprika
1 tablespoon tomato paste
2 teaspoons French mustard
125 ml (4 fl oz/½ cup) dry white wine
60 ml (2 fl oz/¼ cup) chicken stock
185 g (6½ oz/¾ cup) sour cream
1 tablespoon finely chopped flat-leaf (Italian)
   parsley

NUTRITION PER SERVE
Protein 42 g; Fat 28 g; Carbohydrate 9.5 g; Dietary
Fibre 3.5 g; Cholesterol 147 mg; 1970 kJ (470 Cal)

1   Slice the meat across the grain into short, thin pieces. Combine the flour and pepper. Toss the meat in the seasoned flour, shaking off the excess.

2   Heat 2 tablespoons of the oil in a heavy-based saucepan. Cook the meat quickly in small batches over medium–high heat until well browned. Drain on paper towels.

3   Heat the remaining oil in the pan. Cook the onion over medium heat for 3 minutes, or until softened. Add the mushrooms and stir for 5 minutes.

4   Add the paprika, tomato paste, mustard, wine and stock to the pan, and bring to the boil. Reduce the heat and simmer for 5 minutes, uncovered, stirring occasionally. Return the meat to the pan with the sour cream, and stir until combined and just heated through. Sprinkle with the parsley just before serving.

Toss the meat in the seasoned flour, shaking off any of the excess.

Add the mushrooms to the cooked onion and stir for 5 minutes.

Return the meat to the pan with the sour cream, and stir until combined and heated through.

Ham, leek and potato ragu

PREPARATION TIME: 25 MINUTES I TOTAL COOKING TIME: 45 MINUTES I SERVES 4–6

50 g (1¾ oz) butter

2 tablespoons olive oil

250 g (9 oz) piece double-smoked ham, cut
    into cubes (see NOTE)

3 garlic cloves, finely chopped

3 leeks (white part only), sliced

1.5 kg (3 lb 5 oz) potatoes, peeled and cut into
    large chunks

500 ml (17 fl oz/2 cups) chicken stock

2 tablespoons brandy

125 ml (4 fl oz/½ cup) cream

1 tablespoon each of chopped oregano and
    parsley

1   Heat the butter and oil in a large heavy-based
saucepan. Cook the ham, garlic and leek over
low heat for 10 minutes, stirring regularly.

2   Add the potato and cook for 10 minutes,
stirring regularly.

3   Slowly stir in the stock and brandy.
Cover and gently simmer. Cook for another
15–20 minutes until the potato is tender but still
chunky, and sauce has thickened. Add cream and
herbs, and season. Simmer for another 5 minutes.

NOTE: *You can use any type of ham for this
recipe. A double-smoked ham will give a good,
hearty flavour.*

NUTRITION PER SERVE (6)
Protein 15 g; Fat 25 g; Carbohydrate 40 g; Dietary
Fibre 9 g; Cholesterol 70 mg; 1990 kJ (475 Cal)

Heat the butter and oil in a pan, then cook the ham, garlic and leek.

Stir in the stock and brandy, then cover and leave it to simmer.

Once the sauce has thickened, add the cream and chopped herbs.

Seafood and fennel stew

PREPARATION TIME: 10 MINUTES | TOTAL COOKING TIME: 30 MINUTES | SERVES 6

2 tablespoons olive oil
1 large fennel bulb, thinly sliced
2 leeks (white part only), thinly sliced
2 garlic cloves, crushed
½ teaspoon paprika
2 tablespoons Pernod or Ricard
200 ml (7 fl oz) dry white wine
18 mussels, scrubbed and hairy beards removed
¼ teaspoon saffron threads
¼ teaspoon thyme leaves
6 baby octopus
16 raw prawns (shrimp), peeled and deveined,
    leaving the tails intact
500 g (1 lb 2 oz) swordfish steaks, cut into
    large chunks
400 g (14 oz) baby new potatoes
fennel greens, to garnish

1   Heat the oil in a large saucepan over medium heat. Add the fennel, leek and garlic. Stir in the paprika, season lightly and cook for 8 minutes, or until softened. Add the Pernod and wine, and stir for 1 minute, or until reduced by one-third.

2   Add the mussels, firstly discarding any open or cracked ones. Cover and cook for 1 minute, or until opened, discarding any that do not open. Remove from the pan to cool; remove from the shells and set aside.

3   Add the saffron and thyme to the pan, and cook for 1–2 minutes, stirring. Adjust the seasoning and transfer to a large, flameproof casserole dish.

4   Use a small sharp knife to remove the octopus heads. Grasp the bodies and push the beaks out with your index finger; remove and discard. Slit the heads and remove the gut. Mix the octopus, prawns, fish and potatoes into the stew. Cover and cook gently for 10 minutes, or until tender. Add the mussels, cover and heat through. Garnish with fennel greens and serve.

NUTRITION PER SERVE
Protein 65 g; Fat 10 g; Carbohydrate 15 g; Dietary Fibre 5 g; Cholesterol 390 mg; 1840 kJ (440 Cal)

Add the Pernod and wine to the softened fennel, leek and garlic mixture.

Cut off the octopus heads. Grasp the body firmly and push out the beak.

Creamy tomato and chicken stew

PREPARATION TIME: 35 MINUTES | TOTAL COOKING TIME: 50 MINUTES | SERVES 4–6

4 bacon slices

2 tablespoons oil

50 g (1¾ oz) butter

300 g (10½ oz) small button mushrooms, halved

1.5 kg (3 lb 5 oz) boneless, skinless chicken pieces

2 onions, chopped

2 garlic cloves, crushed

400 g (14 oz) tin tomatoes, chopped or whole

250 ml (9 fl oz/1 cup) chicken stock

250 ml (9 fl oz/1 cup) cream

2 tablespoons chopped parsley

2 tablespoons lemon thyme leaves

NUTRITION PER SERVE (6)
Protein 70 g; Fat 40 g; Carbohydrate 7 g; Dietary Fibre 3 g; Cholesterol 215 mg; 2650 kJ (630 Cal)

1 Chop the bacon into large pieces. Place a large heavy-based saucepan over medium heat. Brown the bacon, stirring, then remove and set aside on paper towels.

2 Heat half the oil and one-third of the butter in the saucepan until foaming, then add the mushrooms and cook until they are softened and golden brown. Remove from the pan with a slotted spoon.

3 Add the remaining oil to the pan with a little more butter. When the oil is hot, brown the chicken pieces in batches over high heat until the skin is golden all over and a little crisp. Remove the chicken pieces from the pan and drain on paper towels.

4 Heat the remaining butter in the pan. Add the onion and garlic, and cook over medium–high heat for about 3 minutes, or until softened. Pour in the tomatoes, stock and cream. Return the bacon, mushrooms and chicken pieces to the pan, and simmer over low–medium heat for 25 minutes. Stir in the parsley and thyme, season with salt and freshly ground black pepper, and simmer for another 5 minutes before serving.

When the oil and butter are foaming, add the mushrooms and cook until soft.

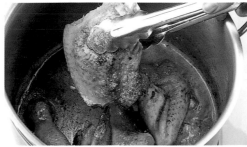

Brown the chicken pieces in batches over high heat until the skin is golden and crisp.

Add the tomatoes, stock and cream to the softened onion and garlic.

Beef bourguignonne

PREPARATION TIME: 10 MINUTES | TOTAL COOKING TIME: 2 HOURS | SERVES 4

1 kg (2 lb 4 oz) stewing beef, cubed
30 g (1 oz/¼ cup) seasoned plain (all-purpose) flour
1 tablespoon oil
150 g (5½ oz) bacon slices, diced
8 bulb spring onions (scallions), greens trimmed to 2 cm (¾ inch)
200 g (7 oz) button mushrooms
500 ml (17 fl oz/2 cups) red wine
2 tablespoons tomato paste (concentrated purée)
500 ml (17 fl oz/2 cups) beef stock
1 bouquet garni (see NOTE)

1   Toss the beef in the seasoned flour until evenly coated, shaking off any excess. Heat the oil in a large saucepan over high heat. Cook the beef in three batches for about 3 minutes, or until well browned all over, adding a little extra oil as needed. Remove from the pan.

2   Add the bacon to the pan and cook for 2 minutes, or until browned. Remove with a slotted spoon and add to the beef. Add the spring onions and mushrooms, and cook for 5 minutes, or until the onions are browned. Remove.

3   Slowly pour the red wine into the pan, scraping up any sediment from the bottom with a wooden spoon. Stir in the tomato paste and stock. Add the bouquet garni and return the beef, bacon and any juices. Bring to the boil, then reduce the heat and simmer for 45 minutes. Return the spring onions and mushrooms to the pan. Cook for 1 hour, or until the meat is very tender and the sauce is glossy. Serve with steamed new potatoes or mash.

NOTE: *To make a bouquet garni, wrap the green part of a leek around a bay leaf, a sprig of thyme, a sprig of parsley and celery leaves, and tie with string. The combination of herbs can be varied according to taste.*

Toss the diced beef in the seasoned flour until evenly coated.

Slowly pour the red wine into the pan, scraping up any sediment with a wooden spoon.

NUTRITION PER SERVE
Protein 65 g; Fat 20 g; Carbohydrate 9.5 g; Dietary Fibre 3 g; Cholesterol 169 mg; 2363 kJ (563 Cal)

Lamb and mustard stew

PREPARATION TIME: 15 MINUTES | TOTAL COOKING TIME: 1 HOUR 40 MINUTES | SERVES 4

750 g (1 lb 10 oz) lean lamb fillets, cut into
    2.5 cm (1 inch) cubes
60¼ g (2 oz/½ cup) plain (all-purpose) flour
1 tablespoon oil
16 baby onions
250 ml (9 fl oz/1 cup) white wine
250 ml (9 fl oz/1 cup) chicken stock
125 g (4½ oz/½ cup) dijon mustard
2 tablespoons chopped thyme

1   Toss the lamb cubes in the flour, shaking off any excess. Heat the oil in a heavy-based saucepan over high heat. Add the lamb in small batches and cook for 3 minutes, or until well browned, turning occasionally. Drain the meat on paper towels.

2   Return the lamb to the pan. Add the onions, wine, stock, mustard and thyme. Bring to the boil, then reduce the heat to low and simmer, covered, for 1 hour, stirring occasionally. Remove the lid and simmer for another 30 minutes, or until the lamb is tender. Serve with pasta.

NOTE: *A small, boned leg of lamb is ideal for making this dish.*

NUTRITION PER SERVE
Protein 46 g; Fat 11 g; Carbohydrate 18 g; Dietary
Fibre 2.5 g; Cholesterol 124 mg; 1655 kJ (395 Cal)

Toss the lamb cubes in the flour, shaking off any excess flour.

Brown the lamb in small batches, turning occasionally, then drain on paper towels.

Add the onions, wine, stock, mustard and thyme to the pan.

Pork and eggplant hotpot

PREPARATION TIME: 20 MINUTES | TOTAL COOKING TIME: 1 HOUR 30 MINUTES | SERVES 4

olive oil, for cooking
375 g (13 oz) slender eggplants (aubergines),
    cut into 3 cm (1¼ inch) slices
8 bulb spring onions (scallions)
400 g (14 oz) tin chopped tomatoes
2 garlic cloves, crushed
2 teaspoons ground cumin
500 g (1 lb 2 oz) pork fillet, cut into 3 cm
    (1¼ inch) thick slices
seasoned plain (all-purpose) flour
170 ml (5½ fl oz/⅔ cup) cider
1 rosemary sprig
2 tablespoons chopped toasted almonds

1 Heat 60 ml (2 fl oz/¼ cup) of oil in a large heavy-based frying pan. Brown the eggplant in batches over high heat, adding oil as needed. Remove and set aside.

2 Quarter the spring onions along their length. Add some oil to the pan and fry the spring onion over medium heat for 5 minutes. Add the tomato, garlic and cumin, and cook for 2 minutes. Remove and set aside.

3 Coat the pork in the seasoned flour, shaking off any excess. Brown in batches over medium–high heat until golden, adding oil as needed. Remove and set aside.

4 Add the cider to the pan and stir well, scraping down the side and base. Allow to boil for 1–2 minutes, then add 125 ml (4 fl oz/½ cup/4 fl oz) water. Reduce the heat and stir in the spring onion and tomato mixture. Add the pork, season, and poke the rosemary sprig into the stew. Partially cover and simmer gently for 20 minutes.

5 Layer the eggplant on top, partially cover and cook for 25 minutes, or until the pork is tender. Just before serving, gently toss the almonds through.

NUTRITION PER SERVE
Protein 30 g; Fat 7 g; Carbohydrate 10 g; Dietary Fibre 5 g; Cholesterol 60 mg; 980 kJ (235 Cal)

Fry the eggplant in batches over high heat until browned on both sides.

Add the cider to the frying pan, scraping the brown bits from the side and base.

Layer the eggplant over the top of the pork and tomato mixture.

French-style octopus

PREPARATION TIME: 25 MINUTES | TOTAL COOKING TIME: 1 HOUR 30 MINUTES | SERVES 6

1 kg (2 lb/4 oz) baby octopus
60 ml (2 fl oz/¼ cup) olive oil
1 large brown onion, chopped
2 garlic cloves
500 g (1 lb 2 oz) ripe tomatoes, peeled, seeded
    and chopped
330 ml (11¼ fl oz/1⅓ cups) dry white wine
¼ teaspoon saffron threads
2 thyme sprigs
2 tablespoons roughly chopped flat-leaf
    (Italian) parsley

1 To clean the octopus, use a small sharp knife and cut each head from the tentacles. Remove the eyes by cutting a round of flesh from the base of each head. To clean the heads, carefully slit them open and remove the gut, avoiding the ink sac. Rinse thoroughly. Cut the heads in half. Push out the beaks from the centre of the tentacles from the cut side. Cut the tentacles into sets of four or two, depending on the size of the octopus. Rinse under running water.

2 Blanch all the octopus in boiling water for 2 minutes, then drain and allow to cool slightly. Pat dry with paper towels.

3 Heat the olive oil in a heavy-based frying pan and cook the onion for 7–8 minutes over medium heat until lightly golden. Add the octopus and garlic to the pan, and cook for another 2–3 minutes. Add the tomato, wine, saffron and thyme. Add just enough water to cover the octopus.

4 Simmer, covered, for 1 hour. Uncover and cook for another 15 minutes, or until the octopus is tender and the sauce has thickened a little. The cooking time will vary depending upon the size of the octopus. Season to taste. Serve hot or at room temperature, sprinkled with parsley.

Carefully cut between the head and the tentacles of the octopus, just below the eyes.

When you have slit the head open, rinse under running water to remove any remaining gut.

NUTRITION PER SERVE
Protein 29 g; Fat 10.5 g; Carbohydrate 4.5 g; Dietary Fibre 1.5 g; Cholesterol 89 mg; 1120 kJ (270 Cal)

Chilli con carne

PREPARATION TIME: 25 MINUTES + OVERNIGHT SOAKING | TOTAL COOKING TIME: 2 HOURS 15 MINUTES | SERVES 6

185 g (6½ oz) dried black-eyed peas

1½ tablespoons oil

900 g (2 lb) trimmed chuck steak, cut into chunks

3 onions, thinly sliced

2 garlic cloves, chopped

2 teaspoons ground cumin

1 tablespoon paprika

½ teaspoon allspice powder

1–2 teaspoons chilli powder

650 g (1 lb 7 oz) tomatoes, peeled, seeded and finely chopped

1 tablespoon soft brown sugar

1 tablespoon red wine vinegar

1   Put the peas in a bowl, cover with plenty of water and leave to soak overnight. Drain well.

2   Heat 1 tablespoon of the oil in a large heavy-based saucepan and cook the meat in two batches over medium–high heat for 2 minutes, or until well browned. Remove from the pan.

3   Pour the rest of the oil into the saucepan and add the onion. Cook over medium heat for 5 minutes, or until translucent. Add the garlic and spices and cook, stirring, for 1 minute, or until aromatic. Add 500 ml (17 fl oz/2 cups) water and stir in.

4   Return the meat to the pan with the peas and tomato. Bring to the boil, then reduce the heat to low and simmer, partially covered, for 2 hours, or until the meat is tender and the chilli con carne is thick and dryish, stirring occasionally. Towards the end of the cooking time the mixture may start to catch, so add a little water if necessary. Stir through the sugar and vinegar, and season with salt to taste. This is delicious served with flour tortillas and grated cheddar cheese.

To peel the tomatoes, score a cross in the base, soak in boiling water, then peel away the skin.

Soak the black-eyed peas in a bowl of cold water overnight.

NUTRITION PER SERVE
Protein 43 g; Fat 10 g; Carbohydrate 54 g; Dietary Fibre 10 g; Cholesterol 100 mg; 2040 kJ (486 Cal)

Easy seafood paella

PREPARATION TIME: 25 MINUTES | TOTAL COOKING TIME: 45 MINUTES | SERVES 6

300 g (10½ oz) skinless firm white fish fillets (see NOTE)

250 g (9 oz) black mussels

500 g (1 lb 2 oz) raw prawns (shrimp), peeled and deveined, leaving the tails intact

200 g (7 oz) squid rings

60 ml (2 fl oz/¼ cup) olive oil

1 large onion, diced

3 garlic cloves, finely chopped

1 small red capsicum (pepper), thinly sliced

1 small red chilli, seeded and chopped (optional)

2 teaspoons paprika

1 teaspoon ground turmeric

2 tomatoes, peeled and diced

1 tablespoon tomato paste (concentrated purée)

400 g (14 oz/2 cups) long-grain rice

125 ml (4 fl oz/½ cup) white wine

1.25 litres (44 fl oz/5 cups) fish stock

2 tablespoons chopped flat-leaf (Italian) parsley, for serving

lemon wedges, for serving

1 Cut the fish fillets into 2.5 cm (1 inch) cubes. Scrub the mussels and pull out the hairy beards and rinse well. Discard any broken mussels or those that don't close when tapped on a work surface. Refrigerate all the seafood, covered, until ready to use.

2 Heat the oil in a paella pan or a large deep frying pan with a lid. Add the onion, garlic, capsicum and chilli to the pan, and cook over medium heat for 2 minutes, or until the onion and capsicum are soft. Add the paprika, turmeric and 1 teaspoon salt, and stir-fry for 1–2 minutes, or until aromatic.

3 Add the tomato and cook for 5 minutes, or until softened. Add the tomato paste. Stir in the rice until it is well coated.

4 Pour in the wine and simmer until almost absorbed. Add all the fish stock and bring to the boil. Reduce heat to low–medium and simmer for 20 minutes, or until almost all the liquid is absorbed into the rice. There is no need to stir the rice, but you may wish to fluff it up with a fork.

5 Add the mussels to the pan, cover and cook for 2–3 minutes over low heat. Add the prawns and cook for 2 3 minutes. Add the fish, cover and cook for 3 minutes. Finally, add the squid rings and cook for 1–2 minutes. By this time, the mussels should have opened— discard any unopened ones. The prawns should be pink and the fish should flake easily

when tested with a fork. The squid should be white, moist and tender. Cook for another 2–3 minutes if the seafood is not quite cooked, but avoid overcooking as the seafood will toughen and dry out.

6 Serve with parsley and lemon wedges. Delicious with a tossed salad.

NOTE: *You can use just fish, or other seafood such as scampi, octopus and crabs. If using just fish, choose one with few bones and chunky flesh, such as ling, blue-eye or warehou.*

NUTRITION PER SERVE
Protein 45 g; Fat 15 g; Carbohydrate 59 g; Dietary Fibre 3.5 g; Cholesterol 217 mg; 2360 kJ (560 Cal)

Pull out the dark vein from along the back of each prawn, leaving on the tail.

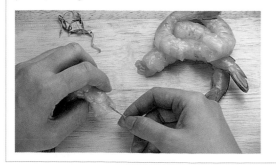

Protect your hands with rubber gloves when seeding the chilli.

Add the paprika and turmeric to the pan, and stir until aromatic.

Moroccan chicken

PREPARATION TIME: 10 MINUTES + 5 MINUTES STANDING | TOTAL COOKING TIME: 35 MINUTES | SERVES 4

1 tablespoon Moroccan spice blend
800 g (1 lb 12 oz) skinless, boneless chicken
    thighs, halved
1 tablespoon oil
60 g (2¼ oz) butter
1 large onion, cut into wedges
1 cinnamon stick
2 garlic cloves, crushed
2 tablespoons lemon juice
250 ml (9 fl oz/1 cup) chicken stock
75 g (2½ oz/⅓ cup) pitted prunes, halved
280 g (10 oz/1½ cups) couscous
lemon wedges, to serve

1   Sprinkle half the spice blend over the chicken. Heat the oil and 20 g (¾ oz) of the butter in a large deep-sided frying pan over medium heat. Cook the chicken in batches for 5 minutes, or until evenly browned. Remove from the pan, then add the onion and cinnamon stick, and cook for 2–3 minutes before adding the garlic. Return the chicken to the pan and add the lemon juice and the remaining spice blend. Season to taste with salt and pepper, then cook, covered, for 5 minutes.

2   Add the stock and prunes to the pan, and bring to the boil. Reduce the heat to low–medium and cook, uncovered, for 15 minutes, or until the chicken is cooked and the liquid has reduced. Before serving, stir 20 g (¾ oz) of the butter into the sauce.

3   About 10 minutes before the chicken is ready, place the couscous in a heatproof bowl, add 375 ml (13 fl oz/1½ cups) boiling water and stand for 3–5 minutes. Stir in the remaining butter and fluff with a fork until the butter has melted and the grains have separated. Serve with the chicken and lemon wedges.

NOTE: *Depending on the quality and freshness of the Moroccan spice blend you buy, you may need to use a little more than specified in the recipe.*

Cook the chicken pieces in batches until they are evenly browned.

When the couscous has absorbed the water, fluff up the grains with a fork.

NUTRITION PER SERVE
Protein 47 g; Fat 32 g; Carbohydrate 56 g; Dietary Fibre 3 g; Cholesterol 213 mg; 2905 kJ (695 Cal)

Lamb meatballs

PREPARATION TIME: 30 MINUTES | TOTAL COOKING TIME: 1 HOUR | SERVES 4

1 kg (2 lb 4 oz) minced (ground) lamb
1 onion, finely chopped
2 garlic cloves, finely chopped
2 tablespoons finely chopped flat-leaf (Italian)
   parsley
2 tablespoons finely chopped coriander
   (cilantro) leaves
½ teaspoon cayenne pepper
½ teaspoon ground allspice
½ teaspoon ground ginger
½ teaspoon ground cardamom
1 teaspoon ground cumin
1 teaspoon paprika

SAUCE
2 tablespoons olive oil
1 onion, finely chopped
2 garlic cloves, finely chopped
2 teaspoons ground cumin
½ teaspoon ground cinnamon
1 teaspoon paprika
2 x 400 g (14 oz) tins chopped tomatoes
2 teaspoons harissa
1 bunch coriander (cilantro) leaves, chopped

1   Preheat the oven to 180°C (350°F/Gas 4).
Lightly grease two baking trays. Place the lamb,
onion, garlic, herbs and spices in a bowl, and mix
together well and then season. Roll tablespoons
of the mixture into balls and place on trays. Bake
for 18–20 minutes, or until browned.

2   Meanwhile, to make the sauce, heat the oil in
a large saucepan, add the onion and cook over
medium heat for 5 minutes, or until soft. Add the
garlic, cumin, cinnamon and paprika, and cook
for 1 minute, or until fragrant.

3   Stir in the tomato and harissa, and bring to
the boil. Reduce heat and simmer for 20 minutes,
then add the meatballs and simmer for another
10 minutes, or until cooked. Stir in the coriander,
and serve.

NUTRITION PER SERVE
Protein 53 g; Fat 37 g; Carbohydrate 10 g; Dietary
Fibre 4 g; Cholesterol 158 mg; 2434 kJ (580 Cal)

Roll tablespoons of the lamb and spice mixture into balls and place on trays.

Add the garlic and spices to the onion, and cook until fragrant.

Beef and peppercorn stew

PREPARATION TIME: 15 MINUTES | TOTAL COOKING TIME: 2 HOURS | SERVES 4

1 kg (2 lb 4 oz) chuck steak, cut into 3 cm
    (1¼ inch) cubes
2 teaspoons cracked black peppercorns
40 g (1½ oz) butter
2 tablespoons oil
1 large onion, thinly sliced
2 garlic cloves, sliced
1½ tablespoons plain (all-purpose) flour
2 tablespoons brandy
750 ml (26 fl oz/3 cups) beef stock
1 tablespoon worcestershire sauce
2 teaspoons dijon mustard
500 g (1 lb 2 oz) baby new potatoes
60 ml (2 fl oz/¼ cup) cream
2 tablespoons chopped parsley

NUTRITION PER SERVE
Protein 60 g; Fat 30 g; Carbohydrate 20 g; Dietary
Fibre 3 g; Cholesterol 215 mg; 2580 kJ (615 Cal)

1   Toss the steak in the peppercorns. Heat half the butter and half the oil in a large heavy-based saucepan. Brown half the steak over high heat, then remove and set aside. Heat the remaining butter and oil, and brown the remaining steak. Remove from the pan and set aside.

2   Add the onion and garlic to the pan and cook, stirring, until the onion is golden. Add the flour and stir until browned. Remove from the heat.

3   Combine the brandy, beef stock, worcestershire sauce and mustard, and gradually stir into the onion mixture. Return to the heat, add the steak and any juices, then simmer, covered, for 1¼ hours.

4   Add the potatoes and simmer, uncovered, for a further 30 minutes, or until the meat and potatoes are tender. Stir in the cream and parsley, and season to taste with salt and freshly ground black pepper. This is delicious served with a green salad.

Cut the steak into 3 cm (1¼ inch) cubes, using a sharp knife.

Add the brandy, stock, worcestershire sauce and mustard to the onion mixture.

Add the potatoes and simmer, uncovered, for a further 30 minutes, or until tender.

Osso bucco

PREPARATION TIME: 30 MINUTES | TOTAL COOKING TIME: 2 HOURS 30 MINUTES | SERVES 4–6

12 meaty pieces veal shank, osso bucco style
40 g (1½ oz/⅓ cup) seasoned plain (all-purpose) flour
20 g (¾ oz) butter
80 ml (2½ fl oz/⅓ cup) olive oil
1 onion, diced
1 carrot, diced
1 celery stalk, diced
1 bay leaf
1 garlic clove, crushed
500 ml (17 fl oz/2 cups) veal or chicken stock
250ml (9 fl oz/1 cup) white wine
80 ml (2½ fl oz/⅓ cup) lemon juice

GREMOLATA
4 tablespoons flat-leaf (Italian) parsley
2 garlic cloves, finely chopped
1 tablespoon grated lemon zest

1   Lightly dust the veal shanks in the seasoned flour. Heat the butter and 60 ml (2 fl oz/¼ cup) of the oil in a large deep-sided frying pan over high heat until sizzling. Add the veal and cook in batches for 5 minutes, or until brown all over. Remove from the pan.

2   Heat the remaining oil in the frying pan, add the onion, carrot, celery and bay leaf, and cook for 10 minutes, or until softened and starting to brown. Add the garlic, stock, wine and lemon juice, and stir to combine, scraping the bottom of the pan to remove any sediment. Return the veal to the pan, bring to the boil, then reduce the heat to low, cover and simmer for 1½–2 hours, or until the veal is very tender and falling off the bone and the sauce has reduced. Season to taste.

3   To make the gremolata, finely chop the parsley and mix together with the garlic and lemon zest. Sprinkle over just before serving. Serve with soft polenta.

Cook the veal shank pieces in batches until they are well browned.

Cook the onion, carrot, celery and bay leaf in oil until softened.

NUTRITION PER SERVE (6)
Protein 53 g; Fat 17 g; Carbohydrate 7.5 g; Dietary Fibre 1.5 g; Cholesterol 205 mg; 1759 kJ (420 Cal)

Braised pork with prunes

PREPARATION TIME: 15 MINUTES | TOTAL COOKING TIME: 35 MINUTES | SERVES 4

4 lean pork loin medallions, about 175 g (6 oz) each
500 ml (17 fl oz/2 cups) chicken stock
2 tablespoons oil
1 large onion, cut into wedges
2 garlic cloves, crushed
1 tablespoon thyme leaves
1 large tomato, peeled, seeded and finely chopped
125 ml (4 fl oz/½ cup) cream
16 pitted prunes

1 Shape the meat into rounds by tying a length of string around the medallions. Tie with a bow for easy removal. Bring the stock to the boil in a medium saucepan. Reduce the heat to a simmer and cook for 5 minutes, or until reduced to 185 ml (6 fl oz/¾ cup).

2 Heat the oil over high heat in a heavy-based frying pan. Cook the meat for 2 minutes each side to seal, turning once. Drain on paper towels.

3 Add the onion and garlic to the frying pan, and stir for 2 minutes. Return the meat to the pan with the thyme, tomato and stock, then reduce the heat to low. Cover the pan and bring slowly to simmering point. Simmer for 10 minutes, or until the meat is tender, turning once. Add the cream and prunes, and simmer for a further 5 minutes. Remove the string and serve with greens.

NUTRITION PER SERVE
Protein 45 g; Fat 25 g; Carbohydrate 20 g; Dietary Fibre 4 g; Cholesterol 138 mg; 2015 kJ (480 Cal)

Shape the pork medallions into rounds by securing a length of string around each one.

Return the meat to the pan with the thyme, tomato and stock.

Creamy garlic seafood stew

PREPARATION TIME: 20 MINUTES | TOTAL COOKING TIME: 20 MINUTES | SERVES 6

12 scallops, with roe

500 g (1 lb 2 oz) skinless firm white fish fillets (see NOTE)

6 raw Moreton Bay bugs/flat-head lobster or crabs

500 g (1 lb 2 oz) raw prawns (shrimp), peeled and deveined, leaving the tails intact

50 g (1¾ oz) butter

1 onion, finely chopped

5–6 large garlic cloves, finely chopped

125 ml (4 fl oz/½ cup) white wine

500 ml (17 fl oz/2 cups) cream

1½ tablespoons dijon mustard

2 teaspoons lemon juice

2 tablespoons chopped flat-leaf (Italian) parsley

lemon wedges, to serve

1   Slice or pull off any membrane or hard muscle from the scallops. Cut the fish into 2 cm (¾ inch) cubes. Cut the heads off the bugs, then use kitchen scissors to cut down around the sides of the tail so you can flap open the shell. Remove the flesh in one piece, then slice each piece in half. Refrigerate all the seafood, covered, until ready to use.

2   Melt the butter in a frying pan and cook the onion and garlic over medium heat for 2 minutes, or until the onion is softened (be careful not to burn the garlic— it may become a little bitter).

3   Add the wine to the pan and cook for 4 minutes, or until reduced by half. Stir in the cream, mustard and lemon juice, and simmer for 5–6 minutes, or until reduced to almost half.

4   Add the prawns to the pan and cook for 1 minute, then add the bug meat and cook for another minute, or until white. Add the fish and cook for 2 minutes, or until cooked through (the flesh will flake easily when tested with a fork). Finally, add the scallops and cook for 1 minute. If any of the seafood is still not cooked, cook for another minute or so, but be careful not to overcook as this will result in tough flesh. Remove the frying pan from the heat and toss the parsley through. Season to taste. Serve with lemon wedges and bread, if desired.

NOTE: *Try using perch, ling, bream, tuna or blue-eye.*

NUTRITION PER SERVE
Protein 39 g; Fat 46 g; Carbohydrate 4 g; Dietary Fibre 1 g; Cholesterol 316 mg; 2460 kJ (585 Cal)

Use strong kitchen scissors to cut through the sides of each bug tail.

Pull back the shell of the bug and remove the flesh in one piece.

Simmer the sauce for about 5 minutes, or until reduced to almost half.

Turkey pot roast

PREPARATION TIME: 20 MINUTES | TOTAL COOKING TIME: 1 HOUR 15 MINUTES | SERVES 6

1 kg (2 lb 4 oz) frozen turkey breast roll
2 tablespoons oil
20 g (¾ oz) butter
1 onion, cut into wedges
125 ml (4 fl oz/½ cup) chicken stock
125 ml (4 fl oz/½ cup) white wine
300 g (10½ oz) orange sweet potato, cut into
    3 cm (1¼ inch) pieces
2 zucchini (courgettes), cut into 2 cm (¾ inch)
    slices
160 g (5½ oz/½ cup) redcurrant jelly
1 tablespoon cornflour (cornstarch)

1   Preheat the oven to 180°C (350°F/Gas 4). Thaw the turkey according to the instructions on the label. Remove the elasticised string from the turkey and tie up securely with kitchen string, at regular intervals, to retain its shape.

2   Heat the oil and butter in a frying pan over high heat, and brown the turkey all over. Transfer the turkey to a 2 litre (70 fl oz/8 cup) casserole dish. Place the onion wedges around the turkey, and pour over the stock and wine. Cover and bake for 40 minutes. Add the sweet potato and bake for 10 minutes. Add the zucchini and bake for a further 20 minutes.

3   Transfer the turkey and vegetables to a plate and keep warm. Strain the remaining liquid into a small saucepan. Stir in the redcurrant jelly. Combine the cornflour and 1 tablespoon water, and stir until smooth. Add gradually to the pan, stirring until the mixture boils and thickens. Slice the turkey and serve with the vegetables and sauce.

Tie up the turkey with string, at regular intervals, to help retain its shape during cooking.

Pour the stock and wine over the turkey and onion wedges.

NUTRITION PER SERVE
Protein 46 g; Fat 12 g; Carbohydrate 21 g; Dietary Fibre 1.5 g; Cholesterol 104 mg; 1630 kJ (390 Cal)

Beef and red wine stew

PREPARATION TIME: 15 MINUTES | TOTAL COOKING TIME: 2 HOURS | SERVES 6

30 g (1 oz) butter

2 tablespoons oil

1 kg (2 lb 4 oz) topside steak, trimmed and cut into 3 cm (1¼ inch) cubes

100 g (3½ oz) bacon pieces, cut into 1.5 cm (⅝ inch) cubes

18 baby onions

2 garlic cloves, crushed

30 g (1 oz/¼ cup) plain (all-purpose) flour

500 ml (17 fl oz/2 cups) red wine

750 ml (26 fl oz/3 cups) beef stock

300 g (10½ oz) small mushrooms, halved

1 Heat the butter and oil in a heavy-based saucepan. Cook the meat quickly in small batches over medium–high heat until browned, then drain on paper towels.

2 Add the bacon, onions and garlic to the pan, and cook, stirring, for 2 minutes, or until browned. Add the flour and stir over low heat until lightly golden. Gradually pour in the wine and stock, and stir until smooth. Stir continuously over medium heat for 2 minutes, or until the mixture boils and thickens.

3 Return the meat to the pan and reduce the heat to a simmer. Cook, covered, for 1½ hours, or until the meat is tender, stirring occasionally. Add the mushrooms and cook for 15 minutes. Delicious served with mashed potato.

NUTRITION PER SERVE
Protein 45 g; Fat 17 g; Carbohydrate 10 g; Dietary Fibre 2.5 g; Cholesterol 105 mg; 1800 kJ (430 Cal)

Cook the meat in small batches until browned, then drain on paper towels.

Add the flour to the bacon, onions and garlic, and stir until lightly golden.

Chicken and cider stew with apple and potato mash

PREPARATION TIME: 15 MINUTES | TOTAL COOKING TIME: 55 MINUTES | SERVES 4

1 kg (2 lb 4 oz) skinless, boneless chicken
    thighs, cut into 2 cm (¾ inch) cubes
1½ tablespoons finely chopped thyme
1 tablespoon oil
90 g (3¼ oz) butter
3 French shallots (eschalots), thinly sliced
375 ml (13 fl oz/1½ cups) apple cider
1 kg (2 lb 4 oz) potatoes, cubed
2 large green apples, peeled, cored and sliced
    into eighths
170 ml (5½ fl oz/⅔ cup) cream
thyme sprigs, to garnish

1   Season the chicken thighs with 2 teaspoons of the thyme and salt and black pepper. Heat the oil and 20 g (¾ oz) of the butter in a large saucepan over medium–high heat. Cook the chicken in two batches for 2–3 minutes, or until evenly browned. Remove from the pan.

2   Add the shallots and the remaining thyme to the pan, and sauté for 2 minutes. Pour in the cider, then bring to the boil, scraping off any sediment that has stuck to the bottom of the pan. Return the chicken to the pan and cover. Reduce the heat to low–medium and cook for 35–40 minutes, or until the chicken is tender and the sauce has reduced (check every now and then to see if any water needs to be added to the sauce).

3   Meanwhile, cook the potato and apple in a saucepan of boiling water for 15–20 minutes, or until tender. Drain and return to the pan over low heat for 1 minute to allow any water to evaporate. Remove from the heat, and mash with a potato masher. With a wooden spoon, stir in 2 tablespoons of the cream and the remaining butter, then season to taste with salt and pepper.

4   Gently stir the remaining cream into the chicken stew and cook for a further 2–4 minutes, or until the sauce has thickened. Garnish with thyme sprigs and serve at once with the potato and apple mash and a crisp green salad.

NUTRITION PER SERVE
Protein 54 g; Fat 60 g; Carbohydrate 56 g; Dietary Fibre 6 g; Cholesterol 333 mg; 4055 kJ (970 Cal)

Pour the cider into the saucepan, scraping off any sediment from the bottom of the pan.

Cook until the chicken is tender and the sauce has reduced and thickened.

With a wooden spoon, stir the cream and butter into the apple and potato mash.

Paprika veal with caraway noodles

PREPARATION TIME: 10 MINUTES | TOTAL COOKING TIME: 1 HOUR 35 MINUTES | SERVES 4

60 ml (2 fl oz/¼ cup) oil
1 kg (2 lb 4 oz) veal shoulder, diced
1 large onion, thinly sliced
3 garlic cloves, finely chopped
60 g (2¼ oz/¼ cup) Hungarian paprika
½ teaspoon caraway seeds
2 x 400 g (14 oz) tins chopped tomatoes,
   one drained
350 g (12 oz) fresh fettuccine
40 g (1½ oz) butter, softened

1   Heat half the oil in a large saucepan over medium–high heat, then brown the veal in batches for 3 minutes per batch. Remove the veal from the pan and set aside with any pan juices.

2   Add the remaining oil to the pan and sauté the onion and garlic over medium heat for 5 minutes, or until softened. Add the paprika and ¼ teaspoon of the caraway seeds, and stir for 30 seconds.

3   Add all the chopped tomatoes and their liquid plus 125 ml (4 fl oz/½ cup) water. Return the veal to the pan with any juices, increase the heat to high and bring to the boil. Reduce the heat to low, then cover and simmer for 1¼ hours, or until the meat is tender and the sauce has reduced and thickened.

4   About 15 minutes before the veal is ready, cook the pasta in a large saucepan of rapidly boiling salted water according to the packet instructions until *al dente*. Drain, then return to the pan. Stir in the butter and the remaining caraway seeds. Serve immediately with the paprika veal.

Brown the veal in batches over medium–heat for 3 minutes.

Cover and simmer until the meat is tender and the sauce has thickened.

NUTRITION PER SERVE
Protein 68 g; Fat 25 g; Carbohydrate 73 g; Dietary Fibre 10 g; Cholesterol 231 mg; 3340 kJ (800 Cal)

Spiced beef and potatoes

PREPARATION TIME: 15 MINUTES | TOTAL COOKING TIME: 1 HOUR 45 MINUTES | SERVES 4

SPICE PASTE
2 onions, chopped
2 garlic cloves, chopped
2 teaspoons grated lemon zest
2 small red chillies, chopped
2 teaspoons ground coriander
2 teaspoons ground cumin
1 teaspoon ground turmeric
½ teaspoon ground cardamom
1 teaspoon garam masala

2 tablespoons oil
1 kg (2 lb 4 oz) lean chuck steak, cut into
    3 cm (1¼ inch) cubes
185 ml (6 fl oz/¾ cup) coconut cream
1 tablespoon tamarind sauce
500 g (1 lb 2 oz) baby potatoes, halved

1   To make the spice paste, combine all the ingredients in a food processor, and process for 1 minute, or until very finely chopped.

2   Heat the oil in a heavy-based saucepan. Cook the meat quickly in small batches over medium–high heat until well browned. Drain meat on paper towels.

3   Add the spice paste to the pan and stir over medium heat for 2 minutes. Return the meat to the pan with the coconut cream, tamarind sauce and 125 ml (4 fl oz/½ cup) water, and bring to the boil. Reduce the heat to a simmer and cook, covered, for 30 minutes, stirring occasionally.

4   Add the potato and cook, covered, for 30 minutes. Remove the lid and cook for another 30 minutes, or until the meat is tender and almost all of the liquid has evaporated.

Trim the meat of excess fat and sinew and cut it into large cubes.

Return the meat to the pan with the coconut cream, tamarind sauce and water.

NUTRITION PER SERVE
Protein 57 g; Fat 25 g; Carbohydrate 25 g; Dietary Fibre 5 g; Cholesterol 168 mg; 2315 kJ (555 Cal)

Spanish meat and chickpea stew

PREPARATION TIME: 25 MINUTES + OVERNIGHT SOAKING | TOTAL COOKING TIME: 2 HOURS 45 MINUTES | SERVES 6–8

220 g (7¾ oz/1 cup) dried chickpeas
1 kg (2 lb 4 oz) chicken, trussed
500 g (1 lb 2 oz) piece lean beef brisket
250 g (9 oz) piece smoke-cured bacon
125 g (4½ oz) tocino, streaky bacon or speck
1 pig's trotter
200 g (7 oz) chorizo
1 onion, studded with 2 cloves
1 bay leaf
1 morcilla blood sausage (optional)
250 g (9 oz) green beans, trimmed and sliced
    lengthways
250 g (9 oz) green cabbage, cut into sections
    through the heart
300 g (10½ oz) silverbeet (Swiss chard)
    leaves, stalks removed
4 small potatoes
2 leeks (white part only), cut into 10 cm
    (4 inch) lengths
pinch saffron threads
75 g (2½ oz) dried rice vermicelli

1   Soak the chickpeas in cold water overnight. Drain and rinse. Tie loosely in a muslin (cheesecloth) bag.

2   Put 3 litres (105 fl oz/12 cups) cold water in a very large, deep saucepan. Add the chicken, beef, bacon and tocino, and bring to the boil. Add the chickpeas, pig's trotter and chorizo, return to the boil, then add the onion, bay leaf and ½ teaspoon salt. Simmer, partially covered, for 2½ hours.

3   After 2 hours, bring a saucepan of water to the boil, add the morcilla and gently boil for 5 minutes. Drain and set aside. Tie the green beans loosely in a muslin (cheesecloth) bag. Pour 1 litre (35 fl oz/4 cups) water into a large saucepan and bring to the boil. Add the beans, cabbage, silverbeet, potatoes, leek and saffron with 1 teaspoon of salt. Return to the boil and simmer for 30 minutes.

4   Strain the stock from both the meat and vegetable saucepans, and combine in a large saucepan. Bring to the boil, adjust the seasoning and add the vermicelli. Simmer for 6–7 minutes. Release the chickpeas and pile them in the centre of a large warm platter. Discard the tocino, then slice the meats and sausages. Arrange the meats and sausages in groups around the chickpeas at one end of the platter. Release the beans. Arrange the vegetables in groups around the other end. Spoon a little of the simmering broth (minus the vermicelli) over the meat, then pour the rest (with the vermicelli) into a soup tureen. Serve at once. It is traditional to serve the two dishes together, although the broth is eaten first.

NUTRITION PER SERVE (8)
Protein 51 g; Fat 27 g; Carbohydrate 26 g; Dietary Fibre 8 g; Cholesterol 158 mg; 2290 kJ (545 Cal)

Using a sharp knife, cut the green beans lengthways into long slices.

Add the chickpeas, pig's trotter and chorizo to the saucepan.

Madrid chicken

PREPARATION TIME: 10 MINUTES I TOTAL COOKING TIME: 1 HOUR I SERVES 4

1 orange
1 tablespoon olive oil
4 chicken breasts (skin and excess fat removed)
2 chorizo sausages (about 200 g/7 oz), cut into 1 cm (½ inch) slices
250 ml (9 fl oz/1 cup) chicken stock
250 g (9 oz/1 cup) bottled tomato pasta sauce
12 kalamata olives
kalamata olives, extra, to garnish
flat-leaf (Italian) parsley, to garnish

1   Using a vegetable peeler, carefully cut 4 thin strips of orange zest (about 1 x 4 cm/½ x 1½ inches). Remove the peel and pith from the orange, and segment the flesh.

2   Heat the oil in a saucepan and brown the chicken and chorizo slices, in batches if necessary. (Leave the meat side of the chicken browning for 5 minutes.) Add the stock, tomato sauce and orange zest. Bring to the boil, then reduce the heat and simmer, covered, for 25 minutes.

3   Remove the lid, turn the chicken over and continue to simmer, uncovered, for about 25 minutes, or until the chicken is tender and the sauce reduced. Season with salt and freshly ground black pepper, and stir through the olives and orange segments. Garnish with extra olives and flat-leaf parsley.

NOTE: *Chorizo sausages can be replaced with any spicy sausages.*

Remove the peel and pith from the orange, and cut the flesh into segments.

Brown the chicken breasts and chorizo slices in the hot oil.

NUTRITION PER SERVE
Protein 75 g; Fat 30 g; Carbohydrate 12 g; Dietary Fibre 3.5 g; Cholesterol 250 mg; 2553 kJ (610 Cal)

Ratatouille

PREPARATION TIME: 30 MINUTES | TOTAL COOKING TIME: 40 MINUTES | SERVES 4–6

100 ml (3½ fl oz) olive oil

500 g (1 lb 2 oz) eggplants (aubergines), cut into 2 cm (¾ inch) cubes

375 g (13 oz) zucchini (courgettes), cut into 2 cm (¾ inch) slices

1 green capsicum (pepper), seeded, cut into 2 cm (¾ inch) cubes

1 red onion, cut into 2 cm (¾ inch) wedges

3 garlic cloves, finely chopped

¼ teaspoon cayenne pepper

2 teaspoons chopped thyme

2 bay leaves

6 vine-ripened tomatoes, peeled and roughly chopped

1 tablespoon red wine vinegar

1 teaspoon caster (superfine) sugar

4 tablespoons shredded basil

1   Heat 2 tablespoons of the oil in a large saucepan and cook the eggplant over medium heat for 4–5 minutes, or until soft but not browned. Remove all the eggplant from the pan.

2   Add another 2 tablespoons oil to the pan and cook the zucchini slices for 3–4 minutes, or until softened. Remove the zucchini from the pan. Add the capsicum to the pan, cook for 2 minutes, then remove.

3   Heat the remaining oil in the pan, add the onion wedges and cook for 2–3 minutes, or until softened. Add the garlic, cayenne pepper, thyme and bay leaves, and cook, stirring, for 1 minute. Return the cooked eggplant, zucchini and capsicum to the pan, and add the tomato, vinegar and sugar. Simmer for 20 minutes, stirring occasionally. Stir in the basil and season with salt and black pepper. Serve hot or cold.

NOTE: *Ratatouille takes quite a long time to prepare and so is traditionally made in large quantities. It is then eaten over several days as an hors d'oeuvre, side dish or main meal.*

NUTRITION PER SERVE (6)
Protein 4 g; Fat 17 g; Carbohydrate 8.5 g; Dietary Fibre 5.5 g; Cholesterol 0 mg; 826 kJ (197 Cal)

Peel the skin away from the crosses cut in the base of the tomatoes.

Cook the eggplant until softened but not browned, then remove.

Seafood stew

PREPARATION TIME: 30 MINUTES + 30 MINUTES SOAKING | TOTAL COOKING TIME: 50 MINUTES | SERVES 4

2 dried mushrooms
1 kg (2 lb 4 oz) firm white fish fillets
375 g (13 oz) raw king prawns
1 raw lobster tail
12 mussels
60 ml (2 fl oz/¼ cup) olive oil
1 large onion, finely chopped
1 green capsicum (pepper), finely chopped
2–3 garlic cloves, crushed
425 g (15 oz) tin chopped tomatoes
250 ml (9 fl oz/1 cup) white wine
250 ml (9 fl oz/1 cup) tomato juice
250 ml (9 fl oz/1 cup) fish stock (see NOTE)
1 bay leaf
2 parsley sprigs
6 basil leaves, chopped
1 tablespoon chopped parsley

1 Soak the mushrooms in boiling water for 20 minutes. Cut the fish into bite-sized pieces, removing any bones. Peel and devein the prawns, leaving the tails intact. Remove the meat from the lobster shell and cut into small pieces. Discard any open mussels; scrub the rest, remove the hairy beards, then soak in cold water for 10 minutes. Drain the mushrooms, squeeze dry and chop finely.

2 Heat the oil in a heavy-based saucepan. Cook the onion, capsicum and garlic over medium heat, stirring, for about 5 minutes, or until the onion is soft. Add the mushrooms, tomato, wine, tomato juice, stock, bay leaf, parsley sprigs and chopped basil. Bring to the boil, reduce the heat, then cover and simmer for 30 minutes.

3 Layer the fish and prawns in a large saucepan. Add the sauce mixture, then cover and leave on low heat for 10 minutes, or until the prawns are pink and the fish is cooked. Add the lobster and mussels, and simmer for 2–3 minutes. Season to taste. Discard any unopened mussels, sprinkle with parsley, and serve with crusty warm bread.

NOTE: *You can make your own fish stock for this recipe by simmering the trimmings from the fish, lobster and prawns in 310 ml (10¾ fl oz/1¼ cups) water for about 20 minutes, then straining the liquid.*

NUTRITION PER SERVE
Protein 100 g; Fat 25 g; Carbohydrate 8 g; Dietary Fibre 3 g; Cholesterol 460 mg; 2905 kJ (695 Cal)

Remove the lobster meat from the shell and cut it into small pieces.

When the onion is soft, add the chopped mushrooms, tomato, liquids and herbs.

Add the lobster and mussels when the prawns are pink and the fish is cooked.

Chicken, artichoke and broad bean stew

PREPARATION TIME: 15 MINUTES | TOTAL COOKING TIME: 1 HOUR 25 MINUTES | SERVES 4

155 g (5½ oz/1 cup) frozen broad (fava) beans
8 chicken thighs (skin removed, optional)
60 g (2¼ oz/½ cup) seasoned plain (all-purpose) flour
2 tablespoons oil
1 large red onion, cut into small wedges
125 ml (4 fl oz/½ cup) dry white wine
310 ml (10¾ fl oz/1¼ cups) chicken stock
2 teaspoons finely chopped fresh rosemary
335 g (11¾ oz) marinated artichokes, well drained and quartered
800 g (1 lb 12 oz) potatoes, cut into large cubes
60 g (2¼ oz) butter

1 Remove the skins from the broad beans. Coat the chicken in the flour, shaking off the excess. Heat the oil in a saucepan or flameproof casserole dish, then brown the chicken in two batches on all sides over medium heat. Remove and drain on paper towels.

2 Add the onion to the pan and cook for 3–4 minutes, or until soft but not brown. Increase the heat to high, pour in the wine and boil for 2 minutes, or until reduced to a syrup. Stir in 250 ml (9 fl oz/1 cup) of the stock and bring just to the boil, then return the chicken to the pan with the rosemary. Reduce the heat to low and simmer, covered, for 45 minutes.

3 Add the artichokes to the pan, increase the heat to high and return to the boil. Reduce to a simmer and cook, uncovered, for 10–15 minutes. Add the beans and cook for a further 5 minutes.

4 Meanwhile, cook the potato in a saucepan of boiling water for 15–20 minutes, or until tender. Drain, then return to the pan. Add the butter and the remaining stock, and mash with a potato masher. Serve on the side of the stew.

Squeeze the broad beans to remove the tough outer skins.

Cook the onion for 3–4 minutes, or until it is soft but not brown.

NUTRITION PER SERVE
Protein 76 g; Fat 47 g; Carbohydrate 43 g; Dietary Fibre 8.5 g; Cholesterol 334 mg; 3845 kJ (920 Cal)

Lamb's liver and bacon stew

PREPARATION TIME: 10 MINUTES | TOTAL COOKING TIME: 30 MINUTES | SERVES 6

1 lamb's liver, about 750 g (1 lb 10 oz) (see NOTE)
30 g (1 oz/¼ cup) cornflour (cornstarch)
¼ teaspoon ground black pepper
6 bacon slices, cut into large pieces
2 tablespoons oil
2 onions, thinly sliced
1 beef stock (bouillon) cube, crumbled

1 Wash the liver and cut it into thin slices, discarding any veins or discoloured spots. Pat the liver dry with paper towels. Combine the cornflour and pepper. Toss the liver slices in the seasoned cornflour, shaking off the excess.

2 Cook the bacon in a heavy-based saucepan until crisp, then drain on paper towels. Heat the oil in the pan and cook the onion gently until golden, then remove from the pan.

3 Cook the liver quickly in small batches over medium heat until well browned, then drain on paper towels. Return the liver, bacon and onion to the pan. Dissolve the stock cube in 250 ml (9 fl oz/1 cup) boiling water, then gradually add to the pan. Stir over medium heat for 10 minutes, or until the liquid boils and thickens. Sprinkle with cracked black pepper and serve immediately.

NOTE: *Soaking the liver in milk for 30 minutes before cooking will result in a milder taste.*

NUTRITION PER SERVE
Protein 36 g; Fat 30 g; Carbohydrate 9 g; Dietary Fibre 0.5 g; Cholesterol 573 mg; 1850 kJ (440 Cal)

Toss the liver slices in the seasoned cornflour, shaking off the excess.

Cook the bacon in a heavy-based saucepan until crisp, then drain on paper towels.

Return the cooked bacon, liver slices and onion to the pan.

Duck with pears

PREPARATION TIME: 20 MINUTES | TOTAL COOKING TIME: 1 HOUR 40 MINUTES | SERVES 4

2 tablespoons olive oil

4 duck breasts

2 red onions, finely diced

1 carrot, finely diced

2 teaspoons thyme

250 ml (9 fl oz/1 cup) chicken stock

2 tomatoes, peeled, seeded and diced

4 green, firm pears, peeled, halved and cored
(leaving the stems intact)

1 cinnamon stick

60 g (2¼ oz) blanched almonds, toasted,
chopped

1 garlic clove

100 ml (3½ fl oz) brandy

NUTRITION PER SERVE
Protein 45 g; Fat 54 g; Carbohydrate 27 g; Dietary
Fibre 6.5 g; Cholesterol 250 mg; 3415 kJ (815 Cal)

1   Heat the oil in a heavy-based frying pan and cook the duck, skin side down first, over medium heat until brown all over. Remove and set aside, reserving 4 tablespoons of the cooking fat.

2   Return 2 tablespoons of the fat to the pan. Add the onion, carrot and thyme, and cook over medium heat for 5 minutes, or until the onion has softened. Add the stock and tomato and bring to the boil. Reduce the heat and simmer for 30 minutes, with the lid slightly askew, or until the sauce has thickened and reduced. Cool slightly, then purée in a food processor until smooth. Return to the pan with the duck. Simmer gently over low heat for 30–40 minutes, or until the duck is tender.

3   While the duck is cooking, place the pears in a saucepan with the cinnamon stick and just cover with cold water. Bring to the boil, reduce the heat and simmer gently for 5 minutes, or until the pears are tender but still firm to the bite. Remove the pears, cover to keep warm and add 125 ml (4 fl oz/½ cup) of the pear poaching liquid to the tomato sauce.

4   Remove the duck from the sauce and keep warm. Grind the almonds, garlic and brandy together in a mortar with a pestle or in a blender to make a smooth paste. Add to the tomato sauce, season, and cook for a further 10 minutes.

5   Arrange the duck pieces on a serving plate and pour the sauce over the top. Arrange the warmed pears around the duck, and serve.

Return the duck to the pan with the processed sauce mixture.

Grind the almonds, garlic and brandy in a mortar with a pestle or in a blender.

French-style beef pot roast

PREPARATION TIME: 15 MINUTES | TOTAL COOKING TIME: 2 HOURS 20 MINUTES | SERVES 6

2 tablespoons oil
2 kg (4 lb 8 oz) rolled beef brisket, trimmed
750 ml (26 fl oz/3 cups) beef stock
250 ml (9 fl oz/1 cup) red wine
60 ml (2 fl oz/¼ cup) brandy
2 onions, quartered
3 garlic cloves, crushed
3 tomatoes, peeled, seeded and chopped
2 bay leaves
1 large handful chopped parsley
2 tablespoons thyme leaves
12 pitted black olives
6 small carrots, thickly sliced
2 tablespoons plain (all-purpose) flour

1   Heat the oil in a deep heavy-based saucepan. Cook the meat over medium–high heat until browned all over, then remove from the heat.

2   Add the stock to the pan with the wine, brandy, onion, garlic, tomato, bay leaves, parsley and thyme. Cover and bring to simmering point over low heat. Simmer for 1½ hours.

3   Add the olives and carrot, and cook for 30 minutes. Remove the meat and leave it in a warm place, and covered with foil, for 10 minutes before slicing.

4   Combine the flour and 60 ml (2 fl oz/¼ cup) water to make a smooth paste. Add to the sauce, stir over medium heat until the sauce thickens, and cook for 3 minutes. Pour over the sliced meat to serve.

Cook the meat in the oil over medium–high heat until it is browned all over.

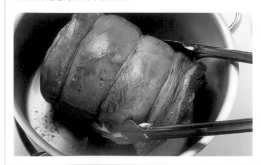

Add the stock to the pan with the wine, brandy, onion, garlic, tomato and herbs.

NUTRITION PER SERVE
Protein 70 g; Fat 11 g; Carbohydrate 11.5 g; Dietary Fibre 2.5 g; Cholesterol 150 mg; 2005 kJ (480 Cal)

Braised chicken and leek in wine

PREPARATION TIME: 15 MINUTES | TOTAL COOKING TIME: 1 HOUR | SERVES 4

2 tablespoons oil
1.2 kg (2 lb 10 oz) chicken pieces
1 leek (white part only), thinly sliced
5 spring onions (scallions), thinly sliced on the
    diagonal
2 tablespoons marjoram
150 ml (5 fl oz) white wine
400 ml (14 fl oz) chicken stock
100 ml (3½ fl oz) cream

1   With a sharp knife, score the thickest part of the chicken drumsticks. Heat 1 tablespoon of the oil in a frying pan and cook the chicken pieces in batches for 3–4 minutes, or until browned.

2   Heat the remaining oil in a large flameproof casserole dish and cook the leek, spring onion and marjoram for 4 minutes, or until soft. Add the chicken and wine, and cook for 2 minutes. Add the stock, cover and bring to the boil. Reduce the heat and simmer for 30 minutes. Stir in the cream and simmer, uncovered, for 15 minutes, or until the chicken is tender. Season to taste. Serve with steamed rice.

NUTRITION PER SERVE
Protein 48 g; Fat 30 g; Carbohydrate 2.5 g; Dietary Fibre 1 g; Cholesterol 190 mg; 2065 kJ (493 Cal)

Use a sharp knife to score the thickest part of the chicken drumsticks.

Add the stock to the chicken and wine mixture, then cover and bring to the boil.

Ponzu chicken and noodle hotpot

PREPARATION TIME: 15 MINUTES + OVERNIGHT REFRIGERATION I TOTAL COOKING TIME: 45 MINUTES I SERVES 4

PONZU SAUCE
1 tablespoon lemon juice
1 tablespoon lime juice
1 tablespoon rice vinegar
1 tablespoon tamari
1½ tablespoons mirin (sweet rice wine)
2½ tablespoons Japanese soy sauce
5 cm (2 inch) piece kombu (kelp), wiped
    with a damp cloth
1 tablespoon bonito flakes

900 g (2 lb) chicken thigh cutlets, cut in half
    across the bone
10 cm (4 inch) piece kombu (kelp)
200 g (7 oz) dried somen noodles
250 g (9 oz) fresh shiitake mushrooms,
    halved if large
1 carrot, thinly sliced
300 g (10½ oz) baby English spinach leaves

1   To make the ponzu sauce, combine all the ingredients in a non-metallic bowl. Cover with plastic wrap and refrigerate overnight, then strain through a fine sieve. Discard any sediment and put the sauce aside.

2   Place the chicken and kombu in a large saucepan with 875 ml (30 fl oz/3½ cups) water. Bring to a simmer over medium heat. Cook for 20 minutes, or until the chicken is cooked, skimming the scum off the surface. Remove the chicken pieces and strain the broth. Transfer the broth and chicken pieces to a 2.5 litre (87 fl oz/10 cup) flameproof casserole dish or Japanese nabe. Cover and continue to cook over low heat for 15 minutes.

3   Meanwhile, cook the noodles in a large saucepan of boiling water for 2 minutes, or until tender. Drain and rinse under cold running water.

4   Add the mushrooms and carrot to the chicken, and cook for 5 minutes. Place the noodles on top of the chicken, then top with the spinach. Cook, covered, for 2 minutes, or until the spinach has just wilted. Stir in 4–6 tablespoons of the ponzu sauce, or to taste. Season with cracked black pepper and serve.

NOTE: *Traditionally, this dish would be served in a ceramic nabe dish, for your guests to help themselves.*

Rinse the noodles well in a colander, under cold running water.

NUTRITION PER SERVE
Protein 32 g; Fat 9 g; Carbohydrate 37 g; Dietary Fibre 6.5 g; Cholesterol 98 mg; 1515 kJ (360 Cal)

Chinese beef in soy

PREPARATION TIME: 20 MINUTES + OVERNIGHT MARINATING | TOTAL COOKING TIME: 1 HOUR 45 MINUTES | SERVES 4

700 g (1 lb 9 oz) chuck steak, trimmed and cut into 2 cm (¾ inch) cubes
80 ml (2½ fl oz/⅓ cup) dark soy sauce
2 tablespoons honey
1 tablespoon wine vinegar
60 ml (2 fl oz/¼ cup) soya bean oil, or cooking oil
4 garlic cloves, chopped
8 spring onions (scallions), thinly sliced
1 tablespoon finely grated fresh ginger
2 star anise
½ teaspoon ground cloves
375 ml (13 fl oz/1½ cups) beef stock
125 ml (4 fl oz/½ cup) red wine
sliced spring onions (scallions), extra, to garnish

1 Place the meat in a non-metallic dish. Combine the soy sauce, honey and vinegar in a small bowl, then pour over the meat. Cover with plastic wrap and marinate for at least 2 hours, or preferably overnight. Drain, reserving the marinade, and pat the cubes dry.

2 Place 1 tablespoon of the oil in a saucepan and brown the meat in 3 batches, for 3–4 minutes per batch—add another tablespoon of oil, if necessary. Remove the meat. Add the remaining oil and fry the garlic, spring onion, ginger, star anise and cloves for 1–2 minutes, or until fragrant.

3 Return all the meat to the pan, and add the reserved marinade, stock and wine. Bring to the boil, then reduce the heat and simmer, covered, for 1¼ hours. Cook, uncovered, for a further 15 minutes, or until the sauce is syrupy and the meat is tender.

4 Garnish with the extra sliced spring onion and serve immediately with steamed rice.

Finely grate a piece of fresh ginger on a wooden ginger grater.

Simmer the beef, marinade, stock and wine until the sauce is thick and syrupy.

NUTRITION PER SERVE
Protein 37 g; Fat 20 g; Carbohydrate 12 g; Dietary Fibre 0.5 g; Cholesterol 117 mg; 1657 kJ (395 Cal)

Mongolian lamb hotpot

PREPARATION TIME: 15 MINUTES + 10 MINUTES SOAKING | TOTAL COOKING TIME: 5 MINUTES | SERVES 6

250 g (9 oz) dried rice vermicelli
600 g (1 lb 5 oz) lamb backstraps, thinly sliced
across the grain
4 spring onions (scallions), sliced

SAUCE
80 ml (2½ fl oz/⅓ cup) light soy sauce
2 tablespoons Chinese sesame paste
1 tablespoon Chinese rice wine
1 teaspoon chilli and garlic paste

1.5 litres (52 fl oz/6 cups) light chicken stock
3 cm x 6 cm (1¼ inch x 2½ inch) piece fresh
ginger, cut into 6 slices
2 tablespoons Chinese rice wine
300 g (10½ oz) silken firm tofu, cut into 1.5
cm (⅝ inch) cubes
300 g (10½ oz) Chinese broccoli (gai larn), cut
into 4 cm (1½ inch) lengths
90 g (3¼ oz/2 cups) shredded Chinese
cabbage (wong bok)

1 Place the vermicelli in a large heatproof
bowl, cover with boiling water and soak for
6–7 minutes. Drain well and divide among six
serving bowls. Top with the lamb slices and
spring onion.

2 To make the sauce, combine the soy sauce,
sesame paste, rice wine and the chilli and garlic
paste in a small bowl.

3 Place the stock, ginger and rice wine in a
2.5 litre (87 fl oz/10 cup) flameproof hotpot or
large saucepan. Cover and bring to the boil over
high heat. Add the tofu, Chinese broccoli and
Chinese cabbage and simmer, uncovered, for 1
minute, or until the cabbage has wilted. Divide
the tofu, broccoli and cabbage among the serving
bowls, then ladle on the hot stock. Drizzle a little
of the sauce on top and serve the rest on the side.

NUTRITION PER SERVE
Protein 36 g; Fat 16 g; Carbohydrate 32 g; Dietary
Fibre 4 g; Cholesterol 68 mg; 1770 kJ (425 Cal)

Cover the vermicelli with boiling water in a
heatproof bowl and leave to soak.

Mix together the soy sauce, sesame paste, rice
wine, chilli and sugar to make a sauce.

Japanese beef hotpot

PREPARATION TIME: 20 MINUTES + 40 MINUTES FREEZING | TOTAL COOKING TIME: 10 MINUTES | SERVES 4

300 g (10½ oz) beef fillet, trimmed

1.5 litres (52 fl oz/6 cups) chicken stock

2 cm x 6 cm (¾ inch x 2½ inch) piece fresh ginger, thinly sliced

80 ml (2½ fl oz/⅓ cup) light soy sauce

2 tablespoons mirin

1 teaspoon sesame oil

200 g (7 oz) fresh udon noodles

150 g (5½ oz) English spinach, stems removed, thinly sliced

400 g (14 oz) cabbage, finely shredded

100 g (3½ oz) fresh shiitake mushrooms, stems removed and caps thinly sliced

200 g (7 oz) firm tofu, cut into 2 cm (¾ inch) cubes

80 ml (2½ fl oz/⅓ cup) ponzu sauce (see page 232), or 60 ml (2 fl oz/¼ cup) soy sauce combined with 1 tablespoon lemon juice

---

NUTRITION PER SERVE
Protein 28 g; Fat 11 g; Carbohydrate 41 g; Dietary
Fibre 7.5 g; Cholesterol 50 mg; 1800 kJ (430 Cal)

---

1 Wrap the beef fillet in plastic wrap and freeze for 40 minutes, or until it begins to harden. Remove and slice as thinly as possible across the grain.

2 Place the stock, ginger, soy sauce, mirin and sesame oil in a 2.5 litre (87 fl oz/10 cup) flameproof casserole dish or hotpot over medium heat, and simmer for 3 minutes. Separate the noodles gently with chopsticks, add to the stock and cook for 1–2 minutes. Add the spinach, cabbage, mushrooms and tofu, and simmer for 1 minute, or until the leaves have wilted.

3 Divide the noodles among four serving bowls using tongs, and top with the beef slices, vegetables and tofu. Ladle the hot stock on top and serve the ponzu sauce on the side.

NOTE: *Traditionally, raw beef slices are arranged on a plate with the tofu, mushrooms, vegetables and noodles. The stock and seasoning are heated on a portable gas flame at the table. Guests dip the meat and vegetables in the hot stock and eat as they go, dipping into the sauce. The noodles are added at the end and served with the broth.*

Shred the cabbage as finely as possible. This will ensure it wilts quickly in the broth.

Using a sharp knife, cut the partially frozen beef fillet as thinly as possible.

Gently separate the udon noodles with your fingers and add to the dish.

Chinese braised chicken

PREPARATION TIME: 10 MINUTES | TOTAL COOKING TIME: 1 HOUR | SERVES 4–6

250 ml (9 fl oz/1 cup) soy sauce
1 cinnamon stick
90 g (3¼ oz/⅓ cup) sugar
80 ml (2½ fl oz/⅓ cup) balsamic vinegar
2.5 cm (1 inch) piece fresh ginger, thinly sliced
4 garlic cloves
¼ teaspoon dried chilli flakes
1.5 kg (3 lb 5 oz) chicken pieces (skin removed)
1 tablespoon sesame seeds, toasted

1 Combine 1 litre (35 fl oz/4 cups) water with the soy sauce, cinnamon stick, sugar, balsamic vinegar, ginger, garlic and chilli flakes in a saucepan. Bring to the boil, then reduce the heat and simmer for 5 minutes.

2 Add the chicken pieces and simmer, covered, for 50 minutes, or until cooked through. Serve the chicken on a bed of steamed vegetables, drizzled with the poaching liquid and sprinkled with toasted sesame seeds.

NUTRITION PER SERVE (6)
Protein 45 g; Fat 10 g; Carbohydrate 16 g; Dietary Fibre 0.5 g; Cholesterol 140 mg; 1420 kJ (339 Cal)

Add the chicken to the simmering soy sauce mixture and cook for 50 minutes.

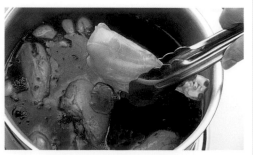

Tofu, vegetable and noodle hotpot

PREPARATION TIME: 10 MINUTES + 20 MINUTES SOAKING | TOTAL COOKING TIME: 15 MINUTES | SERVES 4

8 dried shiitake mushrooms
500 g (1 lb 2 oz) fresh round rice noodles
3 litres (105 fl oz/12 cups) chicken stock
1 carrot, thinly sliced on the diagonal
100 g (3½ oz) fried tofu puffs, halved
800 g (1 lb 12 oz) bok choy (pak choy),
    trimmed and quartered
1–1½ tablespoons mushroom soy sauce
6 drops sesame oil
ground white pepper, to season
100 g (3½ oz) enoki mushrooms, ends
    trimmed

1   Place the shiitake mushrooms in a heatproof bowl, cover with boiling water and soak for 20 minutes. Drain and remove the stems, squeezing out any excess water.

2   Meanwhile, place the noodles in a heatproof bowl, cover with boiling water and soak briefly. Refresh with cold water. Gently separate the noodles with your hands and drain well.

3   Place the chicken stock in a large saucepan, cover and slowly bring to a gentle simmer over low heat.

4   Add the noodles to the simmering stock along with the carrot, tofu puffs, shiitake mushrooms and bok choy. Cook for 1–2 minutes, or until the carrot and noodles are tender and the bok choy has wilted slightly. Stir in the soy sauce and sesame oil, and season with white pepper.

5   Divide the noodles, vegetables, tofu puffs and enoki mushrooms among four serving bowls, ladle the broth on top and serve immediately.

NUTRITION PER SERVE
Protein 20 g; Fat 8.5 g; Carbohydrate 69 g; Dietary
Fibre 9.5 g; Cholesterol 39 mg; 1825 kJ (435 Cal)

To prepare the enoki mushrooms for the hotpot, trim the ends.

Gently separate the noodles with your hands before adding to the stock.

Pork sausage and white bean stew

PREPARATION TIME: 25 MINUTES + OVERNIGHT SOAKING | TOTAL COOKING TIME: 1 HOUR 40 MINUTES | SERVES 4

350 g (12 oz) dried white haricot beans

150 g (5½ oz) tocino, speck or pancetta, unsliced

½ leek (white part only), thinly sliced

2 garlic cloves

1 bay leaf

1 small red chilli, halved and seeded

1 small onion

2 cloves

1 rosemary sprig

3 thyme sprigs

1 parsley sprig

60 ml (2 fl oz/¼ cup) olive oil

8 pork sausages

½ onion, finely chopped

1 green capsicum (pepper), finely chopped

½ teaspoon paprika

125 g (4½ oz/½ cup) tomato paste (concentrated purée)

1 teaspoon cider vinegar

1 Soak the beans overnight in cold water. Drain and rinse the beans under cold water. Put them in a large saucepan with the tocino, leek, garlic, bay leaf and chilli. Stud the onion with the cloves and add to the saucepan. Tie the rosemary, thyme and parsley together, and add to the saucepan. Pour in 750 ml (26 fl oz/ 3 cups) cold water and bring to the boil. Add 1 tablespoon of the oil, reduce the heat and simmer, covered, for about 1 hour, or until the beans are tender. When necessary, add a little more boiling water to keep the beans covered.

2 Prick each sausage five or six times and twist tightly in opposite directions in the middle to give two short fat sausages joined in the middle. Put in a single layer in a large frying pan and add enough cold water to reach halfway up their sides. Bring to the boil and simmer, turning two or three times, until all the water has evaporated and the sausages brown lightly in the little fat that is left in the pan. Remove from the pan and cut the short sausages apart. Add the remaining oil, the chopped onion and capsicum to the pan, and fry over medium heat for 5–6 minutes. Stir in the paprika, cook for 30 seconds, then add the tomato paste. Season to taste. Cook, stirring, for 1 minute.

3 Remove the tocino, herb sprigs and any loose large pieces of onion from the bean mixture. Leave in any loose leaves from the herbs and any small pieces of onion. Add the sausages and sauce to the pan, and stir the vinegar through. Bring to the boil. Adjust the seasoning and serve.

NUTRITION PER SERVE
Protein 39 g; Fat 51 g; Carbohydrate 43 g; Dietary Fibre 20 g; Cholesterol 99 mg; 3195 kJ (765 Cal)

Stud the onion with the cloves by pushing the cloves firmly into the onion.

Twist each sausage tightly in opposite directions so that it forms two short fat sausages.

Beef in beer with capers

PREPARATION TIME: 25 MINUTES | TOTAL COOKING TIME: 3 HOURS 20 MINUTES | SERVES 4–6

1 kg (2 lb 4 oz) gravy beef
seasoned plain (all-purpose) flour
olive oil, for cooking
4 garlic cloves, finely chopped
500 ml (17 fl oz/2 cups) beef stock
375 ml (13 fl oz/1½ cups) beer
2 onions, chopped
3 bay leaves
55 g (2 oz/⅓ cup) stuffed or pitted green
    olives, sliced
6 anchovies
2 tablespoons capers, drained

1   Cut the beef into 4 cm (1½ inch) chunks. Lightly coat in the flour. Heat 60 ml (2 fl oz/¼ cup) of oil in a deep heavy-based saucepan, add the garlic, then brown the beef over a high heat.

2   Add the stock, beer, onion and bay leaves, season well and bring to the boil. Reduce the heat and gently simmer, covered, for 2½ hours, stirring about three times during cooking. Remove the lid and simmer for 30 minutes more. Stir, then mix in the olives.

3   Heat 2 teaspoons of oil in a small saucepan. Add the anchovies and capers, gently breaking up the anchovies. Cook over medium heat for 4 minutes, or until brown and crisp. To serve, place the meat on serving plates, drizzle with the sauce, sprinkle with anchovies and capers, and season with salt and freshly cracked black pepper.

NOTE: *The capers should be squeezed very dry before being added to the pan, or they will spit in the hot oil.*

Using a sharp knife, cut the gravy beef into large chunks.

Add the stock, beer, onion and bay leaves to the browned beef.

NUTRITION PER SERVE (6)
Protein 40 g; Fat 6 g; Carbohydrate 4 g; Dietary Fibre 1 g; Cholesterol 115 mg; 965 kJ (230 Cal)

Lemon and rosemary chicken stew

PREPARATION TIME: 10 MINUTES | TOTAL COOKING TIME: 30 MINUTES | SERVES 4

8 large chicken drumsticks
60 g (2¼ oz) butter
2 garlic cloves, crushed
2 teaspoons finely grated lemon zest
2 tablespoons chopped rosemary
1 tablespoon plain (all-purpose) flour
375 ml (13 fl oz/1½ cups) chicken stock
2 tablespoons lemon juice

1   Using a sharp knife, make two deep cuts in the thickest part of each chicken drumstick.

2   Melt the butter in a large frying pan. Add the drumsticks and cook over medium heat for 2 minutes on each side, or until brown. Add the garlic, lemon zest and rosemary.

3   Blend the flour, stock and lemon juice until smooth. Add to the pan and bring to the boil. Reduce the heat and simmer, covered, for 25 minutes, or until the drumsticks are tender, stirring occasionally. Season, and serve, ladling the sauce over the chicken. Delicious with green beans.

HINT: *To check whether chicken is cooked, insert a skewer into the thickest part. If the juice runs clear, the chicken is cooked.*

NUTRITION PER SERVE
Protein 68 g; Fat 54 g; Carbohydrate 3.5 g; Dietary Fibre 0.5 g; Cholesterol 430 mg; 3205 kJ (765 Cal)

Make two deep cuts in the thickest part of the chicken drumsticks.

Add the crushed garlic, lemon zest and rosemary to the drumsticks.

Pour the stock mixture into the pan, then bring to the boil.

Autumn vegetable stew

PREPARATION TIME: 25 MINUTES | TOTAL COOKING TIME: 30 MINUTES | SERVES 4–6

185 g (6 oz) frozen broad (fava) beans,
    thawed (see NOTES)
150 g (5½ oz) baby onions (see NOTES)
50 g (1¾ oz) butter
2 teaspoons olive oil
400 g (14 oz) small parsnips
150 g (5½ oz) Jerusalem artichokes
2 tablespoons plain (all-purpose) flour
580 ml (20¼ fl oz/2⅓ cups) chicken stock
300 ml (10½ fl oz) cream
2 teaspoons grated lemon zest
1 teaspoon grated orange zest
400 g (14 oz) baby carrots, trimmed
500 g (1 lb 2 oz) baby turnips, trimmed

1 Peel and discard the tough outer skin of the broad beans. Carefully peel the onions, leaving the flat root end attached, then cut a cross through the root end of each onion.

2 Heat the butter and oil in a large heavy-based saucepan until foamy. Add the onions and cook for 7 minutes over low–medium heat, turning often to colour evenly.

3 While the onions are browning, peel the parsnips and artichokes, and cut them into bite-sized pieces. Add to the saucepan and toss well. Scatter the flour over the onion, parsnip and artichokes, toss to coat and cook for 2 minutes.

4 Stir in the chicken stock, cream, lemon zest and orange zest. Bring to the boil, stirring, then reduce the heat and simmer for 7 minutes, or until the vegetables are half-cooked.

5 Add the carrots and turnips, and toss well. Cover the pan and cook for 4–5 minutes, or until the vegetables are just tender. Season well with salt and freshly ground black pepper, stir in the peeled broad beans to heat through, and serve.

NOTES: *Fresh broad beans can be used. Add them with the carrots and turnips.*

Baby vegetables have a sweet, delicate flavour. If unavailable, choose the smallest vegetables and cook them for a few minutes longer.

NUTRITION PER SERVE (6)
Protein 7 g; Fat 30 g; Carbohydrate 25 g; Dietary Fibre 10 g; Cholesterol 90 mg; 1665 kJ (400 Cal)

Peel the broad beans and cut a cross through the root end of the peeled onions.

Peel the small parsnips and Jerusalem artichokes, and cut into bite-sized pieces.

Mexican beef stew

PREPARATION TIME: 30 MINUTES | TOTAL COOKING TIME: 1 HOUR 40 MINUTES | SERVES 6

500 g (1 lb 2 oz) Roma tomatoes, halved
6 flour tortillas
1–2 red chillies, finely chopped
1 tablespoon olive oil
1 kg (2 lb 4 oz) stewing beef, cubed
½ teaspoon black pepper
2 onions, thinly sliced
375 ml (13 fl oz/1½ cups) beef stock
60 g (2¼ oz/¼ cup) tomato paste
    (concentrated purée)
375 g (13 oz) tin kidney beans, drained
1 teaspoon chilli powder
125 g (4½ oz/½ cup) sour cream
flat-leaf (Italian) parsley to garnish

1   Preheat the oven to 180°C (350°F/Gas 4). Grill (broil) the tomatoes, skin side up, under a hot grill (broiler) for 6–8 minutes, or until the skin is black and blistered. Place in a plastic bag and seal. Cool, remove the skin and roughly chop the flesh.

2   Bake two of the tortillas for 4 minutes, or until crisp. Break into pieces and put in a food processor with the tomato and chopped chilli. Process for 30 seconds, or until almost smooth.

3   Heat the oil in a large heavy-based saucepan. Brown the beef in batches, season with pepper, then remove. Add the onion to the pan and cook for 5 minutes. Return the meat to the pan. Stir in the processed mixture, stock and tomato paste, and bring to the boil. Reduce the heat, cover and simmer for 1¼ hours. Add the beans and chilli powder, and heat through.

4   Grill the remaining tortillas for 2–3 minutes on each side, then cool and cut into wedges. Serve the stew with the sour cream, and toasted tortilla wedges on the side.

HINT: *If this stew becomes too thick during cooking, thin it with a little extra stock.*

Grill the tomatoes until the skin is black and blistered and it will peel away easily.

Once the tortillas are crisp, break into pieces and put in the food processor.

NUTRITION PER SERVE
Protein 50 g; Fat 20 g; Carbohydrate 40 g; Dietary Fibre 8 g; Cholesterol 125 mg; 2235 kJ (535 Cal)

Vegetarian chilli

PREPARATION TIME: 15 MINUTES + 10 MINUTES SOAKING | TOTAL COOKING TIME: 40 MINUTES | SERVES 6–8

130 g (4½ oz/¾ cup) burghul (bulgur)
2 tablespoons olive oil
1 large onion, finely chopped
2 garlic cloves, crushed
1 teaspoon chilli powder
2 teaspoons ground cumin
1 teaspoon cayenne pepper
½ teaspoon ground cinnamon
2 x 400 g (14 oz) tins chopped tomatoes
750 ml (26 fl oz/3 cups) vegetable stock
440 g (15½ oz) tin red kidney beans, drained
    and rinsed
2 x 300 g (10½ oz) tins chickpeas, drained and
    rinsed
310 g (11 oz) tin corn kernels, drained
2 tablespoons tomato paste (concentrated
    purée)
corn chips and sour cream, to serve

1   Soak the burghul in 250 ml (9 fl oz/1 cup) hot water for 10 minutes. Heat the oil in a large heavy-based saucepan and cook the onion for 10 minutes, stirring often, until soft and golden.

2   Add the garlic, chilli, cumin, cayenne and cinnamon, and cook, stirring, for 1 minute.

3   Add the tomato, stock and burghul. Bring to the boil and simmer for 10 minutes. Stir in the beans, chickpeas, corn and tomato paste, and simmer for 20 minutes, stirring often. Serve with corn chips and sour cream.

Stir the garlic and spices into the pan with the onion, and cook for 1 minute.

Add the tomato, stock and burghul to the pan and bring to the boil.

NUTRITION PER SERVE (8)
Protein 7 g; Fat 10 g; Carbohydrate 18 g; Dietary Fibre 7 g; Cholesterol 8 mg; 780 kJ (185 Cal)

Basics

Curry pastes

Madras curry paste

MAKES ½ CUP

Place the following ingredients in a small bowl and mix together well: 2½ tablespoons of dry-roasted, ground coriander seeds, 1 tablespoon dry-roasted ground cumin seeds, 1 teaspoon brown mustard seeds, ½ teaspoon cracked black peppercorns, 1 teaspoon chilli powder, 1 teaspoon ground turmeric, 2 crushed garlic cloves, 2 teaspoons of grated fresh ginger and 1 teaspoon salt. Add 3–4 tablespoons of white vinegar and mix to a smooth paste. Will keep in a clean airtight container in the refrigerator for up to a month.

General-purpose Indian curry powder

MAKES ⅓ CUP

Dry-fry the following ingredients separately in a small frying pan, over medium heat for 2–3 minutes, or until fragrant: 2 teaspoons cumin seeds, 2 teaspoons coriander seeds, 2 teaspoons fenugreek seeds, 1 teaspoon yellow mustard seeds, 1 teaspoon black peppercorns, 1 teaspoon cloves, 1 teaspoon chilli powder, 2 teaspoons ground turmeric, ½ teaspoon ground cinnamon and ½ teaspoon ground cardamom. Place in a spice grinder, or use a mortar and pestle or a small food processor with a fine blade to grind to a fine powder. Place in a small bowl with the pre-ground spices and mix together well. Store in an airtight container in a cool, dark place.

Sri Lankan curry powder

MAKES ⅓ CUP

Dry-fry the following ingredients separately over low heat, until fragrant: 3 tablespoons coriander seeds, 1½ tablespoons cumin seeds, 1 teaspoon fennel seeds and ¼ teaspoon fenugreek seeds. It is important to do this separately as all spices brown at different rates. Make sure the spices are well browned, not burnt. Place the browned seeds in a food processor, blender or use a mortar and pestle, add a 2.5 cm (1 inch) piece cinnamon stick, 6 cloves, ¼ teaspoon cardamom seeds, 2 teaspoons dried curry leaves, 2 small dried red chillies and process or grind to a powder. Store in an airtight container in a cool, dry place.

Vindaloo paste

MAKES ½ CUP

Place the following ingredients in a food processor: 2 tablespoons grated fresh ginger, 4 chopped garlic cloves, 4 chopped red chillies, 2 teaspoons ground turmeric, 2 teaspoons ground cardamom, 4 cloves, 6 peppercorns, 1 teaspoon ground cinnamon, 1 tablespoon ground coriander, 1 tablespoon cumin seeds and 125 ml (4 fl oz/ ½ cup) cider vinegar. Mix for 20 seconds, or until well combined and smooth. Refrigerate for up to a month.

Garam masala

MAKES ½ CUP

Dry-fry the following ingredients separately in a frying pan over medium heat, for 2–3 minutes, or until just becoming fragrant: 2 tablespoons coriander seeds, 1½ tablespoons cardamom pods, 1 tablespoon cumin seeds, 2 teaspoons whole black peppercorns, 1 teaspoon whole cloves and 3 cinnamon sticks. Remove the cardamom pods, crush with the handle of a heavy knife and remove the seeds. Discard the pods. Place the fried spices, cardamom seeds and 1 grated nutmeg in a food processor, blender or use a mortar and pestle, and process or grind to a powder. Store in an airtight container in a cool, dark place.

Thai yellow curry paste

MAKES ½ CUP

Mix the following ingredients to a paste in a food processor, blender or use a mortar and pestle: 8 small green chillies, 5 red Asian shallots (eschalots), roughly chopped, 2 chopped garlic cloves, 1 tablespoon finely chopped coriander (cilantro) stem and root, 1 chopped lemongrass stalk, white part only, 2 tablespoons finely chopped fresh galangal, 1 teaspoon ground coriander, 1 teaspoon ground cumin, ½ teaspoon ground turmeric, ½ teaspoon black peppercorns and 1 tablespoon lime juice. Will keep in an airtight container in the fridge for a month.

Thai green curry paste

MAKES 1 CUP

Preheat the oven to 180°C (350°F/ Gas 4). Put the following ingredients in a dish and bake for 5–10 minutes, until fragrant: 1 teaspoon white peppercorns, 1 teaspoon cumin seeds, 2 tablespoons coriander seeds and 2 teaspoons shrimp paste (wrapped in foil). Unwrap the shrimp paste. Mix the above ingredients in a food processor or use a mortar and pestle, and add the following: 1 teaspoon sea salt, 4 finely chopped lemongrass stalks, white part only, 2 teaspoons chopped fresh galangal, 2 teaspoons finely shredded makrut (kaffir lime) leaves, 1 tablespoon chopped coriander (cilantro) root, 5 chopped red Asian shallots (eschalots), 10 chopped garlic cloves, 16 chopped large green chillies. Mix all ingredients to a smooth paste. Keep in an airtight container in the fridge for up to a month.

Thai red curry paste

MAKES 1 CUP

Preheat the oven to 180°C (350°F/ Gas 4). Soak 15 large dried chillies in boiling water for 10 minutes. Remove the seeds and roughly chop the flesh. Put 1 teaspoon white peppercorns, 2 teaspoons coriander seeds, 1 teaspoon cumin seeds and 2 teaspoons shrimp paste (wrapped in foil) in a dish and bake for 5–10 minutes until fragrant. Unwrap the shrimp paste. Mix the above ingredients in a food processor or use a mortar and pestle, and add the following: 5 chopped red Asian shallots (eschalots), 10 garlic cloves, 2 finely chopped lemongrass stalks, white part only, 1 tablespoon chopped fresh galangal, 2 tablespoons chopped coriander (cilantro) root and 1 teaspoon finely grated makrut (kaffir lime) zest. Mix all ingredients to a smooth paste. Will keep in an airtight container in the fridge for a month.

Massaman curry paste

MAKES ½ CUP

Preheat the oven to 180°C (350°F/ Gas 4). Soak 10 large dried red chillies in boiling water for 10 minutes, drain, remove the seeds and roughly chop. Put the following ingredients in a dish and bake for 5 minutes until fragrant: 3 cardamom pods, 1 teaspoon cumin seeds, 1 tablespoon coriander seeds, ¼ teaspoon black peppercorns, 1 teaspoon shrimp paste (wrapped in foil), 5 chopped red Asian shallots (eschalots), 1 finely chopped lemongrass stalk (white part only), 1 tablespoon chopped fresh galangal and 10 chopped garlic cloves. Unwrap the paste. Mix the chilli, roasted ingredients and ¼ teaspoon ground cinnamon, ½ teaspoon ground nutmeg and ¼ teaspoon ground cloves to a smooth paste in a food processor, or use a mortar and pestle or spice grinder. If the mixture is too dry add a little vinegar to moisten it. Will keep in an airtight container in the fridge for up to a month.

Chu chee curry paste

MAKES ½ CUP

Preheat the oven to 180°C (350°F/ Gas 4). Soak 10 large dried red chillies in boiling water for 10 minutes. Drain, remove the seeds and roughly chop. Place 1 teaspoon coriander seeds, 1 tablespoon shrimp paste (wrapped in foil) and 1 tablespoon white peppercorns on a foil-lined baking tray and bake for 5 minutes until fragrant. Unwrap the paste. Mix the above ingredients in a food processor or mortar and pestle, and add the following: 10 finely shredded makrut (kaffir lime) leaves, 10 chopped red Asian shallots (eschalots), chopped, 2 teaspoons finely grated makrut (kaffir lime) zest, 1 tablespoon chopped coriander (cilantro) stem and root, 1 finely chopped lemongrass stalk, white part only, 3 tablespoons chopped fresh galangal, 1 tablespoon chopped Krachai (optional) and 6 chopped garlic cloves. Mix all ingredients to a smooth paste. You may need to use a little lemon juice if the paste is too thick. Will keep in an airtight container in the fridge for up to a month.

Index

Published in 2009 by Murdoch Books Pty Limited.

Murdoch Books Australia
Pier 8/9, 23 Hickson Road
Millers Point NSW 2000
Phone: + 61 (0) 2 8220 2000
Fax: + 61 (0) 2 8220 2558
www.murdochbooks.com.au

Murdoch Books UK Limited
Erico House, 6th Floor
93–99 Upper Richmond Road
Putney, London SW15 2TG
Phone: +44 (0) 20 8785 5995
Fax: +44 (0) 20 8785 5985
www.murdochbooks.co.uk

Chief Executive: Juliet Rogers
Publishing Director: Kay Scarlett

Project manager and editor: Jane Massam
Design concept: Heather Menzies
Design: Heather Menzies and Jacqueline Richards
Photographer: Natasha Milne
Stylist: Kate Brown
Food preparation: Peta Dent, Kirrily La Rosa, Tina Asher
Introduction text: Leanne Kitchen
Production: Kita George

National Library of Australia Cataloguing-in-Publication Data
Homestyle casseroles and one-pots. Includes index.
ISBN 9781741962710 (pbk.)
casserole cookery 641.821

A catalogue record for this book is available from the British Library.
Colour separation by Splitting Image in Clayton, Victoria, Australia.
Printed by i-Book Printing Ltd. in 2009. PRINTED IN CHINA.

IMPORTANT: Those who might be at risk from the effects of salmonella poisoning
(the elderly, pregnant women, young children and those suffering from immune deficiency diseases)
should consult their doctor with any concerns about eating raw eggs.

CONVERSION GUIDE: You may find cooking times vary depending on the oven
you are using. For fan-forced ovens, as a general rule, set the oven temperature
to 20°C (35°F) lower than indicated in the recipe.